UF⊙ENCOUNTERS

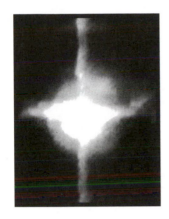

The True Story Behind the Brookhaven and Carp Incidents

J. B. Michaels

Longmeadow Press

Published by Longmeadow Press, 201 High Ridge Road, Stamford, Connecticut 06904. All rights reserved. No part of this book may be reproduced or utilized in any form or by any means, electronic or mechanical, including photocopying, recording or by any information storage or retrieval system, without permission in writing from the Publisher.

Longmeadow Press and the colophon are trademarks.

This Longmeadow Press edition is printed on archival quality paper. It is acid-free and conforms to the guidelines established for permanence and durability by the Council of Library Resources and the American National Standards Institute.∞™

Library of Congress Cataloging-in-Publication Data

Michaels, J. B.
    UFO encounters : the true story behind the Brookhaven and Carp incidents / J.B. Michaels. — 1st Longmeadow Press ed.
        p.   cm.
    ISBN 0-681-00810-5
    1. Unidentified flying objects—Sightings and encounters—New York—Brookhaven (Town)   2. Unidentified flying objects—Sightings and encounters—Ontario—Carp.   I. Title.
TL789.3.M53   1995
001.9'42—dc20
                                                                95-243
                                                                CIP

Printed and bound in the United States of America.
First Longmeadow Press edition.
0 9 8 7 6 5 4 3 2 1

The names of some of the participants involved have been changed to protect their identities. No other facts have been altered.

INTERIOR DESIGN BY LISA STOKES.

There are more things in heaven and earth, Horatio,
Than are dreamt of in your philosophy.
Hamlet Act I, Scene V — *William Shakespeare*

*To Patricia Hansen and Deborah Bell, two
very special women without whose help and
dedication this book would not have been written.
Patricia stood by me in the hardest of times.*

*And Deborah . . .
It was she who first saw the incredible lights that descended
from the sky.*

CONTENTS

Part III
ABDUCTIONS 153

Part IV
HYBRID 185

PROLOGUE

There are two kinds of stories you read about in the media today. The first are common, everyday items reported in your daily newspaper. These events—disasters, earthquakes, floods, famines, wars, and serial killers—are certainly not at all difficult to accept as being true accounts of actual events, events that continue to happen in almost every country all over the world, every single day of the year, and have been happening for thousands of years. Even though few of us have ever witnessed a murder, a rape, seen an ethnic cleansing, or interviewed a serial killer, there is little doubt of the reality of such situations. The second type of story comes from accounts of things that are truly fantastic; the stuff that tabloid journalism, the *National Enquirer*, the *Star*, and other pulp publications thrive on.

As a general rule these stories have no basis at all in fact. If there is a thin thread of reality to be found, it is a thin thread indeed. One of the tabloids' favorite subjects, which can be found in almost every issue, is UFOs. Even decades before the coming of Spielberg's masterpiece, *Close Encounters*

of the Third Kind, the rallying cry of countless, self-proclaimed, "these are the last days and alien contact is imminent" messiahs could be heard from South America to
Scandinavia. Scores of abductees have come forward, flanked
by bespectacled hypnotists and nervous-looking lie-detector
technicians. Dramatically portrayed in such recent films as
Fire in the Sky, individuals relate stories of being taken aboard
alien spacecraft. They tell spine-chilling tales of the intru-
sion of almost every body orifice by cold, sterile instruments,
while large-eyed groups of aliens watched with the cold indif-
ference of human scientists vivisecting a frog. All this can be
and often is very entertaining. Many accounts have been quite
logically explained by individuals seeking attention, notori-
ety, or sums of money for videos of well-thrown hubcaps,
objects clearly suspended by wires, or even flashlights or spar-
klers waved in the dark. With the advent of the camcorder,
the number of such tapes has grown from hundreds to thousands. Camcorders, even some of the cheaper models, can
produce videos of passable quality. Especially in the dark,
they produce some of the most fascinating reflections and
auras, and can often make a simple penlight appear to be a
rather convincing UFO.

Yet, even amid all the skepticism on the subject of UFOs,
a disturbing event alledgedly occurred in July 1947. A news
release at the time stated that an alien spacecraft had crashed
in the Arizona desert near Roswell Army Airfield. The area
was sealed off by the military. Experts were called in from all
over the country, and the hull of the craft was examined and
determined to be unlike any material used in any American
or foreign craft. The Roswell crash set off a chain of events in
the military which lowered a veil of secrecy on all future UFO
investigations. Some of the highest sources in the U.S. government, all the way up to the president himself, no longer

considered UFOs a joke. Frequent radar sightings of bogies, as unknown objects are called, several of which were pursued by jets, supported the theory that they were real enough to be considered a serious threat to our national security, and that fact changed the fabric of our American military. The modern Air Force was formed in response to these sightings to cope with the definite possibility that UFOs were no longer something the military could ignore. In addition, the government did a study on UFOs called Project Blue Book. It was a large, time-consuming effort, and for the most part offered explanations of the majority of UFO sightings. But there was a clear 10 to 15 percent of the sightings that could not be explained by any means.

What you are about to read in *UFO Encounters* is based on facts. It includes not only documented accounts of the crash and the recovery of an alien spacecraft, but of several extraterrestrials as well. It is not fictionalized. It is not dramatized. These are the facts taken from firsthand accounts of individuals present at two events where alien spacecraft not only landed, but were filmed on videotape. The Brookhaven incident, which was the crash at Southaven Park, was witnessed by dozens of people. The roadblock in which the highway was cordoned off and guarded by SWAT teams while unmarked Cobra helicopters swarmed the area was witnessed by a large portion of the small hamlet of Brookhaven. A massive fire that could be seen for miles, as well as the American military weapon that exploded one craft and caused another to crash, was filmed by a fireman. This film was aired on the Fox TV show, "Encounters," on February 26, 1994.

In addition to the Long Island crash, another craft was chased by military helicopters in Carp, Canada. The landing was witnessed by several individuals and a video was also taken. This video has been analyzed by some of the most prominent experts in the field of computer graphics, and even by the CIA. Segments of this video were also aired on Fox, as were interviews with witnesses who saw the landing. According to experts at some of the top video labs in the country, the Carp film is untampered with and genuine, and contains the clearest close-up picture of an alien spacecraft ever captured on film.

Many of the individuals who have been interviewed fear for their lives. As I said during my interview with Fox, "Many people I spoke to were not just scared . . . they were terrified." I personally interviewed over one hundred individuals who had either seen or had evidence concerning the crash in Southaven Park. In my possession, I have a film that clearly shows not only the smoking wreckage of the craft but two alien bodies. There are lab reports of tests done on "alien DNA," and I have discovered that many of the originals of the documents I have copies of have been shredded. The crash site at Brookhaven is still radioactive where the trees were sheared off by the craft.

The dialogues are taken directly from the witnesses and the interview with "the general" is quoted word for word. I have documented reports from UFO researcher Bob Oechsler, video analysts, and the young people who risked a great deal in gathering as much information about Brookhaven National Lab as they did. Much of the information has come from the government, especially the Department of Energy, congressmen, and Mona Rowe at Brookhaven Lab.

So, this is a story of the first kind. It is news. Just as with an earthquake, a famine, an epidemic, or even an interview with a serial killer, it happened. I have interviewed those who saw the crash or the effects of the crash firsthand, from the Air Force lieutenant who heard the boom when the object crashed, to the policeman who admitted the entire town was in an uproar over the fire in the park, to the captain of the special team for handling radioactive fires at Brookhaven. Perhaps our government, which has been extremely helpful in giving me information on Brookhaven Lab and other documentation, will in the near future officially release the facts concerning the Brookhaven crash and the Carp incident.

Not one person whom I have interviewed or who has given me information has received remuneration of any kind. They have shared their experiences and what they observed, and I believe have done so in the most accurate and honest way possible.

For me, it all began with Tom Theophanis, the UFO researcher who shared the Brookhaven crash film with me. This film of an alien ship shot down over Long Island and the body, clearly not human, lying next to the wreckage, was what first compelled me to write this book. It is my hope that by the time you have finished reading this book, you will realize we are not alone in this universe. And that whatever is out there has picked this moment in our history to make contact.

Part I
ENCOUNTERS

one

GRAYS ON FILM

The last thing I expected to see when Tom Theophanis popped the videotape in his VCR was the image of a dead alien lying on the ground amidst the smoldering wreck of a UFO. Tom is an ex-police investigator, a thorough stickler for details, a person who has been trained to deal only in and with verifiable, precise facts. Yet, what I was seeing on the screen was not the typical fare of the typical detective story. Firemen darted about the scene and seemed uncomfortable to be at the fire. The wreckage of whatever had crashed was unlike any hull I had ever seen. And the body was unlike any other body. The most significant difference was that this particular body had a head twice the normal size of a human's and eyes that I had only seen once in a grade B movie called *Killers from Outer Space*. The body could not have been more than 70 or 80 pounds nor could it have been more than five feet tall. The craft, wreckage at this point, was not a jet, private plane, or helicopter. The hull was incredibly thin, much like aluminum, and bubbling from within the structure was a thick greenish cloud, which moved across the ground like dry-ice vapor. Yet I could tell that there must have been heat, something burning inside, because the firemen winced and squinted their eyes as they approached the object.

So there it was, in living color on Tom Theophanis' videotape. A film taken by a fireman on Long Island showing the wreckage of a flying saucer and at least one dead alien on the ground next to it.

"It's the damndest thing I've ever seen," the police-investigator side of Tom said flatly, as if wishing he were not seeing it at all. The other side of Tom Theophanis, the video technician and university-computer graphics teacher, was engrossed by what he saw on the screen. Behind that screen were walls lined with degrees, including ones in biochemistry and computer graphics, that silently attested to the fact that Tom is a clear-thinking, well-grounded person who deals in the facts.

"One thing's for sure," I said. "The thing on the ground is not human and whatever crashed is unlike any type of jet or craft I've ever seen. The head of the creature is like an upside-down pear, with no mouth and just two slits for a nose. And the stuff that the craft is made of is thinner than aluminum."

"Yes, but it's a hell of a lot tougher than aluminum." Tom smiled. "This is a new video but not a new story. That's exactly what the guy at Roswell said in 1947, you know? They called it a weather balloon, claimed it was a special model built to observe from high altitudes if any type of nuclear missiles were being fired. Big difference here though. That gaseous stuff sure the hell isn't helium, and we don't send a lot of little gray men with bulb-shaped heads up with our weather balloons."

A dark figure moved in from the left on the screen. He held an assault rifle stoically and looked very uncomfortable. He kept looking at the body a few feet from him, not all that sure it was dead, and he looked even less sure exactly what course of action he would take if it began moving.

"Who's this guy?" I laughed. "Special Forces, SEAL team?"

"Who knows," said Tom. "I heard they have a special little group kinda like the 'dirty little-gray-men dozen' that are specially trained to handle encounters of this sort. The fireman who's taking the film is scared shitless. You can tell that. He's shooting from the hip. Panning like crazy. One of those autofocus jobs. One of your worst-case home movies of probably what is the most valuable piece of film in the last decade of an alien crash. Just a cheap camcorder, and it's dark. I'd say the film was taken maybe nine to ten at night. What I wanted you to see was this part." Tom grinned. "Look at the expression on that SWAT team guy's face when the thing moves. Even the fireman taking the film staggered back a few feet. Have you ever seen anything move its head like that side to side? Here, let me back it up and slow it down for you. Watch it frame by frame."

I was absorbed by this time. My lit cigarette had burnt to ash without having been touched.

"Look at this," said Tom, pausing the frame. "Look at the thing's head."

He advanced it one more frame. The creature's head moved 90 degrees to the right. "Moves like a goddamned lizard, only faster. No human could move like that. Moves so fast, first it's looking to the side, then straight at you. And those eyes. Yet the rest of the body is completely still, just the head moves." As the camera swung to the right, I could see that there was more than one body; three to be exact. Two sprawled—one of them partially dismembered, missing an arm and part of a leg, and one face down—and the third was sitting up, leaning against a tree. Two SWAT team members spread shiny metallic coverings over the first two bodies. Neither of them seemed particularly anxious to approach the one who seemed to be watching them.

"Okay," I said, turning toward Tom. "What exactly am I seeing here?"

"You're seeing what you're seeing," he said. "I was sent this film by John Ford from Long Island. He claims this is the original footage shot by a fireman at the scene of a UFO crash in Southaven Park. He was even so kind as to blow up a few of the stills." Tom produced a small manila folder containing about a dozen blown-up photographs of some of the more interesting frames. "I know you have a video lab down there and some pretty sophisticated equipment. I don't want to tell you anymore. Just take these stills and the video and take a look."

"Where is Southaven Park?" I said, putting the video and stills in my briefcase. "And what makes this film any different than hundreds like it?"

Tom sighed.

"Southaven Park is near Brookhaven Lab on Long Island, New York," he said. "What makes this film different is there are over a hundred witnesses who either saw the crash, saw the roadblocks put up across the highway after the crash, saw the choppers swarming the skies, or the four firemen who saw the bodies and the craft up close. And most especially the one fireman who took the film.

Also," Tom continued, "this craft did not crash. It was shot down by our military forces. Whatever was used to shoot it down is highly classified, and this whole thing has 'Department of Energy' written all over it."

"John Ford, who has the original film, has personally told me that he is extremely concerned for his personal safety," I said. "And if you talk to the firemen involved you will find they not only are worried about losing their jobs, but that the government might actually 'remove' any and all personnel knowing about or connected with this event.

"Should I be concerned about all this, Tom? I mean, after all, this film is genuine, and we really have a case of not only a downed UFO but a living extraterrestrial that is being kept locked up. This is all pretty dangerous stuff."

"Well, yes," said Tom. "You should be concerned. There are members of the CIA in several of the more well-known UFO groups. Also several of the analysts who look at these films are CIA connected. Also, remember how we got disconnected three times during our phone conversation last night? How bad the quality of the line was?"

"The only way," I said, "is to go to the networks, the media."

"That's right," said Tom, "and on February 26, 1994, the network is coming to you. Fox network to be exact. And as I understand it, you should have a viewership of some 17 million people. Getting this out to the public, writing a damn book about it, talking to congressmen, officials, radio, and TV is the only real protection we have. John Ford will be there with his film, you will have more photographs after you go to the site, there will be over a dozen people on the "Encounters" show talking about the crash and recovery of not only an alien ship but aliens as well."

So, that's how it all started. I saw this film of smoldering wreckage and three alien bodies. In less than a month I would be telling the story on national TV and would begin interviewing individuals who had witnessed firsthand the first videotaped incident in history of an alien spacecraft being shot down by an plasma beam and actual contact with an extraterrestrial.

two

THE CRASH

The following is the combined account of four eyewitnesses who saw the crash at Southaven Park. The dialogue, the events, and the descriptions of what happened are taken word for word from these individuals, who personally saw one UFO explode in the sky, shot down, and the other lose control and crash.

Two teenage boys and their female friend saw the crash. It wasn't as if any of them were UFO aficionados or had any particular interest in science fiction, Richard Corman grade-B movies, psychics, or anything to do with space travel or astronauts. In fact, none of the three had ever seen a UFO or taken any notice of such things, except maybe an occasional glance at a tabloid while waiting in line to buy groceries yet that very night they would be thrown together to witness a "mother ship" from somewhere in the Andromeda galaxy reduced to atoms by a highly classified plasma beam, and then watch as one of the other ship's defense shields collapsed and it plummeted into the nearby public park, setting the surrounding area on fire.

There was something significant about Jennifer Biels, the teenage girl, that would prove to be very helpful in the future investigation of the Southaven Park incident. Her mother worked at the nearby Brookhaven Lab, and this was the "hotly disputed" place where the recovered bodies of the aliens were taken, as well as the craft itself, before later being shipped to the nearby military base.

Because her mother worked at the lab, it was not uncommon to see Jennifer flirting with the security personal; one especially susceptible to her charms was Bob, who was inclined to allow her in areas that normally required a security clearance. Actually, security was difficult, because of the hundreds of corporations, individuals, and scientists with access to the immense, two thousand-acre area of Brookhaven Lab.

Mona Rowe, the public spokesperson for Brookhaven, is about as nice and as charismatic a person as you would ever want to talk to. We spent many hours talking on the phone, and she and the Department of Energy sent me reams of information on Brookhaven Lab as well as some clippings on Brookhaven's involvement with UFOs over the years. When the swarms of newspeople arrived and began asking many, many questions about the crash, Mona Rowe was the perfectly trained, educated, and extremely concise Brookhaven representative, smiling but shaking her head in total sincerity. There had been no crash, no fire, and sorry, there were no aliens in the basement, no craft being analyzed in the lab, nor had anything like that ever occurred. Of course, she had seen a bright formation of lights in the sky while driving to work, and a year earlier there had been talk of an actual battle between the American military and a UFO near the bay, which was later described as just lights produced by an air-sea rescue operation. But of course, that was outside the realm of her position as official spokesperson for Brookhaven Lab.

At the time of this event Jennifer, a good friend of Mona Rowe's, was a 17-year-old straight-A student, sure to be a biochemist, and about to engage in a few activities that would make the security staff at Brookhaven very unhappy. Richard Grayson and Todd Phillips, humble part-time Togo sandwich assemblers, and Jennifer were soon to become three very dedicated and rather adventurous UFO investigators. And this all started the very day that the love of Richard Grayson's life, Joanne, had most indelicately looked Richard straight in the eye and told him their relationship was over.

Togo's sandwich shop was at the base of hill, next to a business complex, just a few blocks from the high school. It was generally busy except in the late afternoons and evenings. There wasn't a whole lot happening in Brookhaven Hamlet on week nights. Richard and Todd worked part time on the five-to-closing shift. Oddly, the time at the shop seemed to pass very quickly. It really wasn't that busy, but Todd had a lot of new "you know you're in trouble when" jokes he had heard on the David Letterman show the previous night. And despite his foul mood, Richard even found himself laughing a few times. The owner of the Togo's shop called at about 8:00 P.M. to ask how business was doing. Todd, who answered the phone, told him the truth. It was dead. Truly dead. They hadn't had a customer in almost an hour.

"Go ahead and close up," said the owner. "I'll pay you two up through nine but no point in staying open if no one's out. Just too damn cold tonight. You'd think it would snow or something. But it's just too damn cold. No one wants to come out when they can order pizza and sit home and watch cable TV."

"Gotcha," said Todd, relieved. Todd hung up the phone and yelled over his shoulder. "Hey, the old man's gonna let us off early. That's great!"

Todd always gave Richard a ride home. They had been friends since second grade. They headed north up the highway. It was cold, bitterly cold. Todd shivered, pulled the fur collar of his flight jacket up around his neck and pulled onto the main stretch of the highway. He adjusted his red baseball cap, lit up a cigarette, and flipped on the CD player. The small cab of the truck was instantly filled with the screeching sounds of Nosferatu.

"Will you turn that racket down!" growled Richard. "I'm not in the mood for it." Todd ignored him, reached out, and turned the volume up.

"I said, turn that shit down!" Richard angrily punched a glowing red button, turning the CD player off.

"Hey," growled Todd. "Don't do that. It's my truck."

"Let's just not talk," said Richard. "Just let me sit here in silence and feel sorry for myself. I'm depressed. And I intend to be depressed for several days. Your music just doesn't fit, that's all."

"Sure," said Todd. He looked over at his friend Richard, who did look genuinely miserable. "Females can sure mess you up," he said sympathetically.

The highway paralleled the bay, which continued for a few miles north of Southaven Park. It was a clear night. There wasn't a lot of pollution on this part of Long Island, and there was a beautiful, cloudless night sky, with brilliant shining stars from horizon to horizon. Richard jumped as he noticed a V-shaped formation of glowing lights moving across the water.

"Holy shit!" said Todd, holding his arm in front of his face. The objects were moving toward Southaven Park. "What are those?" Suddenly he gasped as a huge glowing sphere became visible in the sky.

"I can't watch this and drive!" Todd rammed his foot down on the brake. The truck skidded to a stop at the side of the freeway. Both boys jumped out of the truck.

"Whoa!" said Richard. "I've never seen anything like this." Above the trees of Southaven Park, a glowing ball hung motionless in the sky, streams of yellow, orange, and dark crimson flames swirling around it, the unnatural hue of those colors reflected off the storm clouds moving in from the east. Three smaller craft darted about the shpere, and then were motionless. They were much smaller, each perhaps the size of a commercial plane. They were triangular, with rounded edges like a Stealth jet. But the sphere, or mother ship as Richard later would call it, was immense. It was some 60 to 80 feet in diameter, the size of a four-to-five-story building. What made it all the more unusual was the almost complete silence. The two boys looked up, mesmerized by the bright objects and the magnetic-resonant hum that they felt more than heard. The lights of the truck flickered, blinking in an odd strobelike rhythm to the humming sound. The CD player turned back on, and Todd, looking genuinely scared, pulled the ground wire to shut it off.

"Hey! Hey!" A young girl was jumping up and down on the other side of the road and pointing at the sky. "Do you see that?" Besides a blue Camaro parked on the side of the highway, a tall, slender brunette excitedly motioned then impulsively ran across the road and grabbed Richard's arm, shaking him.

"This is not my kind of thing," said Todd. "But I think we are seeing some type of UFOs, um . . ." he stammered, not knowing the girl's name.

"Jennifer," she said, without turning to look at him. "Jennifer Biels."

"Richard," Todd said, pointing to his friend. "And I'm Todd, the crazy one." He grinned. "But that," he continued, "is definitely no airplane. I don't know if those are our planes circling it or what."

"There's four of them." Jennifer pointed toward the objects, which now seemed to glide above the park. "And they are all moving together."

"It looks like they are looking for something or someone," said Richard. "And they are moving in a definite formation."

Suddenly the air was filled with the sound of helicopters approaching from the north.

"Well, one thing is for certain," said Jennifer. "Our military is not going to like this one bit." A small band of black Cobra helicopter's approached, still keeping a respectable distance from the UFOs. The objects continued to circle over the park, moving slowly in a V formation. From one of the UFOs a shimmering electric blue beam streamed down, barely touching the tops of the trees. As the light appeared, the magnetic-resonant hum rose in pitch and intensity. Jennifer could feel the hairs of her neck bristle as static electricity seemed to sweep over them. The lights of the truck flickered again. The motor of the truck turned on and off, and then suddenly the hum stopped and the scanning light from the craft vanished. Richard, Todd, and Jennifer all jumped as a huge diesel truck pulled up behind the Camaro.

"Hey, Red Eye, you off again on one of your flying saucer hunts!" A coarse female voice came from inside of the cab. They could hear the static of a CB blasting out the double semi. A thin, wiry older man stepped out. He had crew-cut salt-and-pepper hair and intelligent, observant gray eyes. He grinned as he saw the kids and then held up the mike of his CB.

"Gotta go, Hot Stuff. Got a grade-A numero-uno UFO staring right at me. Four of them, in fact. Man, oh man. This is really something." He walked over to the group of teenagers. "I'm Mike," he said, turning toward Todd. "If you have a camera you better grab it. I don't think you realize how exceptional what you are looking at is."

Todd shook his head sadly.

"Me neither," said Jennifer. "But God, I wish I did. This is incredible." She gasped as the sphere became much brighter, as if some type of energy field had been turned on.

"That's the mother ship, guys," said Mike, pulling out his camcorder and fumbling with the digital light sensors. "Jeez, just don't take off on me until I get you on video," he said, looking up, expecting it all to disappear.

"Jeez," said Richard. "That's some camera."

"Yep, almost broke me. My old lady, Hot Stuff, had a fit. But when you are trying to shoot in the dark and you want get something like this, ain't a bit sorry it cost me an arm and a leg." He centered the larger object in the viewfinder. "Man, this is really something else."

Suddenly the lights along the highway dimmed, and began to go out one by one. A wave of darkness swept across the rows of houses that were just a few hundred feet from the highway. "It's a blackout," said Mike. "Somebody's drawing power from the main lines, and I don't think it's those UFOs." There was one last surge of power and then all the lights in the town for several miles around went out. The giant sphere glowed as a beam of energy shot from the ground several miles north of them. There was a low rumble, and the craft shimmered, became incandescent, and then exploded. Two of the other craft streaked across the sky, leaving a shining trail of vapor behind them, and then shot straight up into the night sky.

The remaining craft just hovered, as if whatever was piloting it was completely stunned by the destruction of the larger vessel. Before it could make a move to escape, another beam of light pulsed up from the ground a few miles away at Brookhaven National Laboratory. Energy swirled around the object. The crippled ship veered at a 45 degree angle, and then plummeted down into Southaven Park. The earth trembled as the object crashed and huge flames shot up from behind the trees.

"Sweet Jesus," said Mike, his hands shaking. "I got it! I actually filmed the damn thing." The sound of helicopters was louder now, and they moved quickly over the water toward the crackling flames, where the craft had sheared off the tops of trees and then burst apart. "Military, and I bet they are helluva shook up. This is not all that far from Washington, D.C., you know." As helicopters moved by, two police cars pulled up and a scowling officer approached. The other officer stood by his patrol car, watching the fire in the distance.

"Show's over," said Officer Grisholm. "One of our test aircraft crashed. Nothing more to see."

"Hey, is that your dispatcher I just heard?" said Mike as a wave of chatter echoed from the patrol car.

As the officer turned, puzzled, Mike quickly hid his camcorder and walked rapidly to his truck.

"Hey," said the officer as Mike pulled back on the highway. "You truckers think you can do what you damn well please." He turned to the teenagers. "All right, kids, I got no quarrel with you. You have two choices. We can do license, registration, and a vehicle equipment inspection"—he looked at Todd's tires, which were a bit bare even for an off-road vehicle—"or you can just stay clear of this area for the rest of the night."

"Didn't you see that?" said Jennifer. "That was no test plane."

"I see nothing," said Grisholm, "except three teenage kids who are about to have some very unhappy parents picking them up down at the station."

"Yeah, right," said Todd surlily. "We got the message . . . officer." He said the word *officer* with obvious sarcasm.

"Hey, hey," said Jennifer, poking Richard's arm. "You want to go somewhere for coffee and talk about this?"

"Nah, I don't think I'm up to it. I'm still pretty shook up about a lot of things. This has just been too much of a day for me," said Richard.

"Okay." Jennifer frowned.

"We work at Togo's, weeknights," said Todd, giving Richard a "boy, are you messing this one up" look.

"Well, then," she paused, giving Richard a smile. "See ya, okay?"

"Should we go over and check it out?" said Richard.

"Not too swift an idea," said Todd. "Place is probably crawling with SWAT teams and police and stuff."

"We could send my little brother over on his bike and have him snoop around."

Richard felt strange. Much like after an auto accident when you have to help out and it doesn't hit you until it's all over. And the impact of what had just happened was beginning to hit him.

"Did we just see a flying saucer get shot down by our military and crash right in our very own Southaven Park?"

"Maybe, maybe not," said Todd. "I'm not really sure what I saw."

three

PULSE

What began with the Southaven Park incident and was followed by a UFO landing in Carp, Canada, was an increasing frequency of alien encounters. Obviously either a single race or group of races of extraterrestrials was attempting to make contact with our civilization. There is little doubt of the profound effect such contact, and continued interaction, would have on our nation and the world. There would be serious questions facing the world religions as to whether such entities were to be feared, considered to be heathen, or converted. Were these creatures—previously thought to be gods, angels, or demons—simply curious life-forms from other planets exploring our world?

Whatever the social impact, one thing is for sure. If the aliens were technologically superior to humankind, they would pose a definite threat to the entire human race. To the Pentagon, and throughout the military world, they would represent the greatest potential danger possible, a threat to national security. Since we became self-conscious beings, we have assumed that we are the pinnacle of evolution. Yet now it could be that we are as inferior to this new alien race as cattle and lab animals are to us. There is a great deal of evidence around cases of human abduction to support the idea that aliens simply do not regard us as sentient beings. In several accounts, abductees have described humans being vivisected by aliens—dissected and experimented on while they were still alive. In most cases, these frightening memories have only been discovered by using hypnosis, since they have been erased or suppressed by the aliens before returning the abductees.

Our government, military, and world at large would not welcome an encounter with an alien race. And the attempts to hide the growing mass of information about UFOs from the general public has resulted in the greatest cover-up in history. There have been hundreds of eyewitness accounts of UFOs. Despite the fact that I interviewed over two hundred people who saw or experienced the Southaven crash or Carp incident, all government officials, agencies, and military formally deny either event ever occurred.

The log page of the Fire and Rescue service that recorded the fire on the day of the Southaven crash has since been removed from the records, and Miles Quinn, the spokesperson for that agency, denies that any fires occurred at all. Yet the most incredible evidence came from several persons from Brookhaven Lab to whom I spoke. The narration that follows describes the events inside the Lab that night. The identity of the person who gave me the information I am not at liberty to disclose. Suffice it to say, this is a professional who was present that night and who has had no previous involvement with UFOs. The events have been confirmed by more than one source.

On November 22, 1992, two alien spacecraft were shot down over Southaven Park by a quark-gluon plasma beam. It is a project far ahead of the Star Wars program and can produce a temperature hotter than the surface of the sun. It is the only weapon, the only defense we have against an alien technology vastly superior to ours.

Lt. Colonel Grayson is a Vietnam veteran, decorated for valor with a Purple Heart for a shrapnel wound in combat. His current assignment is in the area of civilian defense contracts, working on top secret projects. There had been more than one embarrassing scenario where hundreds of millions of dollars had been poured into projects that were simply ineffective or actually prone to self-destruct in a combat situation. The colonel was hoping that this would not be one of them. He disliked the know-it-all scientist types and even found intelligence agency personnel particularly difficult to deal with. He was soon to be confronted by one of each.

Sorenson is the head of security with the Department of Energy, and Phil is a scientist who had been working on what he thought was a peaceful application of nuclear physics research.

"Get Sorenson down here! Now!" barked the Colonel to the first lieutenant at his side.

Sorenson entered through one of the side tunnels. He was not the least bit intimidated by Grayson. In fact, Sorenson considered Grayson a generally lesser being, one in a silly uniform with gaudy decorations and medals, but a necessary evil. Hustling to keep up with Sorenson was a young Asian woman. She anxiously peered at her hand-held computer, rapidly making calculations. Grayson disliked Sorenson even more than Sorenson disliked him. But the colonel smiled and lied anyway.

"Always nice to see you, Sorenson. Glad you could spare the time."

"Yeah, glad to see you, too, Colonel," said Sorenson coolly, in slow, measured syllables. "This facility is under the authority of the Department of Energy. They are also involved in the Star Wars project. You will find it somewhat comforting to know that we have already developed an auxiliary device for such a contingency as an alien spacecraft."

"I hate your double-talk bullshit," growled the colonel. "This damn thing better work as some type of weapon. We have a squadron, three to be precise, of alien spacecraft moving toward Washington, D.C., and above them some kind of mother ship. Huge son of a bitch, God knows what kind of armaments and energy it's got. We've got the president on his way to Camp David. This could get real ugly. Just how do you suppose we are going to stop these things before they go and land on the White House lawn?"

"Technology," said Sorenson coolly. "Fortunately for us, we have just had a breakthrough in quantum physics." Sorenson turned toward the particle accelerator. "This supercollider device is quite capable of producing a quark-gluon plasma beam. If we use gold ions that should produce about one hundred billion electron volts for each particle."

"I haven't the faintest idea what you're saying," said the colonel. "All I want to know is, is it going to blow that son of a bitch out of the sky?"

"Yes, it should," said Sorenson. "Such high-energy matter has not existed since the creation of the universe in the Big Bang. It would produce a beam hotter than the surface temperature of the sun. No energy shield or any other type of substance could withstand that much energy."

Phil, the scientist standing next to the colonel, cleared his throat. "Mr. Sorenson, I was not aware of any such application this device. Our facility is no longer part of the Star Wars project. And I must strongly protest any of this being used for some type of weapon. This supercollider was designed for peaceful uses and research."

"And who paid for the damn thing?" said the colonel. "We did. Of course there would be a weapons application."

"Even so," the scientist continued, annoyed at the interruption, "We are ten feet below the ground. How exactly do you plan to aim this beam? Even if we are capable of generating it, it would exist for less than a millionth of a second. How could you possibly direct it at something?"

The colonel's pocket phone beeped.

"Lt. Colonel Grayson here," he said into it, then frowned. "Yes, we are doing everything we can here. Yes, I know the objects will be in range in a few minutes. Uh uh." He shuffled uncomfortably, nodding. "Yes, I understand this could be a very embarrassing situation. I have the matter under control, General."

He clicked off the phone and glared at Sorenson.

"All our asses are on the line here. You're not only going to have to down these craft, but we have to figure out where they will crash. We can't have them going down in the middle of some residential neighborhood. We have to be able to minimize the information leaks on this."

"We've already thought of that," said Sorenson. "They're headed straight for Southaven Park. If we're lucky, we can even get them when they are over the water. No witnesses, very clean. Karen," he said, turning to his assistant, "you about ready?"

"Yes," she said. "I have over-ridden the security access codes ,and the console should be coming up in a few seconds." There was a whir of unseen motors, a panel in the floor slid to the side, and a large console appeared. Karen rushed over to the keyboard, looked at the monitor intently, and began typing feverishly. As the screen flickered to life, a sharp, optically enhanced picture of the four UFOs appeared.

"I'm activating the grid diversion and the alternate accelerator path module," said Karen.

The research scientist moved up next to Sorenson and looked suspiciously at the console. "I was never even aware that this was installed or interfaced with our accelerator. You avoided answering my question. Just exactly how do you propose to aim this beam?" he said.

"That's a 'Need to Know.' I am afraid that's classified. Besides," he gave the scientist a scornful look, "we wouldn't want to confuse your peaceful-applications mind."

"I have a need to know," said the scientist flatly. "And you know I have clearance. Tell me."

"We deflect it at a precise instant," said Sorenson. "And we have modified the circular accelerator at one point to convey the beam to the surface."

"That is very dangerous," said the scientist. "This plasma is highly unstable. It is more dangerous than a nuclear bomb. If there were some type of chain reaction that would create other plasma, such as occurs in a nuclear explosion, you could wind up vaporizing Long Island, and maybe half of the East Coast."

"We have several other highly competent physicists on it. They have assured us it is impossible for what you are saying to occur. I talked to them at Stanford Linear Accelerator yesterday. They assured me there was no danger whatsoever."

The colonel's phone beeped once more.

"Yes, yes," he hissed into it. "We're on it!" He turned around, glaring at Sorenson. "Those goddamned things are almost on top of us."

"Okay," said Karen. "I think I'm into the alternate particle grid." The magnetic hum of the accelerator began to increase. A portion of the circular accelerator slid away and a huge cylindrical object descended from a hidden panel in the ceiling.

"Give me an Eye Sky look," said Sorenson.

"Got it," said Karen. "Patching into satellite. On screen."

The view was from an altitude of one hundred miles above the North American continent. As it continued to zoom in, they could see the East Coast and finally the shape of Long Island. Several miles to the south, four specks of light and a large, more luminescent globe of light were moving toward the lab.

"Hell," the colonel gasped. "They are moving fast, maybe Mach 8 or 9?"

"Yes, I'm aware of that. I believe they are also aware that it is our intent in a few moments to vaporize them," said Sorenson. "So probably one of their prime objectives will be to neutralize this target first. We don't have much time. Karen . . ." he said, his voice not as confident as it had been before.

"I have to wait for the pulse to build. We will have two beams, plus the primary laser to cut a path for the plasma. At the crucial moments, we will divert the beam through our alternate accelerator." She sighed. "Just two shots. That's all I can give you."

As the objects approached Southaven Park, the colonel, watching the Eye Sky aerial view, noticed two cars by the highway, a large diesel truck, and a group of teenagers staring at the sky.

"Damn," said the colonel. He turned to the first lieutenant at his side. "Get the SEAL team over here and some choppers, contact the Fire Emergency and Rescue people, and send some P.D. Get those fucking roads blocked off." The lights in the tunnel flickered.

"I can't get enough power," moaned Karen. "We're going to lose it."

"Give me your phone," said Sorenson, grabbing the colonel's pocket phone. He tapped out a number.

"Is this the main energy grid at the power company? Yes, this is Special Agent Sorenson here. Hit those switches. Divert all your power to the Brookhaven research facility. Now."

There was a long pause as the supervisor came to the phone.

"The Op code is FLASH. Now do it!"

In a few seconds, the lights brightened and the hum grew to a deafening roar as the cyclotron began to vibrate. "They're shutting the power down to a large part of Brookhaven Hamlet and diverting it here," said Sorenson. "That should give you enough power."

"I have a lock on the mother ship," said Karen. "Full charge. Diverting . . . now."

The plasma beam shot up into the sky, vaporizing ten feet of earth, producing a brilliant flash on the glowing blue sphere of the mother ship. For a moment, the ship seemed to be resisting, as some type of force field flowed around the craft, then suddenly there was a rumble and the ship exploded.

"Yes!" said Karen, her hands shaking as she typed in the next fire sequence.

The colonel scowled. The other craft were darting about. Two of the alien ships glowed briefly and shot straight up into the sky. The remaining object hesitated, hovering several hundred feet above the ground.

"Get that other bastard, before he gets away," the colonel shouted.

"The other vessels are moving away, sir," said Karen. "I don't think it will be necessary. . ."

"Use a lower power setting," said the colonel. "Let's just cripple this one. I want one of these bastards to take apart. I'm sure our people would like to get a closer look at that craft."

"Should I?" she said, looking at Sorenson for approval.

"Proceed," said Sorenson, nodding his head.

"Locked," said Karen. "Reducing power to thirty percent but it is for a smaller craft. I think this will do it."

Another beam shot up into the sky. The remaining saucer wobbled drunkenly and then crashed into the park. A huge wall of flame shot up into the night sky, and the ground shuddered as it hit.

The colonel's phone beeped.

"Damn, yes," he said into it. "Yes, I saw it, too. We vaporized the bastard and knocked the other one out of the sky. The other two got away, but we should be able to salvage the wreckage. Send some Cobra choppers over there and we'll be right on over."

"They were probably not even hostile," said Phil, the scientist. "We didn't even try to communicate with them."

"We communicated exactly what we wanted to say," growled the colonel. "Get your sorry asses home and don't come back."

The wave of helicopters moved over the waters toward the burning wreckage. One chopper landed near the site, and the SEAL team began jumping out and running toward the craft. That night, seven separate fire stations and dozens of government agencies were notified that an unidentified object had crashed in Southaven Park. Later, on national TV, every single one of them would deny anything had ever happened.

There are a few problems with this story: the more than two dozen people who either saw the objects in the sky or the roadblocks put up and the Special Forces teams guarding the highway.

The fire engines were turned away at the gates when they arrived. The area was "hot," meaning radioactive, and a special team had to be called to handle that type of fire. It was not the first time the American military had shot down an alien spacecraft or recovered alien bodies. Yet after the object hit and split apart, one of the extraterrestrials survived the crash, and was sitting near the flames rising from the craft, still very much alive.

four

INFERNO

There were two fires documented in the Fire and Rescue log on the evening of November 22, 1992. One of these, at 8:32 P.M. in the Brookhaven Hamlet area, occurred less than thirty minutes before the UFO crash at Southaven Park. The other, which occurred at 9:04 P.M., was the crash itself. The times and locations of these fires were read to me by Miles Quinn, spokesperson of the Department of Fire and Rescue. They concurred with information given to me by three firemen who were present at the crash site whom, I later interviewed. They did not agree with the formal statement given by Miles Quinn to the Fox network on the show "Encounters." In his interview, he stated vehemently that there had been no fires on the night of the crash. My next step in researching the Long Island incident was to find out more about the first fire reported only minutes before the UFO was shot down.

Reverend Stanley is a local minister at a fair-sized congregation in the Brookhaven area. The fire occurred when his car attempted to start itself and then burst into flames. It was fairly difficult for me to get an interview with Reverend Stanley. Because of a barrage of media attention, he was not answering his phone. Also, he had been seriously mistreated by the local law enforcement officials and government. I was fortunate in that he did return my call, and with the understanding that I would tell the whole story of what happened on that evening, he agreed to an interview.

The following is a narration of the event as related to me by Reverend Stanley.

Reverend Stanley is a good man. He has been preaching the gospel for many years. The event had occurred several days before Thanksgiving. He had spent most of the day at the church office preparing his sermon. After locking up the church and returning home, Reverend Stanley lay back on his recliner chair. He was breathing irregularly. He felt a cold wave of fear wash through him.

"Not yet, Lord. I'm not ready." Reverend Stanley had a good soul and a good heart, but God, in his infinite wisdom, had not seen fit to give him a good body. He reached over and filled the hypodermic, measuring the insulin precisely. Too much or too little could kill him. God had seen fit to give the reverend a curse, and his curse was diabetes.

He lay back, exhausted from working on his sermon. As he was slipping off to sleep, he hardly noticed a strange sound outside. In the driveway, with a click and then slow churning, his car was trying to start itself.

"I'm dreaming," he mused, ignoring the sound. As his eyelids flickered open, he noticed his clock had stopped. The old grandfather clock's pendulum hung silent, the hands frozen on 8:33 P.M. With a shrill sound the telephone rang, rousing him to full consciousness.

"Hello," he said, picking up the receiver. Yet there was only silence at the other end. He stumbled back as a blinding flash of light streamed through his window, bathing the room in tungsten brilliance, and outside his car burst into flames. As he ran outside, he could see the rising wind driving the rapidly growing inferno within inches of his house.

Reverend Stanley rushed to the phone and dialed 911.

"911 Emergency," said a bored female voice.

"My car is on fire!" he yelled. "Send the fire trucks. Please hurry, my house is about to go up, too!"

Several minutes after the fire department had arrived, he stood numbly staring at his car. The fire had been put out and his once beautiful new car was a charred, smoking mess of melted metal. Two policemen had arrived. Officer Grisholm stared at the minister as the reverend rambled on nervously.

"It was all so strange, Officer. First my wall clock just stopped. My car tried to start itself and then burst into flames . . . and the phones were ringing and nobody was there. . . . I tell you, nobody was there at the other end."

Officer Grisholm gave him a worried look.

"Do you have any history of psychiatric problems?" he said coldly. "Are you on any prescription medications?"

"No, I don't have any such history," said the reverend, annoyed. "And yes, I take insulin. I am a diabetic."

"Of course," said the officer, picking up a syringe on the coffee table.

The policeman was treating him like some sort of mental case. Reverend Stanley didn't have much experience with law enforcement. In fact, he had never even gotten a citation or been in court. His congregation and other ministers treated him with respect and sometimes even admiration.

"You're bleeding," said Grisholm, pointing to an oozing patch of crimson on the minister's sweater.

"Oh," said Reverend Stanley numbly. "I didn't notice." The minister looked dazed. The room began to swim about him.

"That's it," said Grisholm, giving a grunt of annoyance. He led the minister to a chair and sat him down. "No drugs, my ass." He rushed to the door and shouted. "Jack! Call ER. We got a problem here. Tell them we're en route."

"Maybe you should call an ambulance," said the minister, his voice shaking.

"Don't think so. We'll handle this."

The minister began to panic and stood up.

"I said SIT!" The officer pushed Stanley down roughly. "I don't want to have to put the cuffs on you."

As the minister stumbled into the Emergency Room reception area, he was flanked by two-stern looking officers, one on either side. The reception nurse looked appalled.

"God, someone get a wheelchair for this man."

"The man's in custody," said Grisholm gruffly. "We just need a private room. This is a government matter. Somewhere isolated. Do you understand?"

The nurse looked at him defiantly. "No, I don't understand. This man is ill. He needs treatment."

The minister's heart was pounding.

"I need my insulin," he said weakly.

"First, we have some questions for you. And we need to get you secured. Then we'll talk about insulin."

The minister was placed in a small sterile room and left for almost six hours. Most of that time he spent on the cold tile floor on his knees, praying. "God, please don't let me die."

The officers entered the room finally, accompanied by a man in a dark suit.

"It's simple," said Sorenson. "We can hold you for 48 hours observation in the psych ward, or you can sign this release."

"I don't understand," said the minister.

Sorenson looked annoyed. "Don't make this tough on both of us. You've been ranting about UFOs for almost two hours, claiming they blew up your car."

"I never said anything about UFOs," whispered the minister. "I don't know what blew up my car."

"Look," barked Sorenson. "Sign this. It says the fire was caused by a frequently occurring electrical short in your car."

The minister took the pen and reluctantly scrawled his signature.

"Good," said Sorenson, stepping in the hall. "Nurse," he called out, "get this man some insulin."

The Reverend Stanley is currently in the process of filing suit against the county law enforcement department. In other UFO reports, frequently power and electrical appliances are affected by the passage of UFOs overhead. It has been speculated that the form of propulsion or engine used by many UFOs produces a strong magnetic field that plays havoc with radios, televisions, and even car electrical systems. The officers that were involved in the incident with Reverend Stanley mentioned several times that he had attributed the explosion and fire in his car to UFOs. This was not the case. In fact, the only mention of UFOs was by the officers themselves, who seemed more than casually informed about the crash that had happened that evening. Other nearby residents, one family in particular, observed and reported to local officials the formation of UFOs flying overhead at the time when Reverend Stanley's car caught fire.

The next step in my investigation would be to verify the second fire, which occurred in the park. In this case, I was even more fortunate, for I was able to contact and interview three firemen who were actually present at the fire.

five

CRASH SITE

During the course of the Southaven Park investigation, I interviewed more than a dozen firemaen. I also spoke to the fire chiefs at Brookhaven Hamlet and Yaphank fire departments. One of the firemen has since moved to another state. There were actually two films taken of the crash, along with several photographs. Although most of the fire engines were turned away and the Brookhaven radioactive fire team handled the blaze, the lime-green trucks of the local fire department, as well as the SWAT teams guarding the highway, were seen by several witnesses. The remaining wreckage of the UFO at Southaven Park was placed on trucks and taken to a barge, which conveyed it to the nearby military base. The following is the firsthand account of the scene of the fire at Southaven Park by two of the fire fighters who were there. Details of this report were reconfirmed in another interview on December 4, 1994.

Jeff Collins pulled the fire engine onto the highway and was moving at more than eighty miles an hour with neither siren nor lights on. The fire chief, another truck, and two other fire fighters were already at the scene of the UFO crash. They passed several parked cars, their drivers standing outside, watching the raging fire at Southaven Park in the distance. The sound of helicopters filled the air as a squadron of black, unmarked military choppers moved swiftly, barely skimming the water a few hundred feet above the bay. They sped by two green troop carriers heading toward the scene.

"If the chief wasn't so insistent, I would never go this fast. Especially without lights or a siren," said Jeff Collins. "We'll be lucky if we even get there without getting in an accident." The fire fighter at his side, Jo Beth, nodded in agreement and poked curiously at the bulge in Jeff's jacket.

"Video camera," he said. "If anyone says anything, I will say it's for that training seminar I teach." He looked toward the south, where flames rose above the trees and huge clouds of oddly colored smoke billowed up into the night sky. "That is some fire. I can see why they called out so many departments. It's going to be a bitch to contain it."

Jo Beth frowned. "Certainly looks serious. The chief was the most stressed I've ever seen him. And that document he read to us. That was weird."

"I know," said Jeff. "I can't believe we actually have an SOP for a UFO crash right there in the manual. Been there for years. Why would the government go to the trouble of including provisions for handling such a thing if they didn't exist? And he certainly was adamant that we not discuss what we see with the press or reporters."

"So you brought a camera," said Jo Beth. "You realize our chief got a call from the government and you realize they stated everything about this is classified. They are not going appreciate you taking a video of it."

"I don't plan to be that obvious about it. Who else has been called in on this?" said Jeff.

"Over seven fire departments and the unit for handling radioactive fires at Brookhaven Lab. Very high-tech team over there." It was 9:07 P.M. on November 22, 1992. and it was very cold and very dark.

As Jeff and Jo Beth reached the main entrance to Southaven Park, they could see three other trucks had already arrived. Having a real problem seeing the road, Jeff flicked on his headlights. A small group of Special Forces wearing black jumpsuits and carrying automatic weapons stood blocking the entrance to the park. The highway had also been blocked off and was guarded by a dozen or more National Guard.

"Turn off your lights," hissed one of the soldiers, and waved them past. Jeff could see the flames licking above the treetops as they proceeded down the main road toward the fire. As they neared the site, Jeff could see that limbs had been sheared off and some of the upper branches had caught fire. Ahead they could see a smoldering metallic object. It was broken in several large pieces. A milky white cloud flowed from the interior of the craft.

"Jo Beth!" The chief walked briskly towards them as they stopped the fire truck and got out. "Start hosing down some of the surrounding trees. Jeff, I want you over here with me. I have something to show you."

As Jeff entered the clearing, scrambling to keep up with the chief, he gasped in amazement. On the ground were two bodies wrapped in shiny Mylar. By the craft, another figure was slumped over, but still moving. The figure was badly injured but watching everything. As they approached, its head turned quickly. It had large dark eyes that followed their movement.

"What in the hell is that?" said Jeff, moving closer and looking at the creature.

"It's one of the pilots of the craft who survived," said the chief.

"It's not human." Jeff shuddered.

"Obviously," said the chief, annoyed. "What would you expect? This ain't no Stealth jet. And I'll tell you what else. This sure the hell ain't no ordinary fire. Never seen anything like it."

Shit, thought Jeff, fumbling under his jacket. *I got to get this on film. And I've got to keep the damned record light off so no one will know I've got a camcorder.* Anticipating how difficult it would be to shoot from the hip without being able to used the view finder, Jeff had preset the recorder for autofocus. As he turned on the camera and moved to get closer to the alien, he spoke a little louder than usual to cover up the whir of the camera. "Why did you want me to see this?"

"This whole incident presents me with a major problem," said the chief. "You're my number two man, Jeff. The others have a lot of respect for you. I figure they'll listen to you. No one is to say anything about what they saw this evening to anyone. Even to their families. As far as the outside world is concerned, this is nothing more than a standard rescue and recovery operation. Not a word of this gets out to anyone, understand? What we don't need is a lot of wild stories about UFOs and alien bodies hitting the newspapers. I need your full cooperation on this. Do I have it?"

"Of course. That goes without saying," said Jeff. "I can see your point. I certainly won't say anything about this and I'm sure the other fire fighters will understand the situation and do the same."

Jo Beth ran up to the men, her face covered with sweat.

"We need to clear a firebreak," said Jo Beth breathlessly. "I don't know what that craft was made of, but it is burning a hell of a lot hotter than anything I've ever dealt with before. The surrounding trees are just going up in flash burn. If we don't contain this fire in the next few minutes, it's going to spread throughout the whole park."

The chief shook his head. "No firebreak. Don't even think about getting near that craft. It's highly radioactive. Brookhaven team told me that. They're the only ones with radiation suits." The chief looked at several SWAT team members who were guarding the extraterrestrial and shook his head. "I wonder if they were told that this is a radioactive fire. Well, that's really too bad. They are probably getting quite a dose just standing that close to the craft, but I have my own people to worry about. We don't have any suits and I don't want any problems cropping up later with you people. We'll be out of here in a few minutes anyway. We got a copter coming up dumping chemical on it. That should do the job."

Jo Beth turned and shuddered as she noticed the bodies on the ground and then the surviving alien, who seemed to return her stare with large liquid, black eyes.

"Whatever that is, it's not from this planet," she said.

"No, it sure the hell isn't. Here comes that damn special agent, Sorenson." A man entered the clearing and signaled for them to join him and two other military types.

"So," whispered Jo Beth to Jeff as the chief walked toward the agent. "I suppose you are filming this."

"Yes," said Jeff. "Absolutely. Wish I had brought another videotape."

"Well," Jo Beth said. "I haven't seen anything with a head like that." Despite the chief's instructions, she moved closer to the smoking wreckage. The three SWAT team guards gave her a hostile look but did not speak. Whatever the original shape of the craft had been, it was difficult to make out its shape now. It was scattered in heaps of glowing aluminumlike debris about the clearing.

A van pulled up and several figures wearing radiation suits emerged.

"Brookhaven special unit," mumbled Jeff to Jo Beth, "or government. Kinda hard to tell in those suits."

They approached the two Mylar bundles on the ground that were the bodies of the dead aliens. Once those had been transferred to the canvas-enclosed truck bed, they stood looking at the remaining alien. The arms of the creature were held part way up and seemed to rest on an invisible cushion. They did not remain still but instead floated up and down a few inches at irregular intervals. None of the team was that anxious to touch the creature, even with the radiation suit and thick gloves between human and alien flesh. As one of the braver members took a step forward, the creature's head whipped around in the disturbing lizardlike fashion they had observed before. It moved very quickly, so quickly that one moment it was sitting against the tree, and the next it was lying on the stretcher. The figure that was going to assist it stepped back, relieved that it would not be necessary to actually touch the creature.

"It is intelligent," said Jeff.

"Of course," said Jo Beth. "After all, they built the craft that must have carried them light-years from their home. They probably underestimated our military forces, poor things."

After a brief exchange of words with the chief, Sorenson turned toward the remaining personnel and shouted in a clear and commanding voice.

"Okay, I would like all of you, except for the rad unit, to clear out. This is now a secured area and will be for the next few days. The fire chief has informed me that several choppers will be here to cover the area with chemicals. The Brookhaven team can handle it from here." He then turned toward Jeff and Jo Beth.

"Now let me tell you precisely what has just occurred here." He paused, looking into Jeff's eyes intently. "Nothing. Nothing has occurred. There hasn't been a fire in the Southaven Park area for several years. If anyone inquires about this, you are to do two things. First, you are to emphatically and convincingly assure them that you have checked the reports for today and there were only two incidents, one involving a faulty electrical system in the vehicle of a Reverend Stanley, and one false alarm. And second, you are to write down the name, phone number, and source of the inquiry so we can check it out."

"I see," said Jeff coldly. He wondered if his camera was still getting all this. What would happen if this special agent Sorenson discovered he was filming the whole thing?"

"No fire?" said Jo Beth, stunned.

"That is correct, Miss. Do you know what the term 'breach of national security' means?" said Sorenson.

"Well, yes," said Jo Beth, "but I don't get it."

"Well, let me make it perfectly clear," said Sorenson, becoming annoyed. "We have two scenarios here. The first is very simple. You both get on your fire truck and head back to the station. You remember today exactly as I have described it. You go on with your lives, keep working your jobs, living where you are."

"The second scenario?" said Jeff.

"Fighting fires is a dangerous profession, isn't it?" said Sorenson. "Local fire fighters get hurt, even killed quite frequently. So let us say that at a particularly nasty blaze in the near future they find two charred bodies, two fire fighters who just happened to be overcome by smoke and burned to death while trying to rescue someone trapped inside. How unfortunate, and yet that would solve the problem of two very serious security leaks. Do we understand each other?"

"Only too well," said Jeff.

As per instructions, most of the firemen and agencies have repeated Sorenson's version of the events of the evening of November 22, 1992. The caretaker for the park has restated that there have been no fires at Southaven Park for ten years. The park was closed for almost a week after the crash and no one was allowed to enter. Scars on the trunks of trees and residual ash indicate the presence of a fire two, not ten, years ago in the park.

The three teenagers who saw the crash, especially Jennifer, would begin the second part of the investigation. With the removal of the craft itself to several different locations, the most obvious path to follow in the investigation would be to search for two things at Brookhaven Lab: a particle accelerator capable of producing the quark-gluon plasma beam and some type of evidence that the aliens, both dead and alive, had passed through the underground labs. Jennifer and her friends were about to discover both of these.

SIX

BROOKHAVEN

The Southaven Park incident was witnessed by people of all ages. The youngest witness I spoke to was only eleven years old and had actually ridden his bicycle through the park and saw the fire. Being quite an accomplished artist, he was kind enough to draw me a picture of one of the craft.

The second part of the drama, as told to me by Jennifer, begins at a small sandwich shop at the base of the hill near the park.

"Hi, guys!" Jennifer Biels entered the sandwich shop.

It was a truly cold December day, and she was the first customer to enter the shop in almost an hour. The owner had called just minutes earlier and told the boys to close early. They were just about to turn on the security system and leave when Jennifer arrived.

"Well, I said I'd drop in. I need a favor."

"What kind of favor?" said Richard.

Jennifer fiddled with her purse and held out several color brochures for the boys to look at.

"I gathered some information on Brookhaven National Laboratory. You remember what we saw that night. Well, apparently Brookhaven Lab produced the technology for whatever shot that object in the sky."

Richard stepped forward. "Yes, I remember the UFO crash. Why?"

Jennifer pulled out a folder that contained a large sheaf of newspaper clippings.

"Well," she said, showing a photocopied clipping to Richard, "looks like this is not the first time something like this has happened. Listen to this." Jennifer began reading aloud.

Mona Rowe, who is a spokesperson for the Brookhaven National Laboratory, said she was driving home that evening and off to the south, in the night sky she saw what looked like flares.

"But maybe they weren't flares," she told a reporter. "Maybe my perception was colored by the fact that I work in a very scientifically minded environment."

"And this," said Jennifer, holding out another clipping. "A writer named Michaels called me last night and was talking about something called a quark-gluon plasma beam. He said he had talked to Mona Rowe personally and she had described to him how the plasma was produced." She continued, reading the second article.

Ms. Rowe actually made enquiries about this before answering. There is, indeed, a Star Wars program at the lab, but all the scientists she did ask said they knew nothing about alien bodies, spacecraft, or supercomputer weapons. In fact, there was no way, one of them ventured, to hook up such a weapon to a superconductor.

"Well, I heard my mom and dad talking the other night. They were fighting. You know Dad is always stressed about something, but he seemed really upset. Anyway, although Mona Rowe denies the fire or the crash, I am positive they are keeping an alien there."

"No!" said Richard, choking on the root beer he was drinking.

"Anyway, I need a favor. That writer guy keeps asking a lot of questions about Brookhaven. You know he even talked to a man who was driving on the highway right near the park. The man says he saw a UFO get hit with something and then crash in the park. Just like what we saw. He also said that Fox is producing a show called 'Encounters.' They sent a reporter down there who did an interview with Mona. Anyway, the writer guy said it would sure be interesting to go under the facility and look around. There are tons of tunnels down there."

Jennifer paused, taking a deep breath. "So what do you say? Are you game?"

"Why are you doing this?" said Robert, giving Jennifer a critical look. "Is this guy paying a lot of money or something?"

"No, it's not about money," she said. "I just think people should know what happened. And besides, aren't you just a little curious?"

"Well, I am," said Todd. He locked the register and flipped the open/closed sign in the sandwich shop window. We'll need a flashlight. It's going to be real dark at Brookhaven by the time we get there, and there's no way we have a prayer of getting in the front entrance."

Alison Wyer is an employee working at Brookhaven Lab. I have withheld her true identity to protect not only her job but to shield her from possible CIA or government reprisals. Combined with the information given by the three teenagers, Alison and her friend Carol were very helpful in establishing the presence of the alien as well as confirming diagnostic tests that were done on alien tissue and DNA. Alison is highly trained, with a master's degree in microbiology and chemistry. Unfortunately, she is overqualified for her job, which is basically sterilizing and destroying petri dishes and maintaining blood and agar specimens in the ovens. The trail to her small corner of the world in the basement of Brookhaven Lab would lead not only to evidence that alien bodies and tissue had been analyzed at the lab, but to records and documents that would indicate a live alien had been kept there as well.

"Terrific," said the woman, looking at the smoking mass of fused plastic as huge clouds of hot steam billowed out of the autoclave. What had once been a neatly stacked tray of petri dishes filled with blood and agar was now one formless, sterile blob. Alison Wyer had worked at Brookhaven Lab for almost three years. Between her classes at a nearby college to finish her master's degree and her night-shift job at the lab, she simply had no life. She worked alone in her small corner in the dimly lit basement. She washed slides, autoclaved thousands of cultures, and for excitement she would take breaks with her friend Carol, who worked in the pathology lab. Alison Wyer was completely unprepared for the three teenagers who burst into her tiny, tiled room, and in a few moments, eliminated the word *boredom* from her vocabulary.

"What am I going to tell my parents?" said Jennifer, and then turned and gave Alison a desperate look. "You've got to help us. If you don't, we're going to be in a lot of trouble. My mom could even get fired."

Call Security, thought Alison. But for some reason she didn't. "How can I help you?" she said.

"I am not sure," said Jennifer. "Go close the door, Richard." She turned back to face Alison. "But we better think of something fast, or that security guy is going to find us. He almost got us upstairs but we beat him to the elevator."

"And he's too lazy to take the stairs." Todd grinned. "He actually waited for the next elevator."

Down the hall and to the right, just around the comer, the elevator opened. They listened as the click of Bob Whitaker's overly polished black regulation shoes echoed in the hallway. "We better do something quick," said Richard, watching through a tiny window in the door and seeing the security guard round the corner.

"The oven," said Alison, motioning toward a chrome door in the back of the room. "That's the only place you can hide. I'll do my best to get rid of him."

"The what!" said Richard, his eyes widening. "No way."

"No, no, no!" Alison took his arm, pulling him toward the back of the room. "It's where we incubate the blood cultures. It's body temperature. A little warm, but that's all I can think of."

Alison opened the large door and the teenagers hesitantly stepped in.

"I don't like this." Todd's voice was silenced by a loud click as the door swung shut.

There was a dim, sixty-watt bulb illuminating the interior in a ghostly yellow hue. On either side of them, racks of round red petri dishes fermented in the semidarkness. It was warm, uncomfortably warm, almost stifling.

The security guard knocked. "Yes?" said Alison, briskly dipping a large basket of slides into an alcohol bath.

The guard entered. His eyes scanned the room suspiciously.

"We have some teenagers that broke into the facility," he said. "You must have heard them running down the hall. I know they passed this way."

"Nobody ran by here." Alison held up a slide and rubbed it meticulously with a cotton cloth. "It's dead quiet at night. I would have heard them. I sure heard you coming."

"Are you positive?" The guard looked around the bleak room, trying to imagine where the teenagers could be hiding. "They didn't have time to make it all the way down the hall. There isn't another door until the pathology lab. They had to come in here."

Alison clicked her fingernails nervously on the metal counter. "Don't know what to tell you. I have a phone. I know the security extension. If I see or hear anything, you'll be the first one to know."

"You know . . ." he said, seeming to lose track of his words. "You know, we had some other kids on the grounds with their damn three wheelers. Tried to set one of the buildings on fire. I really get tired of this. We need better outside security instead of those damn cameras."

Alison, without thinking, nervously glanced at the door to the oven.

The guard smiled. "I see. How could I have missed it?" He seemed incredibly pleased, the way only a policeman or security officer can be pleased when they catch a person in a lie. "And what exactly is in there?" he said, moving up to Alison, looking her squarely in the eye.

Alison remained silent.

"I'm going to give you one last chance to level with me, Ms—" He looked at her badge. "—Alison Wyer. What's in there? You realize this is a secured area now. You could lose your job."

"I wasn't aware this was a secured area," she said. "Since when did that happen?"

"It's not important," he said, losing his patience. "What's in there?"

She moved toward the door.

"It's an incubation room for blood cultures. You are welcome to go in."

The guard moved swiftly toward the door. As his hand grasped the handle, Alison said, "But up to now, I'm the only one that will go in there."

"And why exactly is that, Ms Wyer?"

"Well, I don't really understand it. You know all the evidence we have indicates that the AIDS virus is not airborne."

The security guard whipped his hand back. "AIDS virus! Shit, are you people experimenting with AIDS down here?"

Alison wanted to laugh. The man's expression had changed from one of contempt and total confidence to one of pure, undisguised fear.

"We are not experimenting. But those are blood cultures and they are part of the screens we do." She sat back on her stool, smugly crossing her arms. "Like I said. According to most of our data, it is not airborne."

"No, thanks," said the guard. "If you see those kids, you call me."

As Alison opened the door, she did laugh this time. All three teenagers looked horrified.

"Not to worry," she said. "We don't do any work with AIDS and none of those plates have even been inoculated. So exactly what are you doing here? I just risked my job. Tell me, and it better be good."

No one spoke for several moments. They all jumped as there was a loud knock on the door.

"Ally," said a female voice. "You in there?"

A tall, dark-haired Hispanic woman stepped in. "Ah." Carol laughed. "The fugitives. So this is where they are."

Richard looked puzzled. "How did you know?"

Carol smiled. "El Jerko. That guard came by Pathology. I think he's given up. He took the other elevator back to the main floor."

Alison looked at her watch. It was 3:30 A.M. "Is it that late? God, I'm hungry."

"Me, too," said Carol. "Come on over to the morgue. I promise you, no one will come looking for you there."

The morgue was one of the "doesn't exist" areas in Brookhaven. When it came to the UFO crash at Southaven Park, the laboratory offered a varied assortment of items and places that were categorically denied to the press and emphatically stated, "I'm sorry. This item or place simply doesn't exist."

One could start with a fire that never happened, and Day-glo green fire trucks exclusive to Brookhaven. Fire trucks that were seen responding to that fire by more than a dozen witnesses. This was followed by a radiation suit discovered in the park, which officials denied knowing. Then there was a fleet of unmarked black helicopters that rushed to the scene. The official military statement was "There have been no experimental air crashes in the last eleven years." There was a quark-gluon plasma beam, which one scientist sincerely stated could not be used as a weapon. There was a statement that they were no longer part of the Star Wars project, when it was still clearly indicated in their budget that they were.

But most singularly, and relevant to this particular part of the Southaven Park story, was a pathology department, a genetic analyzer, and most hotly denied, a morgue. A morgue that some sources say an alien corpse briefly resided in, and for this reason alone, the morgue never existed.

CAROL SAT on a stool, eagerly munching on a medium-rare roast beef sandwich.

"I don't see how you can eat in here," said Todd dryly, observing a human brain in a glass jar. "Pretty weird looking," he said. "Biggest one I've ever seen." Todd really hadn't seen all that many brains in his life, but the organ did appear considerably larger than normal. "At least there are no bodies here."

"There are sometimes," said Carol, her voice muffled by roast beef. "In fact, last week this place was completely secured. They had some kind of body in here. A lot of those organ samples and tissue slices weren't here when I left. I am surprised they didn't take them with them. Probably someone just forgot. Anyway, last week I couldn't even come in here. They gave me a few days off."

"Yeah, me too," said Alison. "I thought that was pretty strange. I have to beg them even to give me my sick days . . . like I'm pulling teeth. Then they just up and give me a whole week off."

Richard and Jennifer remained silent. They had never been in a morgue before. They certainly weren't hungry. The whole placed reeked of formaldehyde. The multitude of human organs, the butcher-shop scale where they weighed those organs, and the vast assortment of cutting tools, especially the circular saw, were bad enough. Yet on several trays were laid out thinly sliced sections of hearts and other unfamiliar internal organs, much like the cold meats at Togo's.

Jennifer stared at one tray and mumbled, "God, you slice up people's hearts."

"I forget," said Carol, finishing her sandwich and taking a swig

of her Diet Pepsi. "I'm pretty much used to it. When I was in training some of the interns and students would come in here . . ." She
picked up the circular saw. "We used this to cut open the skull and
remove the brain. Some of the students would get pretty pale, even
nauseated. Doesn't bother me."

"Enough," said Jennifer, waving her arm and feeling her stomach heave. "Can we leave now?"

"Can't leave yet," Carol said. "I would guess, if that guard is
like the rest of our night security, about 4 A.M., he will take a serious snooze. Lot of them have day jobs. If you take off your shoes,
and take the far corridor which doesn't go past his desk, you
shouldn't have any problem." She looked at the teenagers, her voice
becoming more stern. "Now, why exactly are you here?"

Jennifer told the two women the story of how they had seen
the crash and had heard that they were keeping two aliens they
had recovered at Brookhaven.

Carol laughed. "You sure you don't work for the *National
Enquirer?*" she said. "I don't want to burst your bubble, but I have
been here for a hell of a long time and I have yet to do an autopsy
on a little green man."

Todd grunted. "Well, I've had it. What a wild goose chase. We
went up and down those tunnels for half the night and I didn't see
anything that looked like a weapon. Then that security guard
chased us and finally we end up here, in a morgue."

Jennifer had recovered from her nausea and was examining a
set of slides on the counter. "What exactly are these?" she said,
holding out a slide.

"Oh," said Carol, looking at the slide thoughtfully. "Government stuff. Who knows. Maybe some serial killer the CIA is tracking. They want a gene analysis. We do that."

Jennifer reached out and pointed to the label on the slide.
"NTL," she said. "That's what my mom and dad were fighting about
last night." She stared at the slide incredulously. "Nonterrestrial
Lifeform."

seven

TOP SECRET

Jennifer Biels, after seeing the Nonterrestrial Lifeform slides in the Brookhaven Lab, continued to secure additional documents for me concerning the dissection and lab tests done on the aliens, and also several "Top Secret" documents from the Departments of Defense and Energy dealing with government involvement in the UFO cover-up, as well as specific instructions to our national defense organizations on dealing with UFOs. We have secured a declassification release to print the following information. Although it is a bit out of character for the government to actually release this type of information, the current administration, the Department of Energy, and the CIA have taken a much more positive and realistic approach to UFOs. All documents are reproduced exactly as received, with misspellings and inconsistencies intact.

AUTOPSY REPORT ON NTL ANALYSIS

Photo number 1 showed an alien being on an autopsy table which is a metal table with runnels and traps underneath to trap fluid and feces. Body appeared to be a little short of 4 feet. Table about 7 foot. No clothing on body, no genitalia, body completely heterous, head was a rounded cranium, slightly enlarged, eyes almond shaped, slits where nose would be, extremely small mouth, receding chin line, holes where ears would be. Photo was taken at angle, side view, looking at body from 45-degree elevation, left hand was visible, head was facing to left, body was right to left (head on right, feet on left), eyes were closed and appeared to be oriental looking and almond shaped, left hand slightly longer than normal, wrist coming down just about 2 to 3 inches above the knees. Wrist appeared to be articulated in a fashion that allowed a double joint with 3 digit fingers. Wrist was very slender. There was no thumb. A palm was almost nonexistent. The three fingers were a direct extension from the wrist.

Color of the skin was a bluish gray, dark bluish gray. At the base of the body there was a darker color, indicating body was dead for some time. Body fluids or blood had settled to base of body. This indicated that body had been examined before beginning autopsy.

Pictures showed beginning stages of autopsy, following standard procedure, body was slit from crotch to just under chin and green viscous liquid was in evidence. There were internal organs but these could not be identified. Photos thereafter concerned specific areas of internal organs of what appeared as small cluster of multi-valve heart or at least two hearts within the cadaver. No accurate description of autopsy report or what was found with corpse accompanying photos. Indications that there was no stomach or digestive tract per se. Later analysis showed that fluid within the body was chloropyhyl-based liquid which apparently dealt with photosynthesis or similar process. The report theorized that nourishment was taken in through mouth; however, since there was no digestive tract or anything of this nature, the waste products were excreted through skin.

One section of the report did specify that cadavers were extremely odorous, but this could be accounted for by either deterioration or a number of things, but theory was that waste was excreted through pores of skin. They could only theorize in report because there was no xenobiology.

Other photos dealt with a body that was vivisectioned in various ways. At one point, the head was removed from the body and photographed and autopsy was performed on head The cranium was opened and brain matter was photographed and evident. Interesting thing about photo was that there was a ridge bone or dividing partition-type bone running directly through center of skull, from front to back, as though dividing two brains, one from the *other. This seemed apparent from the picture. The skin was completely removed from the cranial structure and the skull was laid bare as much as possible.*

At one point the skull was cut directly in half and photo showed underdeveloped esophagus and nasal cavities. No clear photo of eye orbs as we know them, just complete vivisection of skull itself. Numerous photos of flesh of the being starting with cutaneous and subcutaneous microphotographic plates. Appeared to be cellular studies done under microscopic and electronmicroscopic type photos. Extreme magnification of tissue samples.

PROJECT BLUE DOCUMENTS NOT PUBLISHED
TOP SECRET

Publication was withdrawn from pouch. It measured approx. 8" by 11" with grey cover. Heavily bound, paper back style similar to technical manuals. Across the center front it read, "Grudge / Blue Book Report No. 13." It was dated 1953-(1963). In the lower right-hand corner was AFSN 2246-3. In upper left-hand corner was the word "annotated." Across the front upper right-hand corner to lower left-hand corner was red tape indicating code red security measures. Across the front was stamped in red ink "Top Secret Need to Know Only Crypto Clearance 14 Required." Inside front cover upper left-hand corner were handwritten notations in ink which were blacked out by black felt pen.

Inside cover sheet was basically the same information as the cover. Second page was a title page. Next page after that was an appendix with numerous notations made in it. Notations dealt with inserts of what appeared to be photos and additional notes. At bottom of third page it read G / BV Page 1 of 624 pages. Title page was subject letter. Complete list of appendix not remember. Title. Some notes on the practical applications of the Worst Nemo equations.

Table of contents, Part 1. "On the design of generators to accomplish strain free molecular translation." Part 2, The generation of space time discontinuums, closed, opened and folded." Part 3, on the generation of temporary pseudo acceleration locas." Part 1, Chapter 1, "design criteria for a simple generator and control system referring to equation 17 appendix A." Part 2, Chapter 1, *"Continuation of Einstein's Theory of Relativity to final conclusion."* Part 3, Chapter 1, *"Possible applications of Einstein's theory of relativity at conclusion."*

Part 1, Chapter 2, *reports of UFO encounters, classifications "Close Encounters of the 1st Kind," subtitle sightings and witnesses.* Part 2, chapter 2, *"Close Encounters of the 2nd," subtitle UFO sightings witnessed within close proximity. Part 3, chapter 2 "Close Encounters of the 3rd Kind," subtitle UFO encounters and extraterrestrial life forms witnessed and personal encounters. Subtitle, "Colonies, relocation thereof." Case histories. Chapter 3, Part 1, titled "military Encounters with UFO's." Part 2, Chapter 3, "Military Reports Concerning Sightings on Radar and Electronic Surveillance of UFO's." Subsection 2, Analysis Report, J. Allen Hynek, Lt. Col. Friend. Appendix continued on for about 5 pages. Opening subject page consisted of a report of the findings as written by Lt. Col. Friend and his analysis.*

Must stress at this point that the version seen was annotated. **There were inserts that were added to this copy after it had been initially printed.** *Sections remembered very vividly are the photographs and the reports concerning captive sights of various UFO's to include Mexico, Sweden, United States and Canada. There were also what was then classified Close Encounters of the 3rd kind. It was made very clear that these people whom it was determined had genuine CE 3's were moved in the middle of the night by Air Force personnel and relocated to various sites in the Midwest and Northwest parts of the United States. In many cases these people experienced physical ailments from exposure to various types of radiation.*

One case especially noted and remembered very vividly was entitled "Darlington Farm Case" out of Ohio. Case apparently took place in October 1953. Man, wife and 13-year-old son were sitting down at dinner table. As they sat there the lights in the farm house began to dim. Dogs and animals raised ruckus on outside. 13-year-old boy got up from dinner table to see what was going on. Called his mother and father to come look at the funny light in the sky. Father and mother went out onto the porch. When they got out on the porch one of the dogs broke loose from leash beside house and came running around front. Boy began chasing it into the open field.

As mother and father watched the light come down from the sky. They described it as a round ball of fire and it began to hover over the field where the boy and dog had run to. As they stood and watched, the mother and father heard the boy start screaming for help whereupon the father grabbed his shotgun which was right next to the door and began to run out into the field with the mother following. When the father got to the field he saw his son being carried away by what looked like little men, into this huge fiery looking object. As it took off the father fired several rounds at the object, to no avail. They found the dog, its head had been crushed but no sign of the boy or any other footprints of the little men who apparently carried him off. Father immediately called the Darlington police and they immediately came out to investigate. The official report read that the boy had run off and was lost in the forest which bordered the farm. Within 48 hours the Air Force made the determination that the family was to be relocated and the mother and father were picked up by Air Force Intelligence and all personal belongings and possessions were loaded into U.S. Air Force trucks and moved to a northwestern relocation site.

The mother was in shock and had to go through a great deal of psychotherapy and deprogramming as did father. One interesting aspect about this case was classification under Air Force report which read it was a genuine CE 3 and that for the good of national security the mother and father had been relocated to relocation zones Z21-14. Not sure whether this indicated map grid coordinates or latitude longitude. According to the report there were at least four relocation sites across the United States. Depending upon which type of encounter these people had, the report indicated that there were extensive medical facilities available at the relocation sites to deal with all medical emergencies up to and including radiation poisoning. The report mentioned a site located in the Utah-Nevada area, but no indication of its purpose or what it was for.

Report gave clear indication of reports of human mutilations, most notably was a case witnessed by Air Force personnel in which an Air Force Sgt. E-6 by the name of Jonathan P. Lovette was observed being taken captive aboard what appeared to be a UFO at the WHITE sands Missile Test Range in New Mexico. This abduction took place in March of 1956 at about 0300 local and was witnessed by Major William Cunningham of the United States Air Force

Missile Command near Holloman Air Force Base.

Major Cunningham and Sgt. Lovelle were out in a field down-range from the launch sites looking for debris from a missile test when Sgt. Lovette went over the ridge of a small sand dune and was out of sight for a time. Major Cunningham heard Sgt. Lovette scream in what was described as terror or agony. The Major, thinking Lovette had been bitten by a snake or something ran over the crest of the dune and saw Sgt. Lovette being dragged into what appeared to him and was described as being a silvery disk-like object which hovered in the air approximately 15 to 20 feet. Major Cunningham described what appeared to be a long snake-like object which was wrapped around the sergeant's legs and was dragging him to the craft. Major Cunningham admittedly froze as the sergeant was dragged inside the disc and observed the disc and observed the disc going up into the sky very quickly. Major Cunningham got on the jeep radio and reported the incident to Missile Control whereupon Missile Control confirmed a radar sighting. Search parties went into the desert looking for Sgt. Lovette. Major Cunningham's report was taken and he was admitted to the White Sands Base Dispensary for observation.

The search for Sgt. Lovette continues for three days at the end of which his nude body was found approximately ten miles down-range. The body had been mutilated; the tongue had been removed from the lower portion of the jaw. An incision had been made just under the tip of the chin and extended all the way back to the esophagus and larynx. He had been emasculated and his eyes had been removed. Also, his anus had been removed and there were comments in the report on the apparent surgical skill of the removal of these items including the genitalia. The report commented that the anus and the genitalia had been removed "as though a plug" which in the case of the anus extended all the way to the colon. There was no sign of blood within the system. The initial autopsy report confirmed that the system had been completely drained of blood and that there was no vascular collapse due to death by bleeding. Sub-comment was added that this was unusual because in any body who dies of bleeding or in the case of a complete blood loss there is always vascular collapse. Also noted was that when the body was found there were a number of dead predatory type birds within the area who apparently had died after trying to partake of the sergeant's body.

There were a number of extremely grisly black and white photo-graphs. From all indications the body had been exposed to the ele-ments for at least a day or two. The New Mexico sun in the desert is extremely hot and debilitating under normal circumstances.

TOP SECRET GOVERNMENT DIRECTIVES FOR MILITARY INTERACTION WITH UFOS
Document 3

(Declassification and permission to publish secured by author J.B. Michaels)

THE JOINT CHIEFS OF STAFF

JOINT COMMUNICATIONS-ELECTRONICS COMMITTEE

Washington, D. C.

7. This document contains information affecting the National Defense of the United States, within the meaning of the espionage laws, title 18, U.S.C., sections 793 and 794. The transmission or the revelation of its contents in any manner to an unauthorized person is prohibited by law.

102. Scope.

a. This publication is limited to the reporting of informa-tion of vital importance to the security of the United States of America, its territories and possessions, which, in the opinion of the observer, requires prompt defensive and / or investigative action by the U.S. Armed Forces.

Chapter 2 CIRVIS REPORTS SECTION I — GENERAL

201. Information to be reported and when to report.
(1) immediately (except over foreign territory—see Art. 215)
(b) Unidentified flying objects.

205. Precedence (priority of transmission).
Transmission of CIRVIS reports will be preceded by or in-clude the international "URGENCY SIGNAL," military precedence of "EMERGENCY," or "EMERGENCY U.S. GOVERNMENT," as appropriate for the communications means, system of service employed.

206. Addressing.
A. All CIRVIS messages will be multiple addressed to:
(1) CG, AIR DEFENSE COMMAND, ENT AFB, COLO-
RADO SPRINGS, COLORADO. (commanding general, air
defense command, ent air force base, Colorado Springs,
Colorado.)
(2) SEDEF WASHINGTON D C (SECRETARY OF
DEFENSE, WASHINGTON, D.C.) who will transmit copies
of the reports to the CENTRAL INTELLIGENCE AGENCY
and other appropriate agencies.
(3) Nearest U.S. Military Command with which communi-
cations may be effected.

208. Acceptance of Responsibility for CIRVIS Reports.
(a) All military communications activities described in para-
graph 206, when receiving or being asked to relay or deliver
CIRVIS reports, shall accept, forward and / or deliver
immediately without question, the contents of such reports
EXACTLY AS RECEIVED by the most expeditious means
available, in strict accordance with the instructions con-
tained herein. All civilian communications activities will
be urged to follow the same procedure. Insofar as is practi-
cable, military facilities of the United States of America or
those under United States control will be utilized.

(e) Fixed and mobile military communications facilities, and
military personnel having occasion to handle CIRVIS reports
are responsible, and all civilian facilities and personnel are
urged to lend assistance in all cases required in expediting
CIRVIS reports. Maximum care must be taken by all per-
sons handling CIRVIS reports to insure positive immediate
delivery.

SECTION 3 — SECURITY

209. MILITARY AND CIVILIAN.
(A) All persons aware of the contents or existence of a CIRVIS
report are governed by the Communications Act of 1934 and
amendments thereto, and espionage laws.

(2) CIRVIS reports contain information affecting the National Defense of the United States within the meaning of the espionage laws, 18 U.S. Code 793 and 794. The unauthorized transmission or revelation of the contents of CIRVIS reports in any manner is prohibited.

LIST OF ALIEN BODIES RECOVERED
Document 4

22	July	1947	Roswell New Mexico	4	Bodies
13	Feb	1948	Aztec New Mexico	12	Bodies
7	Jul	1948	Mexico So. of Laredo Texas	1	Body
1952			Spitzbergen Norway	2	Bodies
14	Aug	1952	Ely Nevada	16	Bodies
10	Sep	1950	Albuquerque New Mexico	3	Bodies
18	Apr	1953	S.W. Arizona	No	Bodies
20	May	1953	Kingman Arizona	1	Body
19	Jun	1953	Laredo Texas	4	Bodies
10	Jul	1953	Johanisburg S. Africa	5	Bodies
13	Oct	1953	Dutton Montana	4	Bodies
5	May	1955	Brighton England	4	Bodies
18	Jul	1957	Carlsbad New Mexico	4	Bodies
12	Jun	1962	Holloman AFB New Mexico	2	Bodies
10	Nov	1964	Ft. Riley Kansas	9	Bodies
27	Oct	1966	N.W. Arizona	1	Body
1966-1968			5 Crashes in Kentucky / Ohio Area (one UFO intact removed)	3	Bodies
18	Jul	1972	Morroco Sahara Desert	3	Bodies
10	Jul	1973	NW Arizona	5	Bodies
12	May	1976	Australian Desert	4	Bodies
22	Jun	1977	NW Arizona	5	Bodies
5	Apr	1977	SW OHIO	11	Bodies
17	Aug	1977	TOBASCO MEXICO	2	Bodies
	May	1978	Bolivia	No	Bodies
	Nov	1988	Afghanistan	7	Bodies
	May	1989	South Africa	2	ET living

June 1989	*UFO & 2 ET Transported in*	
	2 Galaxy Transports—Wright-Patterson	
	AFB from South Africa.	
July 1989	*Siberia*	*9 ET living*
Nov 1992	*Brookhaven Hamlet, Long Island*	*1 ET living*
		2 Bodies

THE UFO CRASH/RETRIEVAL SYNDROME (STATUS REPORT II: NEW SOURCES, NEW DATA) by Leonard H. Stringfield is published by MUTUAL UFO NETWORK INC., 103 Oldtowne Road, Sequin Texas 78155. It has a January 1980 copyright date. The report interviews several medical doctors who did autopsies on ET bodies from UFO crash sites. ET had large heads and were around 4 ft tall. They have small noses and mouths with no ears or hair. The ET photo that I have was taken by an ET and has an eye diameter of an inch. He has his left hand raised in a salute. That hand has 4 fingers on it with one finger twice as long as either outside finger. The photo was taken at a range of 3 ft from the waist up. Brain capacity is 1800 cc versus 1300 cc for the average human. The skin is grey or ashen and under the microscope appears meshlike. This meshlike appearance gives it the reptilian texture of granular skinned lizards like iguana or chameleon. There was a colorless liquid in the body without red cells, no lymphocytes, no hemoglobin. There was no digestive system, intestinal, alimentary canal, or rectal area in the ET autopsy.

The preceding documents relate to the Southhaven Park and Carp, Ontario incidents as follows :

1. The first document specifically describes the government's method in conducting an autopsy on an alien lifeform as well as a detailed description of the exterior and interior anatomy of the NTL.

2. The second document lists technology possibly recovered from the downed craft and how such technology coupled with an extension of Einstein's Unified Field Theory was used by the U.S. Military to understand the design of the propulsion system used by the craft. It also details two unexplained Close Encounters of the Third Kind and documents the method the government uses for individuals and families contacted by NTLs.

3. The third document is a Top Secret CIRVIS directive for handling UFO Encounters by the National Defense System.

4. The fourth document is a previously classified list of recovered craft and alien bodies.

All of these events, including Brookhaven, have one thing in common, in none of the events did the extraterrestrials attempt to make contact. The exception occurred at the landing of a UFO in Carp, Ontario. These extraterrestrials did make contact. In fact, they not only were in direct contact with an individual who is known as Guardian, but abducted a female government employee who actually has described the interior of the craft. Except for the Long Island incident, the Carp crash is probably the best documented UFO Encounter in the last fifty years.

eight

THE LANDING

Don Echer is one of the most interesting people I talked with. Perhaps that is because he is a talk-show host. His show, "UFO Tonite," has a wide listening audience all across the United States. He is also the Director of Research for *UFO Magazine*, a former police investigator, and a solid, methodical UFO researcher. The following document, with his introduction, is printed word for word as he received it, with an excellent 20-minute videotape of the landing of a UFO in Carp:

To All CIS and ParaNet members:

This file is uploaded exactly as I received it. The file came to me unsigned and in the proverbial brown paper envelope. It was postmarked from Canada, and had no return address. In the file you will see reference to two photo's that were included. What these were: a xerox of an aerial photo of the Carp, Ontario region and a very poor xerox of what was supposed to be an alien. No detail was observed. Just a poor shot of what appeared to be a "Grey." All in all, this is extremely "suspect" and the only reason that I uploaded it was that there had been much comment regarding it, not only here but on ParaNet. So: read it at your own risk.

Don Ecner

The Alleged C / R of the 11 / 89 "Alien Starfighter"

"Canadian and American Security Agencies are engaged in a conspiracy of silence, to withhold from the world the alien vessel seized in the swamps of Corkery Road, Carp, in 1989.

UFO sightings in the Ontario region had intensified in the 1980's, specifically, around nuclear power generating stations. On Nov. 4, 1989 at 20:00 hrs Canadian Defense Dept. radars picked up a globe-shaped object travelling at phenomenal speed over Carp, Ontario. The UFO abruptly stopped, and dropped like a stone.

Canadian and American Security Agencies were immediately notified of the landing. Monitoring satellites traced the movements of the aliens to a triangular area (see aerial map) off Almonte and Corkery Roads.

The ship had landed in deep swamp near Corkery Road. Two AH-64 Apaches and a UH-60 Blackhawk headed for the area the following night. The helicopters carried full weapon loads. They were part of a covert American unit that specialized in the recovery of alien craft.

Flying low over Ontario pine trees the Apache attack choppers soon spotted a glowing, blue, 20 metre in diameter sphere. As targeting lasers locked-on, both gunships unleashed their full weapon loads of 8 missiles each. All 16 were exploded in proximity bursts 10 meters downwind from the ship.

The missiles were carrying VEXXON, a deadly neuroactive gas which kills on contact. Exposed to air the gas breaks down quickly into inert components. Immediately after having completed their mission the gunships turned around, and headed back across the border.

Now the Blackhawk landed, as men exploded from its open doors. In seconds the six man strike team had entered the UFO through a 7 metre hatchless, oval portal. No resistance was encountered. At the controls, 3 dead crewman were found.

With the ship captured, the US Air Force, Pentagon, and Office of Naval Intelligence were notified. Through the night a special team of technicians had shut-down and disassembled the sphere. Early the next morning Nov. 6, 1989 construction equipment and trucks were brought into the swamp. The UFO parts were transported to a secret facility in Konata, Ontario.

As a cover story the locals were informed that a road was being built through the swamp. No smokescreen was needed for the military activity as Canadian forces regularly train in the Carp region. Officially nothing unusual was reported in the area. Although someone anonymously turned in a 35mm roll of film. It was received by the National Research Council of Canada, in Ottawa.

The film contained several clear shots of an entity holding a light (see photo). At this time the photographer is still unidentified. The humanoids were packed in ice and sent to an isolation chamber at the Univ. of Ottawa. CIA physiologists performed the autopsies.

The reptilian, fetus-headed beings, were listed as CLASS 1 NTE's (Non Terrestrial Entities). Like others recovered in previous operations, they were muscular, grey-white skinned, humanoids.

The ship was partially reassembled at the underground facility in Kanata. Unlike previous recoveries this one is pure military. Built as a "Starfighter" it is heavily armed and armored. In design no rivets, bolts, or welds were used in fastening, yet when reconstructed there are no seams. The UFO itself is made up of a matrixed dielectric magnesium alloy. It is driven by pulsed electromagnetic fields generated by a cold fusion reactor. All offensive capabilities utilize independently targeting electronic beam weapons."

I viewed the Carp film many times. Unlike most UFO films, it included a sound track, and one could hear the sound of a barking dog in the background. The shots clearly depicted a saucer-shaped object, producing a strobelike light, with a dome. On the ground, left by the person who shot the film, was a series of flares to signal to alien craft where to land.

The film was sent to several film analysts, including an individual who worked with the CIA. It was very important that I ascertain the validity of this film, and to do so, each frame needed to be analyzed for any evidence that it had been tampered with or modified. Since special effects and computer graphics can be used to produce a fairly believable UFO video to the untrained eye, it was necessary to check for all the telltale signs of a fake.

The recovery of the vessel and the bodies of several aliens at Carp was impressive. But far more interesting, and definitely the next step in my research, would be to investigate information that a live alien was being kept confined at Brookhaven Lab.

Part II
EVIDENCE

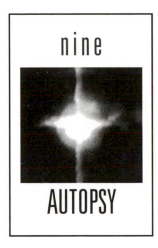

nine

AUTOPSY

The following narration is a continuation of information given to me by sources at Brookhaven Lab. The colonel is the same individual present when the craft was shot down.

Parts of the town of Brookhaven Hamlet were plunged into blackness as the weapon fired from beneath Brookhaven, literally sucking the power out of the surrounding area. The Emergency Air Rescue Center was notified, and at least seven fire departments were called to the scene.

Sorenson watched the lime-green fire trucks of Brookhaven Hamlet pull away. The colonel stood at his side, surveying the smoking wreckage of the UFO.

He looked a few yards away, where another body lay. He knew what the sickly sweet odor of barbecued human flesh was like. This was much different. It was pungent, smelling of strange esters and burning ketones. But that was to be expected, the different smell. What was lying dead, smoking on the ground, was very different. It wasn't human.

Carter, a military pathologist, joined the two men looking down at the body, and frowned.

"I hope there is enough there for me to do a decent autopsy. The boys at the top are very curious to know what these are."

Sorenson signaled the SWAT team members guarding the body to cover it up.

"Don't worry, Carter," Sorenson said smugly. "We just sent away another body in much better condition. That one is alive."

Carter winced. "You don't want me to vivisect this thing . . . do you?"

This bothered the pathologist. In his late seventies, he probably should have retired years ago. In fact, he had once. But he had been with the military a long time, and besides being highly skilled, he also had a much more important quality. He would keep his mouth shut. He would not leak information to the media. They had called Carter in because he was an expert in dissecting Nonterrestrial Lifeforms and also had an "Eyes Only" clearance.

The actual instances that Carter knew of where the U.S. had captured and secretly held an NTL could be counted on the fingers of one hand. Carter had been involved or directly performed the autopsy in three of them.

Two of the guards stood back as several of Carter's assistants moved in and wrapped the body in metallic Mylar.

"I recently received a memo indicating we have secured the services of a technician who was attempting to use symbols to communicate with the aliens. Is that so?" asked the colonel.

"In a way," said Sorenson. "You remember all those experiments where we developed symbolic communication with chimps and orangutans? The simians don't have the capacity or larynx structure to do human speech, but they can learn what certain symbols mean. We set up a button board with a whole set of such symbols, and the beasts can actually join several symbols to form simple sentences."

The colonel snorted and then laughed.

"Damn monkeys. But what does this have to do with that thing over there?"

"The primary purpose of the project was not to teach monkeys to talk. The objective was to develop a form of communication we could use when dealing with NTLs. The lab personnel were pretty surprised the first time one of our interrogators handed the symbol board to an alien and it began immediately pushing buttons. Apparently, they monitor us closer than we had realized."

The colonel was annoyed.

"We come in peace?" Carter grinned.

"Something like that." Sorenson smiled. "But what are they

supposed to say? That they are a race fleeing from a dying planet looking for a new home?"

A man in a radiation suit rushed up, waving a digital rad detector. He was a member of the team from Brookhaven, specially trained to fight radioactive fires and hazardous-waste spills.

"You are in no immediate danger," he said, his voice muffled by the suit. "Two or three roentgens an hour. But I suggest you not stand around here too much longer. We have put out all of the surrounding fires, but we are having a hell of a time getting whatever is burning inside the craft under control."

"I have noted your recommendation," said Sorenson tersely. "I am still in charge here."

The man nodded and headed toward the wreckage, continuing to wave the sensor for the rad scan in the air.

The colonel's pocket phone rang. He listened to it for a moment. "It's for you," he said, handing the phone to Sorenson.

"Uh huh. Yes. Okay." Sorenson seemed to be listening to a long, precise explanation of something. "Yes, be sure to relay this to the head of the D.O.D." He clicked the terminate call button and handed the phone back to the colonel.

Carter shifted about, looking anxious. "Listen, they have secured the lower lab at Brookhaven for me. Put everyone down there on administrative leave," he said.

"Good," said Sorenson. "I suggest you hustle on over there and get started ASAP. We don't want to keep the bodies there for more than a day or so. They have very poor security over there. After all, it's over six thousand acres and a lot of it is wilderness. And don't be an idiot like the tech who just called me and told me his report over the phone. Damn." He glowered. "Where do they get these people?"

"I'll get right on it, sir," Carter said sarcastically and headed toward the ambulance, where his assistants were loading the second body.

"Smart ass, isn't he?" said the colonel.

"Doesn't matter," said Sorenson. "He's damn good. I want to show you something, colonel. It has to do with the report I just got on the phone." He walked toward the wreckage.

The crash had taken its toll on the park. As it came down, it had sheared off the tops of several trees, caused multiple small fires, and then exploded as it impacted in the field. Apparently, even to the last moment, the aliens had been desperately trying to control the craft.

"This is what I wanted to show you," he said, pointing to a small piece of the wreckage smoldering on the ground. "Notice how thin the hull was. Whatever metal they used is very unique. According to the lab, that's who I just talked to, this substance is thinner than aluminum foil and harder than diamond."

"I wish we had something like that," said the colonel, kneeling down to look at the crumpled metal. "Where exactly do you think these spacemen come from?"

"I would assume," said Sorenson, "that they are from the same civilization that we had at Roswell. Of course, that was way before my time."

This was all very disturbing to the colonel. Because they had shot down these craft, it was certain that others would return. And if they had any notion of military strategy, they would be far more cautious, and keep their fighter craft in space just outside the range of our weapons. Yet, there had been no choice. The formation of UFOs had been headed directly toward Washington, D.C. That was a "terminate with extreme prejudice" situation if he had ever heard of one.

"You say they've talked to these aliens?" said the colonel.

"Not talked. But we have communicated through the symbol boards."

The colonel looked up at the night sky. It was unusually clear that night. It was now 9:35 P.M., and instead of standing around talking, they should be checking with the local police and making sure that the highway was not only secured, but blocked to all traffic.

"I bet they traveled a long way to get here," he said, imagining that somewhere around one of those diamond pinpoints of light in the sky, there was a planet where a strangely alien civilization existed.

"About 6 million light years away," said Sorenson, little awed by the thought. "If we had started from here at the speed of light in the time of the dinosaurs, we wouldn't even be half way there by now. "He paused letting the idea sink in. "Somewhere very far away, in a constellation known as the Pleiades."

IT HAS BEEN said that dogs have a natural fear of danger. Joanne had only had Brutus, an Irish setter, for a few weeks. Brutus sat looking out a window. Across the street there were two other dogs, with owners much more permissive than his, wandering down Gerrard Road. Brutus paid no attention as the strange lights slowly moved across the sky in a triangular formation. Nor did it matter to him when two of the lights exploded and one plunged in the park, fingers of crackling flames reaching up above the treetops.

Of much more importance was a different phenomenon. A phenomenon that in his short dog life had not happened all that often. There, only a few feet away, both the door and the screen door were open. Freedom!

It was Cheryl, a friend of Joanne's visiting from California, who had left the door open. And it was a very upset Cheryl who greeted Joanne, returning from work, with the simple words.

"He got out."

"I just don't need this," said Joanne. "I needed the time tonight to go shopping. Thanksgiving is in a couple of days and our clan is coming for the holidays. And I only have four days off from work and so much I have to do, and Brad will be mad if he has to go to that sandwich place down the road again. They never make his sandwiches right, you know, and he get's so mad, and then he goes home, and he's in a bad mood and—"

"Don't worry," said Cheryl. "We'll find him. Let's just take the car and go looking around the neighborhood. I have a dog, too, you know. They always have places they go and visit their other dog friends."

"I hope he's all right. He probably headed for the park, but I know another place he went when he got out before. Okay, let's go." She rushed out of the door.

Cheryl felt strange. She felt a lot worse than she should for just letting the dog get away. As they drove slowly along the suburban streets, the feeling got worse. She didn't want to say anything to Joanne. She would think it was because Cheryl, who was just a bit psychic, knew that Brutus had been run over by a car or something. It was very cold that night. It was hard to say how long it had been since the dog had escaped, but he could be fairly far

away by now, maybe two or three miles. After 45 minutes of looking up and down the streets near Joanne's house, they headed out
toward the park. They were traveling up the road toward the main
highway. Just as they came over the hill and could see down on
Brookhaven Hamlet, Cheryl cried out. "My God! Did you see that!
Over there, just above the lake, I think I just saw a UFO."

The road was curvy at that point and Joanne was intent on
driving. She didn't like this part. She never did. And if she were to
start gawking around trying to see what Cheryl saw, they would
wind up going through the guard rail, and plummeting down the
hillside.

"I can't look," she snapped. "Really, I am worried about Brutus."

Cheryl continued to watch the glowing ball in the sky.

"Well, I see it. It's not a plane. And it's moving really fast, like
it's running away from something."

Joanne exhaled, relieved as they neared the main road.

"You know," she said. "I haven't seen a single car. That is really
strange. The stores are still open, couldn't be much past nine
o'clock."

"You think that is strange." Cheryl pointed toward the north.
"Take a look at this."

They were just nearing the Brookhaven Hamlet fire station.
Just to the right was the sandwich shop. A man in a black SWAT-
team uniform stood directly in of front them in the middle of the
road, waving his arms wildly. In back of him were several fire
trucks, police cars, and firemen. The highway was completely
blocked off.

"Look at that," said Cheryl. She pointed to a red fire truck. "No
lights. And it's not one of ours. They must have called another
department in. I wonder where the fire is."

"The real question is," said Joanne, peering through her wind-
shield, "why do they have some guy in a black jumpsuit directing
traffic?"

SORENSON AND THE colonel stood behind the military transport vehicle
and watched the approaching car.

"Another damn car," mumbled the colonel.

"We're ready, sir." Another of the small group of armed swat
team approached. "We have the wreckage on transport. We should

be at the barge in a few more minutes. We need to get this road open before more cars see this roadblock."

"Did you get the license number of that car?" said Sorenson as he turned toward the Colonel. "Tell your people to get their asses in gear. I want that to be the last car that sees this roadblock."

ten

BLUE LIGHT

Each year, tens of thousands of sightings are reported. They range from simple lights in the sky to detailed accounts of persons abducted by aliens. A great number of these reports flow through MUFON, CUFON, and KUFON, computer UFO bulletin board networks that have members from Alaska to Venezuela, from the U.K. to the outback of Australia. Some reports are sincere accounts of actual UFO sitings; some are incredibly ludicrous hoaxes.

A director friend of mine, Kathyrn Cahill, who worked on the "Encounters" program, called most videos submitted "penlights in the dark." Now I sat with reams of printouts, a dozen videos, hours of recorded conversations, and numerous signed statements from well-known authorities in the field. The most difficult part of this for me was to follow those tracks, interview key witnesses, and try to separate the truth from what was either bad research or deliberate misinformation. The task at hand was to separate the real gold, the material that would explain the incidents on Long Island and in Carp, from the penlights in the dark.

In addition, there is a small group of UFO messiahs, self-proclaimed researchers in the UFO field, moving across the U.S.A., giving seminars and interviews, flanked by hungry reporters, disseminating information at warp speed, with no one to really cover their tracks, to check their stories.

In an age where President Clinton's head can be superimposed on a body next to an eggheaded Gray (a frequently reported type of alien with light gray skin and large eyes), with headlines proclaiming "Clinton consorts with aliens," the art of video forgery is rampant. Fortunately, most of the creators of such preposterous hoaxes are not all that educated or sophisticated in their methods.

Many prominent experts in the UFO field are very hesitant to come forward and expose the few vocal researchers in the industry. Tom Theophanis was not such a person. He had patiently and with great precision gathered information on the Carp film and landing, and now on the phone told me, in no uncertain terms, he was about to go public with what he knew.

"I know you have some great analysis equipment down there in California," he said. "I want you to take this film and tell me what you think of it. You also mentioned something about someone named Video Dave who has several video experts who could help us."

I settled back, listening to Tom's voice. He was angry and expecting me to find that the film was a complete fraud.

"Listen," I said. "I have always been straight with you. I came into this with no conclusions. I certainly have never said that any of these objects were extraterrestrial. In fact, until I gather more information, I still don't know exactly what happened in the encounters. I have tried to research this in a methodical, precise way."

He remained silent. Something was very wrong. I could feel this. The friendship and enthusiasm were no longer there. There was no excitement in his voice. He was like a small child who had seen an animal die: a child who had lost the ability to see magic in the world.

"It's a hoax," he said flatly. "Just like the Loch Ness Monster, or Bigfoot. In the case of Loch Ness, 50 years later, we find the guy used a toy submarine with a model head of a dinosaur. As for Bigfoot . . ." He paused. "People running around with plaster of paris feet making footprints in the mud."

For a few moments I sat there, letting his words sink in.

"I don't think so," I said. "I have watched the film over and over. There is this one part, the part where a bright light flashes from the UFO. The key is there. The proof is there."

"I don't know what the hell you are talking about," he said.

"You're right," I said, and hung up the phone.

I shuddered as a black, unmarked helicopter slowly made its way over the ocean while I looked out my window at the sea. It was perfect, I thought. A prominent authority in the world of UFOs comes forward and proclaims the sightings a hoax. I was sure that Tom Theophanis believed that what he was doing was right. I was also sure that the CIA and probably most of the top brass in the military were breathing a collective sigh of relief.

The phone rang.

"It's Dave," said the voice, excited, out of breath. "It's the blue light. You know on the film. I just ran an RBG comparative. You aren't even going to believe this."

"NOW THIS WILL be a surprise. You're gonna love this," said Video Dave.

I sat watching another blank screen, much as I had with Tom Theophanis. Video Dave is impressive, with a fierce moustache, penetrating dark eyes, and a quick wit. He has a distinctive gaucho look to him, as if he had just dismounted from a horse and would fit better in a Marlboro commercial. He is a legend in the UFO community. Major television producers, movie companies, and thousands of members of his UFO Audio-Video Clearing house knew him to be *the* source for anything on film related to UFOs. Watching the grin on his face, I knew he was up to something, and knowing his reputation for unusual films, I was ready for just about anything.

Ralph McCarrin, who was sitting in a nearby chair, was smiling, too. He is probably one of the best video analysts around. Tall, thin, dark hair to his shoulders, and piercing dark eyes. He can take apart the best picture pixel by pixel. He has enemies. For he is also well known for being able to spot a bogus Polaroid or film clip within seconds. I wanted to ask him what he had found out about the bright light in the Carp film, but this was Video Dave's show, and I knew he would be irritated if I didn't at least watch and appear to be mildly fascinated.

Still no picture, but the sound track began. A man and a woman were talking. They had just seen a UFO land on the grass, just beyond a grove of trees less than 50 yards from their mobile home.

"Okay! Okay! I got the camera. Let's go!" an excited male voice said.

Still blackness on the screen.

"Go where?" said a female voice.

"Outside! I want to go outside and get a shot of whatever that was."

I looked at Video Dave and wondered, Was this a joke? A film that was only voices and no pictures. Penlights in the dark with no penlights.

Finally the screen came to life. The camcorder panned the stairs as the couple made their way across the unkept area of faded grass.

"Do you see where it came down?" said the man.

"It's over there. I see something by those bushes." She paused, her voice suddenly wavering with fear. "I think we should go back in the house."

They proceeded, or I should say, the camera proceeded, for neither of them had come into view. The powerful beam of the flashlight scanned the area ahead of them, almost swallowed by the darkness of the dense woods. Suddenly, there was a stir of motion just beyond a clump of trees less than 20 feet away.

"There's something in those bushes," said the man. The camera lens turned to face the area of dense woods, where branches continued to dance wildly while some unseen entity watched them approach. "Let's zoom in on it," said the man. More violent shaking of the bushes and then a menacing growl.

"Oh my God!" the man cried out. "It's horrible."

The woman shrieked, her high-pitched screams barely louder than the thing in the shadows. And then, stepping into the clearing with a look of smug confidence, was the grinning visage of our very own Video Dave.

"Really. That is so tacky," I said, looking at the real Dave as he grinned with fond admiration at his video.

"Great, isn't it?" he said. "Then I go on to talk about the footage I supplied for the Roswell movie."

"I really wonder how many of the so-called UFO films are just like this, and how difficult would it be to disprove this particular footage if Dave had not stepped forward at the very end?

"So, Ralph," I said, turning to the video expert. "What about the Carp film? What was it that you wanted to tell me?"

He settled back down in the chair, pulled a sheaf of papers from his briefcase, and looked at me intently.

"You may have something there," he said. "Of course, I would need to run some more video analysis on the clip to be sure. But so far, looks like it's the real item," he said.

"Not so fast," said Video Dave. "There are lots of criteria here to consider." He took a deep breath and continued. "One, the source of the film. You looked over that statement that Guardian, the individual who took the film, made. It's pretty strange stuff. Doesn't do a hell of a lot to add credibility to the video. Two, the sound track doesn't seem to match, and three, what are all those flares to the left of the object?"

Video Dave was beginning to sound a lot like Tom Theophanis.

"Before you shoot the film down too much," said Ralph, "let me add a few things here. As far as Guardian's very unusual statement, it is quite possible that Guardian may have had contact with the aliens or at least that the encounter may have affected him quite a bit. As for the sound track, I do hear dogs barking in the background. But what I had called J.B. about was the bright blue flash in the middle of the film, the flash coming from the object. Now, it's pretty hard to overload a camcorder with that much light to produce that kind of effect on the electronics. I spoke to Jeff Ronan, a real tech guy on video, and he said that the RGB on this was very strange. Comparative ratings were Red 4, Green 5, Blue 42."

"What exactly does that mean?" I said.

Ralph looked deeply disturbed by this. I was sure he had probably analyzed thousands of video in the last ten years. It sounded like he had never encountered this phenomenon on a tape before.

"It means that whatever was out there aimed an incredibly powerful beam of almost pure blue, laserlike light, at the person holding the camera. The intensity of this light, to produce that kind of effect on the tape, would have to have been enormous."

I could see where this was leading. Tom Theophanis had told me that he had taken an ordinary strobe, which he had bought at Radio Shack, measured the light put out, and then matched it to the film. He had claimed they produced the same spectrum of light. It was obvious from Ralph's data that this was not the case.

"So, what you're saying, Ralph, is that no ordinary type light source, such as from an emergency vehicle floodlight, could ever produce that flash?"

"Took you long enough." Ralph smiled. "Did you see the colors and shape of that object? I can tell you for one, it was not reflected off anything. Sometimes hoaxers will shine a light on a wall or screen and take a picture of the reflection. I did a ray trace, and you can see the strobe, which by the way is pulsing up to 17 times a second, reflected off the ground."

There was still one thing I could not understand. To the left of craft was a circle of flares. Ordinary highway emergency flares.

"Ralph, one problem with all this. When I talked to Theophanis, he was insistent that he had run a spectral analysis of the light coming from the bright objects to the left of the craft. He is absolutely certain they are highway flares." Ralph did not seem to be the least bit pleased by what I was saying. He continued listening, but already I could tell he knew exactly what I was about to say. "Why would you have this incredible UFO with all the unusual light phenomena and then just a bunch of flares?"

"Why don't you tell him?" said Ralph, turning to Video Dave.

"Something you have overlooked here," said Dave. "It is often the case where direct contact is made between extraterrestrial craft and a human, that some sort of mind control comes into play. Have you examined the last part of that film carefully? I understand you have a third generation copy, which is pretty decent in this business."

I tried to remember all the parts of the film, and finally it hit me. At the very end, I had seen the face of some type of creature on the film and something moving from the saucer toward the person taking the video. But I still didn't get his point. What would these frames I had of the alien have to do with flares?

"Simple," said Ralph. "The letter, written by Guardian, which accompanied the tape, was so strange because Guardian had actually had direct contact with the aliens and it messed him up pretty bad. And the flares? This particular landing was no chance encounter. Guardian had known precisely where and when the extraterrestrials would land. Those flares weren't put there by the aliens, they were put there by Guardian. They weren't the result of fire or radiation burning the ground. Those flares were to show the aliens where he would be waiting for them. They were the best Guardian could do to provide the craft with a primitive but effective beacon."

eleven

PARTICLE BEAM

Brookhaven Lab does research for over three dozen of the largest companies as well as hundreds of top scientists in the United States. Much research is being done in the area of particle physics. In addition to new sources of energy, such research also provides insights into the atom that can be used for military as well as peaceful applications. In interviewing physicists concerning the existence of quark-gluon plasma, I found a host of vastly conflicting opinions. The formal defense releases deny the existence of such a substance. Other individuals describe methods that can be used to produce such a beam—specifically, documents sent to me by the Department of Energy. The following is from an interior source at Brookhaven and describes the test and an unfortunate incident with such a weapon.

"Well, I've got good news and bad news," said Earl Voyt, a physicist with the Texas Accelerator Project.

He was tired. They had hit turbulence on his flight to Long Island somewhere over Salt Lake City.

"Bad news first," said Miles Pritchard.

Miles was almost used to it. Ever since the night when he had learned they had a high-powered weapon at Brookhaven, and then witnessed them shoot down an alien spacecraft with that weapon, there had been a lot of problems at the lab. A group of teenagers had gotten into the secured lab and stolen a slide that supposedly had a tissue smear from one of the NTLs recovered. The government had beefed up security and added surveillance cameras, and there had been several internal memos forbidding any persons involved in the incidents from talking to the press, even from talking to their own families about what had happened.

"Okay," said Earl. "They have shut down the Texas accelerator. Literally scraped the entire project. Everybody is very worried about what is going to happen to other, similar linear accelerator projects in the U.S. It certainly will affect us all." His face grew dark as he stared at the memo. "It says here that even though they had already invested seven to eight billion dollars, the Department of Energy and Congress felt it to be a really big money saver to can the project."

"They can't do that," said Miles, taking the fax and reading it over. "You know, they dug a five-mile-long tunnel 200 feet underground. My God, didn't the planners know what it would cost to put it that far below the surface? I don't get it. Our accelerators here are only ten feet or so underground. What was their point? If they had cuts costs, perhaps they wouldn't have snuffed the project."

"Listen, we can talk about this in the control room," said Earl. "We are going to do a very special collide in about 15 minutes. That's why I am here."

"That's just fine," said Miles. "Just great. No one ever tells me about these things."

"I'm telling you," said Earl sternly. "It's a classified test. I heard that some pretty important people will be here to see this. They didn't want you to know in advance. Just standard security bullshit. That's all."

As Miles followed Earl down the long, dimly lit tunnel, they reached a small, unimpressive-looking elevator marked "Maintenance Personnel Only."

"I don't get it. You know you said before you had bad news and good news. Well, so what is the good news?"

"This is it," said Earl, pressing the button. The doors slid open. "Or to be more precise, it's several hundred feet down below us. What I am about to show you is the reason they terminated the accelerator in Texas."

The device Earl was taking Miles to is the RHIC. The RHIC is Brookhaven's most powerful particle accelerator. It enables the ions to achieve much greater velocities, and it can accelerate much larger particles. Miles had heard about the project. Yet his information had been that this device would not be completed until 1997. Now he realized the dream of a lot of his physicist friends had become a reality.

"Put your thumb on the glass," said Earl, pointing to a small black rectangle on the wall. "The people upstairs just fed in your print codes a few minutes ago for 'Eyes Only' on this, the same as mine. This is going to be a big part of your life for the next year. In fact, it will *be* your life for the next year."

As they entered the small room, Miles noticed a dozen or so military types, what looked to be a congresswoman and her assistant, and another gentleman.

"As you know," Earl began, "I work with the Stanford group in California. We are linked by network to Texas, Comsak, and most of the defense nodes. One of my primary functions here is to give you a brief background on what is about to take place, in layman's terms. Some of it may be a bit complex, but we have simplified this briefing as much as possible.

"This device is a major project of the Department of Energy. It is the largest and most powerful accelerator ever constructed. Most accelerators are designed to collide particles and then study the subparticles and effects created by those collisions. This device is unique. It is a one-of-a-kind accelerator with a new capacity. It will collide large particles—atomic nuclei—at high energies to create a quark-gluon plasma—a form of hot, dense matter that has not existed since moments after the Big Bang.

"In the RHIC, Relativistic Heavy Ion Collider, two beams of heavy ions—atoms stripped of their electrons, leaving bare nuclei —will whirl in opposite directions around a 3.8 kilometer circular tunnel at nearly the speed of light and then collide. As this happens, an incredible amount of energy, approximately 100 billion electron volts per nucleon, will be produced. At this moment, a substance called quark-gluon plasma will be produced.

"To reach this explosive point of impact, ions as heavy as gold will begin their journey to the RHIC through a series of three increasingly more powerful accelerators, beginning with the Randem Van de Graaf, then the Booster, and finally, the AGs. From there, the ions will be extracted in bunches and transferred to one of the two collider rings. At six points, where the beams cross, particles will collide head on at the rate of tens of thousands of collisions per second. One of the breakthroughs is that these collisions can be made to occur outside the accelerator by crossing several beams. There are six alternate tunnels and particle conduits that extend to the surface."

"It's a damned weapon," said the congresswoman breathlessly.

"I see a problem here," said Miles flatly.

"Poor timing," said Earl, looking annoyed. "I suggest we discuss this 'problem' later in private."

"I think not," he said. "In fact, before you start this demonstration, I have something to say that I think should be considered. Seriously considered."

Miles turned to face the group. He could tell that none of them, except for possibly the congresswoman, was really that interested in hearing about any problems.

"I am sure you are all familiar with the initial test of the nuclear bomb. Several physicists there were very concerned that the reaction might not be able to be contained, or that it would initiate some even larger, more devastating reaction that would destroy everything. We were fortunate. It didn't. As predicted, as the atoms affected were spaced further and further apart, at a certain point, the reaction stopped. What hasn't been told to you is that we still do not entirely understand the physics involved in black holes or even concerning what is happening with our own sun. The amount of energy being produced when this plasma is generated is beyond your imagination. It is insignificant if it only involves a few particles, but if for some reason it spreads, begins to internally generate more plasmas, we are looking at a chain reaction that would make Hiroshima look like a firecracker. This chain reaction could create a rift in the space-time continuum. The effects of such a rift, are beyond the abilities of modern-day physics to comprehend."

"With no disrespect intended, Dr. Pritchard," said Earl, "there is absolutely no chance of such a thing occurring here. There is a small amount of plasma regeneration, but we can control that. All of our subparticle traces indicate the reaction will terminate in several milliseconds."

"Has this ever been tested before?" said the congresswoman gravely.

"Yes, it has," said Earl. "Special Agent Sorenson, with the Department of Energy, and Karen Brown, a qualified nuclear physicist, were able to successfully use this device to terminate two alien craft."

"I thought we were using one of the accelerators closer to the surface that night," said Miles.

"That's what you were supposed to think. Karen Brown was actually linked to this control center by the console you saw her operating."

"And the structure coming down from the ceiling?" said Miles, still confused.

"One of the six particle conduits I mentioned earlier."

The rest of the group remained silent. Most the military brass had been thoroughly lost since the beginning of Earl's briefing. It certainly wasn't simplified to them. The only thing that had made them perk up their ears was the word *weapon*. And if this thing was capable of producing a beam hotter than the surface of the sun, it would undoubtedly be the most powerful weapon on the face of the planet. It was almost as if Earl Voyt could read their minds, for he continued.

"As you all know, since we have uncovered two double agents recently who were directly responsible for the deaths of at least a dozen others, most of our technology that we had assumed was unknown to Russia has now been compromised. This technology was not available to those two agents, and so the RHIC represents a major step to the U.S. regaining our lead in the arms race."

"Enough of this horseshit," said the colonel, stepping forward. "Are we going to see this or not? I have to meet with the president in a few hours. Get on with it."

"Exactly," said Earl, extremely grateful for an opportunity to end the discussion.

The group watched for several minutes while Earl initiated the program that would control the acceleration of the particles. They could feel the floor vibrate and hear a rising magnetic hum as the huge magnets around the perimeter of RHIC began to pulse.

"There is a shielded camera that will visually monitor the point of collision. We should get a substantial amount of light generated when the plasma is produced."

"Okay," said Earl, pointing to a monitor. "At precisely 1:04:00

A.M. by the digital clock on this console, the computer will change the path of the ions and the collision will occur."

1:03:57 . . . 1:03:58 . . . 1:03:59 . . .

There was a brief, incredibly brilliant flash of light on the monitor, and then the screen went black. The flash was brief because the plasma reaction continued several thousandths of a second too long before the plasma dissipated, and the camera as well as the surrounding area were vaporized.

"Oh, hell," said Earl, as several heat-monitor alarms along the length of the tunnel went to red.

"What is going on?" said the colonel. "Are we in danger or what?"

"No danger," said Earl, trying to sound convincing. "But we've got about a quarter mile of molten earth where part of the accelerator used to be, according to my readouts here. Shouldn't take too long for that to cool and solildify again. The heat dampers have activated and there is coolant being pumped into the adjoining areas." Yet while he was talking, Earl Voyt was thinking. What if that reaction had continued even for just a few moments longer? The area they were now standing in, and most of Brookhaven, would have rapidly been transformed from a quiet town on a cold winter night to a pool of fire very much resembling the center of an active volcano.

"Now do you understand why the accelerator is located two hundred feet below the ground?" said Earl, turning to Miles.

"I understand only too well," said Miles. "One more demonstration like that, and none of us will be around to discuss anything."

twelve

THE GENERAL

The following is the text of an interview with a retired three-star general concerning the government's interaction with UFOs. If the general's comments are accurate, our military is not only aware of the presence of UFOs, but has developed several top-secret agencies to deal with them.

The man looked ordinary enough. He wore a sweater, smoked a pipe, and had close-cut gray hair. He was retired now, but not too many years before, he had held the rank of a three-star general. What was unusual about this interview was not that this man had been such a high-ranking officer, but that he was about to relay information to me concerning direct government contact with extraterrestrials.

"Around four months ago I called in several favors. I was given documents, allowed to view videotapes, given photographs and base locations, and I was even asked to participate in the 'Awareness Program'... which is to disseminate information about alien contact to the public."

I thought it very strange that he was reading this from several typed pages he had laid on his desk. "Where were the bases located?" I asked. He continued reading, ignoring my question.

"I turned down the offer. When I did, I was sort of an outcast, and I found that friends of 30 years had no time for me. I soon was limited to all forms of information. Hell, every time I requested anything through normal channels, it was either lost or delayed for 'higher approval.' These were normal, everyday decisions, which were *never* questioned before. I gave over 30 years of faithful and loyal service to this great country of ours. Who in the hell do those political bastards think they are, anyway?" he said.

"Has there been alien contact?"

"I always had my suspicions, and I had heard the rumors about alien spacecraft that crashed, bodies found, alien craft shot down, UFO evidence stored in special buildings on certain military bases. I just never really took it seriously. Now I know it is true. I have seen the evidence, I have seen the alien craft, the frozen bodies from the Roswell site, and I have seen on videotape the live alien that is a guest of the U.S. government. From all the documentation and information that I have seen with my own eyes, as well as the physical evidence, there have been several crashes of UFOs over the years.

"The aliens really do not have any sort of invasion planned for this planet. They have visited off and on for thousands of years. Our U.S. guest is over three hundred years old. There are both 'good and bad' aliens just as there are good and bad humans. They are not all that different from us. The aliens utilize around 55 percent of their brain capacity or ability and have DNA, just like we do. The guest alien is five feet three inches tall and weighs 96 pounds, and has a large head (no hair) and large, slanted eyes. Some of the aliens' abilities include moderate telepathy and telekinesis.

"The purpose of alien visitation to this planet is one of curiosity and scientific research, not world domination, as some would have you believe. Cattle and humans have been used in alien and U.S. research for various biological applications. Most humans are not hurt in this research and experimentation. Some, however, have died due to complications and downright carelessness.

"Several crossbreed young have been born to both human females and alien females. We as humans seem to be biologically compatible with most visiting aliens. More than one type or species of alien has visited this planet. They are listed by category . . . this information I could not retrieve.

"The U.S. and British governments have made secret treaty agreements with the aliens in exchange for technology and so-called 'recon missions' during times of human conflict. The aliens have basically agreed not to concern themselves with the wars or con-flicts of humans. Not to interfere in society, thus letting govern-ments rule and decide for themselves. Exactly what the aliens get in return was not exactly made clear or available.

"The Awareness Program that I mentioned earlier was designed to inform the public about alien contact, landings, crashes, the Roswell incident, and UFOs. All of this is filtered to the public in a systematic, logical way. This is coupled with the increased alien-human abductions and contacts. It is a joint government and alien program. If done correctly, there will be extremely little or no panic and no resistance. Ruling nations will retain control and chaos will be avoided."

The general paused. I could see he was used to talking for quite a long time without being interrupted. That the government wanted the public to know made a lot of sense to me. I had received docu-ments from the Department of Energy and other anonymous pack-ages that were obviously from the government. Yet, on the other hand, that same government had been also very hesitant and secretive in their dealings. And why was that same government trying to hush up the Brookhaven crash, monitoring statements by the fire chief, the park ranger, and Brookhaven Lab? Perhaps the government actually had several splinter groups, some of which wanted the public to know, some of which did not.

"Why exactly do you think the government has instituted the Awareness Program?"

"The Awareness Program calls for the funding of movies, series on TV, specials, and books. All of the front money will filter its way to fund a TV series or movie if it is deemed worthy of friendly, helpful alien contact. An idea is passed along to the big-name producers and directors, and if it takes hold, everything will fall in place and the funding starts. It is really unique how it all works. No way to trace it to the government. And the people involved truly believe it is their own creative work. Everyone gets into the act with no problems. After the movie hits the public, the reaction and interest of the masses are carefully monitored."

"So how would I know whether or not you are still working for the government and if this entire interview will be leaked to the public, to the computer networks, and to prime researchers in the UFO field?"

"I never said this was an exclusive interview. Now, may I continue?" He frowned.

I was sorry I had interrupted him. "Please continue," I said.

"Abductions of humans are both random and selective. Influential people are selected to either explain and guide the public or to serve some political need or requirement."

Suddenly I realized the reason the government was being so cooperative with me. "So, actually they are aware of exactly what I am doing. It's hard to believe after all these years, they finally want the public to know. So what are these UFOs like? Have you ever seen any?"

"The alien craft are disc, triangle, cigar shaped. They range from 30 feet in diameter for the smaller recon discs to over 730 feet in diameter for the larger 'mother' discs or flying saucers, if you will. The triangular-shaped craft are 210 feet. This does not seem to change, as you can see in the photos that show three different triangular craft that all measure the same and are identical in shape and appearance.

"The basic propulsion system or drive is a fusion reactor, which ranges from about the size of a medicine ball, you know, the kind tossed around in gym class, to about the size of a large van or station wagon. It is a magnetic drive surrounded by an aura of bright white light. This is for the disc and triangle-shaped craft. The cigar-shaped craft does not have this aura of light. All craft are almost totally silent, although there is some noise."

I still was thinking of what he had said before, that this was not the first time this information had been released. "You were saying, this information has been sent out before?"

"Several times. I am only repeating to you what I have said to several other UFO people," he said. "That's why much of it I have read to you word for word from this paper here."

"Well, I do appreciate your time. I doubt I can use all of this material."

"I am well aware that there are no guarantees when this information hits the media. I just hope that the people involved with this whole UFO, alien, and government connection will come forward and let the world know the truth."

thirteen

CONTACT

Linda King is a researcher in the field of linguistics and communication through the use of symbols. She certainly had no idea that the results of her research were soon to be used in communication with an extraterrestrial.

"Linda, we need you. We're all set," said Emma Travis, the other zoologist involved in handling the chimps and orangutans. "Brutus has pressed the human button about twelve times and he's getting very impatient. He really looks forward to your talks, you know." Emma grinned.

"I know. I do, too," Linda said, heading toward the low olive-drab building behind the monkey cages. "It is amazing, the more I work with these animals, the more I see how very intelligent they really are. It makes you wonder what they think of us." She picked up the communication symbol punch board and frowned.

"I know," said Emma. "They wanted all those extra weird symbols put on the board. The sun symbol." She pointed to a yellow ball with a bright aura around it. "What looks like an explosion, and all that other crazy stuff. We had to redesign the whole board. Now we have about 66 symbols on it."

Linda sighed. "Doesn't matter, I guess. Without the government funding this project, we'd have to go back to 'adopt a zoo animal' again. They certainly have been putting a lot of money in lately."

"Yes," said Sorenson, entering with his assistant and two military officers. "We certainly have."

"Hello," said Linda, standing up and extending her hand. "I am Linda King, head zoologist on the SymCom program. This is Emma, who also works with the apes."

Sorenson shook Linda's hand briefly, gave a cursory nod to Emma, and studied Brutus, who was now looking him over suspiciously.

"We'll need a briefing for the colonel here. I read the faxes you sent, but going over it again would be a good idea."

"No problem," said Linda. She turned the SymCom board so the group could see the symbols more clearly.

"This is certainly not an original technique or concept," she said. "In fact, several prominent researchers in this field have been communicating with apes and chimpanzees for decades using similar devices." She handed several stapled packets to the group and then continued. "As you can see, we started with just a few basic symbols, such as a picture of a banana, water, the images of a gorilla and a human. We have been able to teach the apes to associate the symbol with the object it represents. In addition," she made a gesture, pointing to herself, "we have also been able to use body language along with the symbol board to provide some concept of verbs and actions. It is somewhat difficult to have a pictograph for an action."

The colonel grinned. "So what you're saying is, if I point to myself and then to the symbol for human, that ape will understand me. Or at least, he will understand the symbol stands for me."

"Something like that," said Linda. "Are you going to use this to train gorillas for some type of combat scenario?" she said.

"What we are going to use this for is classified," said Sorenson. "But I can assure you, at least for the present, it will not involve any type of military action."

Linda moved over to the cage, and Brutus lumbered toward her. "Okay, now," she said, crossing her arms over her chest. "This one wasn't too hard. You will notice on the board there is a picture of two arms crossed. At first this just meant 'bringing something to you' or 'wanting something.' This is a bit primitive," she said, handing the board to Brutus, "but it will illustrate my point." She walked over and pulled a banana from her lunch bag. "Now, I know he wants this. Watch what he does."

Brutus did not even hesitate. He quickly punched the symbol of the gorilla, the crossed arms, and then the banana symbol.

"I'll be damned," said the colonel. "He actually thought that out."

"It gets better," said Linda. "Remember, I said at first the crossed arms just meant 'wanting something.' Now watch." She reached through the bars and held her arms out, giving Brutus a crude hug.

The gorilla punched the symbol for gorilla, the crossed arms, and then the human symbol.

"You see," she said. "That symbol, like many of our words to us, now has a context for Brutus. I know that when he uses it that way, it means something more than just wanting, it means affection or caring. It is his expression that he likes or cares for me."

"You better hope that's what it means," said the colonel, grinning.

"Anyway," said Linda, "we have put these other symbols on here as you have requested. I doubt Brutus will be able to comprehend this sun symbol or some of these other images."

Sorenson looked restless. "Fine," he said. "And in these documents, it describes all the symbols, the techniques you used to train this beast to use them, and so forth. Well, thank you for your time, Ms. King."

"Are you going to try and train other apes? I would find that very interesting. I could come to wherever you are going and implement these techniques."

Sorenson remained silent, deep in thought for quite some time. "Well, that really hadn't been part of the scenario. But perhaps you are correct. You could be of some use in implementing this SymCom board."

Linda still didn't understand. Yet she wanted to know how this knowledge would be used. Maybe, if she were there, and they were going to do something bad with it, she could be sure the experiment failed.

"What kind of apes will I be working with?" said Linda.

"You won't be working with apes," said Sorenson.

fourteen

EVIDENCE

At the request of Bob Oechsler and several other noted researchers, the RCMP, Royal Canadian Mounted Police, did a formal investigation on the UFO landing in Carp, Canada. The final report generated by this agency as a result of this investigation is very interesting. I downloaded the report from a computer network run by a good friend, Mike Christol. Mike runs the Kentucky UFO Network, KUFON. And the particular gem of evidence he considered very interesting is a statement made by the Canadian military giving the results of their investigation.

"It's the final word on Carp," said Mike. "I really think you should consider this information before this all comes out, and the Canadian UFO landing turns out to be the Canadian UFO hoax."

"You realize," I said, "this is not the first time that the military has come up with this kind of pat, perfect explanation for a UFO phenomenon. I believe in the Roswell case, the military announced we had shot a 'flying saucer' down. Later they completely changed their story. Backed by a team of scientists, they claimed it had only been a weather balloon."

"Look, J.B.," he said. "I'm not saying that it was a helicopter. I just want you to read this over."

The following document is included in its entirety as received.

Message #7722 "LOCALMSG"
Date: 09-Apr-94 17:10
From: MIKE CHRISTOL
To: J.B. Michaels
Subj: CARP: FINAL WORD 2/9

* Forward from "LOCALMSG"
* Originally by Jacques Poulet
* Originally to All
* Originally dated 4 Apr 1994, 9:54

* Message originally:
    From: Benjamin Leblanc
    To: All
    Date: 04-Apr-94
    Area: "MUFONET UFO echo"
* Forwarded by Jacques Poulet using Remote Access 2.01+

RCMP GRC
Information Access Directorate
720 Chemin Belfast Rd.
OTTAWA, Ontario K1A 0R2
RCMP GRC - INVESTIGATION REPORT

Security classification : PROTECTED A
RCMP File References : 93A-0735

Division: A
Date: 1993-APR-01
Sub-division: Federal Policing Section
Detachment: F.I.U.

Reference: Unsolved Mysteries
                Assistance to General Public   1993-FEB-07

1.0 INDIVIDUALS & ORGANIZATIONS SUBJECT OF INVESTIGATION

5. (N.J. PATTERSON) Mjr.
Canadian Forces Base Ottawa
Base Information Officer
ph: (613) 991-4457

7. (P. FRASER), Sgt.
Add: R.C.M.P. H-Q, Audio Visual Enhancement
ph 993-8448

ORGANIZATIONS

1. TOWNSHIP of WEST CARLETON
Municipal Offices
ph: (613) 839-5644

2. Huisson Aviation Ltd.
Add: Carp Ont.
ph: (613) 839-5868

3. Department of Transport (D.O.T.)
Add: Ottawa Ont.
ph: (613) 990-1189

4. National Research Council (N.R.C.)
Flight Research
ph: (613) 998-3071

5. Ottawa Weather Office
ph: (613) 998-3440

2.0 HISTORY OF THE COMPLAINT

2.1 On February 02nd 1993, a television broadcast entitled "Unsolved Mysteries" was aired. In this broadcast Diane LABENEK alleges that on August 18th 1991, at approximately 22:00 hrs, she observed a UFO (Unidentified Flying Object), approaching, land-

ing then departing from the back fields of her residence.

2.2 Ten minutes after the departure an unidentified helicopter passed over her residence at an altitude close enough to cause some damage to a few roof shingles.

2.3 At the time Mr. LABENEK was reported to be on an errand and as a result he did not witness the incidents. The broadcast also indicated that the UFO incident had been captured on video tape by an unknown individual identified only as, "THE GUARDIAN." The video and correspondence was then sent ########### [text blanked out in document] some six months after the incident.

2.4 On February 10th 1993, "A" Division F.I.U. received information from a source stating that the incident ############# [text blanked out in document]

3.0 PURPOSE OF INVESTIGATION

3.1 A: To ascertain if sufficient evidence is available to support a prosecution under the Aeronautics Act, Section 534(2)(b), for flying below 500 feet.
   B: To ascertain if in fact the object observed is an aircraft.
   C: To ascertain if the craft observed is a UFO.

4.0 INVESTIGATION

4.1 On FEB. 15th 1993, Cst. DE HAITRE conducted an enquiry with the following results.

4.2 One source interviewed (A) had not observed the reported occurrence, however on February 14th 1993, he did video tape a sign ############# of where the incident had occurred. This sign was approximately five feet square, made of steel, painted in yellow with the phrases; "DEFECE CAAA" "KILLING TECHNOLOGY" "TEST AREA," in black paint with a hand drawn picture of a tank and an airwolf type helicopter at the bottom of the sign. A copy of the video was made for the writer.

4.3 One observation made of the sign, is that the general character-istics of the lettering closely resembled that of the correspondence sent by "THE GUARDIAN," ############# along with the video taping of the UFO.

4.4 The source had in 1991 and 1992 observed several more such signs in that area, one even had the word "NUCLEAR" spelt as "NUCLEEAR," with two "E"s. It appears that at the present time these signs are either gone or buried under the snow.

4.5 The source ############# further stated that low flying heli-copters with no observed identifiable markings have been in the area at different times of the day and night. As a result it was agreed that the source would keep a daily diary until further notice. An attempt to photograph and/or video tape future helicopters flying over would be made, as an assistance to the writer.

4.6 At approximately 10:00 hrs Cst. DE HAITRE attended at the location where the video of the sign was made. Four more signs were located and photographed for the file. These signs were simi-lar to signs previously mentioned in 4.4 but smaller in size, with only the word "WARNING" on one and the word "ONE" on the other. Nothing of further value was found. These signs had been severely damaged by gun shots likely as a result of hunters using them as target practice.

4.7 At approximately 11:00 hrs a red and white helicopter was observed and photographed by the investigator who was at the in-tersection of Corkery Rd., and Old Almonte Rd. The helicopter was travelling in a north to south direction crisscrossing ###### ##################### well above the 500 feet limit required by law.

4.8 Another source interviewed (B) did not observe any UFO sight-ing as mentioned on the broadcast. This individual has lived in the area #################### and has had occasion to observe helicopters flying in a south-west direction. He stated that a mili-tary base exists in Carp, and that there is also a training school at the Carp airport about seven miles away.

4.9 This source further stated that around 1988 / 1989 a helicopter was sighted in the field behind #########. A few months later it was rumored that a farmer in that area had been missing a few cows. No comments was made regarding the Unsolved Mysteries showing.

4.10 Another source interviewed (C) did not observe the UFO sighting, however did say that helicopters do fly low in the area, further, that there is a medical helicopter described as being white and orange-red in color that does the Carp to Kingston run. The helicopter's flight path is directly over their residence. It was not mentioned if the medical helicopter was the suspected low flyer.

4.11 Another source interviewed (D) who has resided in the are ########## did not see the program in question ############### This person ########### indicates that there are many helicopters flying usually out of the Carp Airport, but not at low altitudes.

4.12 Another source interviewed (E) has resided in the area ######## (same area visited by the first source and the investigator). He further stated that almost every night at approximately 21:00 hrs, for the last couple of years, helicopters have been flying over the residence.

4.13 Another source interviewed (F) has lived in the area ### ########## has seen several helicopters fly over, noticed nothing out of the ordinary and added that this is a quiet area. The source did view the Unsolved Mysteries program.

4.14 Another source interviewed (G) has lived in the area many years (same area visited by the investigator). He is aware of the signs erected saying, "NUCLEAR TESTING" etc.

##
###
###
##
[section 4.15 completely lined out]

4.16 When questioned about the red and white helicopters the source indicated that this was the new emergency helicopter which for the last two years has been flying over the house when making its runs to and from Barrys Bay. At times it even flies three times a night.

4.17 As a final piece of information the source indicated that a person living in the area,
###################
############### ###################
############################## ####################
##

4.18 Another source interviewed (H) has lived in the area many years and indicates that for as long as he can remember their (sic) have bee odd grass formations, approximately ten feet in diameter. They could be found #################################### ##

4.19 Another source interviewed (I) has lived in the area #### ######## and could only say that ########################## ######################
##################
##################################
##
##

[section 4.20 also lined out]

4.21 Attendance made at the West Carleton township clerks office where it was learnt that a similar letter much like the one aired on Unsolved Mysteries had been received about a year ago. Since it made reference to the military it was subsequently handed over to the Military Police at the Carp military base.

It was also learnt that pictures had been taken of various signs on the previously mentioned property, by a by-laws officer who subsequently handed them to the military. To date this information has not been made available to the writer.

4.22 On February 17th 1993, another source interviewed (J) ####

################## *advised that the air ambulance has been in operation for the last two years, it covers all of Eastern Ontario and the flight path from Carp to Cornwall takes it directly #######################. The helicopter has a white strobe light which at night can look blue and can flash several cycles per second much like the one seen on Unsolved Mysteries.*

4.23 The air ambulance helicopter was in operation from 20:35 hrs on the 18th of August 1991, till 00:22hrs on the 19th. At the time of the sighting the helicopter was on route from Cornwall to N.D.M.C. (National Defence Medical Center) in Ottawa and therefore eliminated as a subject.

*4.24 The writer heard rumors that the military, the RCMP S.E.R.T. teams and the N.R.C. (National Research Council) had each been conducting helicopter exercises and training sessions during the same period of time. This information was later denied by the Military and RCMP. The NRC flight research lab with facilities in Carp has been experimenting with different means of commanding a helicopter, a Bell 205 Red and Yellow. **Such tests are usually during the day and originate from Uplands Airport, furthermore no such flights were recorded on the 18th of August.***

*4.25 On February 18th information was received from the D.O.T., revealing that Military helicopters have in fact been conducting exercises at Connaught Ranges, #########################
and that often helicopters land in farmers fields. The exercises consists of night vision goggles (NVG) flight training, in which the pilot flies the helicopter without lights in total darkness using only special night vision equipment, the purpose is to fly as close to the ground as possible. It is conceivable that the pilot may by design or by error stray from the designated area. When such activities are to take place a Notice to Airmen should be sent out advising of same and that red flares will be used as markers, in a "T" formation.*

4.26 The D.O.T. also advises that it is not uncommon to see the U.S. military making unscheduled or unspecified flights into Canadian Air Space, without alerting Canadian authorities. Such patrols would never be admitted by U.S. authorities. These flights are likely out of Fort DRUM, N.Y. They will often participate in Cnd. Armed Forces manoeuvred, for an exchange of experience and information during training sessions, and sometimes although rarely, "just for a ride." It has also been learnt that the Canadian military's actions are not governed by the Civil Aeronautics Act but rather by parallel military air regulations. Should the military be found flying in a manner dangerous to the public safety, the D.O.T. procedure is to advise the Ministry of Defence who will then investigate the matter. In the source's opinion it is an accepted practice that until something happens the infractions are ignored.

4.27 Mjr. PATTERSON admits that helicopters do fly in the area but not at tree top level. That N.V.G. flights are made but in designated areas. He further admits that he may not be aware of all unscheduled or unspecified flights. He further stated that it is not uncommon to have U.S. helicopters in the area for reasons such as refuelling etc.

4.28 Mjr. PATTERSON who had received a copy of the video tape and a letter relating to the incident ########## provided same to the writer for investigational purposes. ################# ### PATTERSON has viewed the video and in his opinion, the event appears to be real but the location where it occurred is not certain. ## ##

4.29 On February 18th three experts from the D.O.T. viewed the video and as a result a letter expressing a personal opinion was provided to the writer, indicating the following.

Note that the letter has been condensed

The main rotor, the tail bottom assembly, the bright white light under the object is consistent with helicopter high intensity hover lights, the red and green lights which could be navigation lights that are low and close to the body again consistent with a helicopter. The flickering light could be a "masthead light," which is a white light shinning on the rotor mast of a helicopter for inspection purposes. This light shines on the rotating portion of the flight control rods of the main rotor and gives the impression that the light is pulsing. The frequency of the flicker, 7 cycles per second as stated in the television video, would be consistent with the rotation speed of a helicopter rotor (360-400 RPM). As a result the helicopter is likely a SIKORSKY S-76 commercial or a SIKORSKY UH60 U.S. Military helicopter.

4.30 On February 19th at approx. 10:00 hrs Cst. DE HAITRE spoke ################################### made reference to several individuals he had apparently interviewed regarding the incident and who the GUARDIAN might be.

##
##
##

[section 4.31 masked out of document]

4.32 Fraudulent Cheque Section at H-Q was provided a copy of the correspondence as seen on the broadcast, to compare with any similar material. This resulted with a negative reply.

4.33 On February 22nd the writer obtained the weather conditions for the 18th AUGUST 1991, for the general area including Carp.
   High 23.5 C Low 15.8 C   Precipitation nil
   At 20:00hrs: 18.7 C - wind East 11Km - mild
   At 21:00hrs: 17.3 C - wind East North East 11Km - mild
   At 22:00hrs: 16.9 C - wind North North East 9Km - mild
   At 23:00hrs: 16.1 C - wind East North East 11Km - mild
   At 24:00hrs: 15.9 C - wind North East 11Km - mild
No clouds from 20:00hrs to 24:00hrs clear visibility 15 miles+

4.34 On February 25th at approx. 15H00hrs ################ scaled photograph of the fingerprint found on the "GUARDIAN's" video cassette. However without a suspect print to compare t, A-Div. Ident. was not able to provide any results.

4.35 On February 26th at approx. 09:30hrs Cst. DE HAITRE con-

tacted the complainant and was advised that low flying helicopters had been recorded in a diary and video taped. On the 02nd of March attendance was made to view the diary and the video. Unfortunately the quality was so poor that the helicopter could not be identified. However the daily diary has no less than six separate sightings of a low flying white helicopter between February 15th and 25th.

4.36 At approximately 13:15 hrs Mjr. PATTERSON was informed of this new development and provided a response for only two of the sightings. He states that they are UN helicopters, white in color, on manoeuvred and should be no lower than 500 feet.

4.37 D.O.T. advised that the helicopters refereed to here are likely RCMP S.E.R.T. TEAMS doing scenarios, flown by the military. The bottom line is that the civil air regulations does not apply in this case, but these flights may be bordering on illegal low-flying.

4.38 The Ottawa Intl. airport could not provide information regarding the UFO and would not ordinarily know of any incident in the Carp area unless advised. As for the Carp airport it is a limited operation, operated by the township. Basically one can come and go at will without anyone knowing.

4.39 On March 02 at approx. 10:30 hrs the writer attended HUISSON Aviation in Carp where pictures were taken of the air ambulance and the Bell 205 helicopter. ################# the maintenance crew and pilots were allowed to view the video. Their conclusion is that the aircraft in question is likely a SIKORSKY UH-60, Black Hawk. One person mentioning that it sounded like one. Their opinions mirror that of the Dept. of Transport. These helicopters including the Bell 205 all resemble each other with very minor differences.

4.40 Attendance was made at the ####### residence at approx. 12:30hrs. In conversation with ########### it was learnt that on the date in question he remembered that at approx. 14:00hrs he saw a dark colored possibly green helicopter in the third field, and observed people jumping out. He stated "they don't bother me I don't bother them." He admits it may be that they were doing the same

*thing later that evening. His concern is that helicopters fly so close
to his house that they damage the shingles.*

*4.41 On March 03 at approx. 13:30 hrs ##########################
In the conversation he indicated that there was no STRONTIUM
residue in the area and that there should have been since it is a
component of red flares. This residue remains in the ground for
years and years and should therefore have been present. #########
also made mention to the writer and to Mjr. PATTERSON,
that TITANIUM had been found in some of the soil samples he had
taken from the area. He did not explain how the samples were taken
and if any precautions were made against contamination.*

*4.42 On March 03rd at approx. 14:45hrs Cst. DE HAITRE was
advised by H-Q chemistry section that time and knowing where to
look is an important factor when attempting to find strontium. All
traces of the material would disappear in a very short time especially when exposed to the elements. This information contradicts
########### theory that because strontium was not found, that
the red flares were from a U.F.O.*

*4.43 At approx. 10:30 hrs ############### contacted the investi-
gator by phone. He refused to be interviewed in person stating that
he had no time. ################ ################ ##########
######### ################## ########### and further does not
wish to be involved with the investigation. When asked about the
alien pictures in the video ######### immediate response was that
it was a picture of a mask taken in the dark. "It's that simple to do."*

*4.44 On March 8th a voluntary statement was obtained from a source
(K) who said that, after hearing of the Unsolved Mysteries crew
being in the Carp area filming a UFO incident, he provided the
name ############################## as a possible reference,
simply because of his knowledge on the subject. The source also
advised that ############################## ##########
############# ########################## ################
also claims that the GUARDIAN tape has been poorly edited. That
it has several of what is called "jump cuts," poor edits throughout.*

In his opinion there is nothing in the video to suggest it was filmed in Corkery and he also suspects that the Allen pictures were from another video tape.

4.45 On March 05th at approx. 09:30hrs Sgt FRASER RCMP Video Analysis viewed the video in question. The video provided appeared to be a third or fourth generation and there is an attendant decrease in the quality of the video recording with each successive genera-tion. As a result of this viewing certain characteristics of a helicop-ter were noted, ie:

    A: Tail end
    B: Lights at front
    C: Two sets of windows

Prints of the above were provided to the writer. The following two observations were equally as interesting.

    D: The flares appear at the beginning of the video with the UFO then they disappear not to be seen again. This is contrary to #################### the Unsolved Mysteries program which show the UFO leaving then the flares extinguish.

    E: The UFO shown on Unsolved Mysteries was seen approach-ing, landing then departing the scene as the flares went out. This is contrary to the actual GUARDIAN video which shows the UFO sta-tionary throughout the filming and the red flares disappearing at the beginning.

4.46 On March 30th 1993 at approx. 08:00 hrs Cst. DE HAITRE interviewed ########### ################### ################ ###### ################## ############################### ###### ########### ############ ############################# #############

5.0 INVESTIGATOR'S COMMENTS

5.1 It is worth noting that to this date there have been no further re-ported incidents of low flying white helicopters, as indicated in 4.35.

6.0 IN CONCLUSION

6.1 The purpose of the investigation is stated in paragraph 3.1. In reviewing the facts pertaining to the incident ################### ########### it has been determined that ;
    A: Not enough evidence has been brought forward to support a prosecution under Section 534(2)(b) of the Aeronautics Act.
    B: The object observed was a helicopter but could not be identified due to a lack of sufficient details ie; markings.
    C: See B above.

Unless further information regarding this incident comes to light this file will be as here undernoted.

CONCLUDED HERE.
                                    (JRD DE HAITRE), Cst.
                                    Reg. #: 34529
(JCP BISSON), Sgt.
"A" DIVISION
Federal Investigation Unit
Distribution: - original to General Enforcement Branch H-Q
                - copy to the file

[END OF DOCUMENT]

So in the final analysis in section 6.1b of the document, the object that landed at Carp, Ontario was never positively identified. In addition, there were no low-flying helicopter flights sighted in the area, and according to military schedules, none were present at the time of the sighting. None of the three independent video experts I consulted were able to identify or locate the craft features noted in the report by the RCMP. Also, the strobe rate of the light above the craft was significantly different than that of a helicopter propeller. The controversy was certainly not over. In fact, Bob Oechsler was soon to release a document completely refuting the RCMP report and giving additional information that would strongly suggest the craft was a UFO.

fifteen

GODS

There is an old saying that the gods of one nation are the demons of another. So the deities worshipped by the ancient Babylonians, the Romans, the Greeks, and the Egyptians were readily incorporated in the pantheon of Jewish and Hebrew evil entities to be feared rather than worshipped. One might further observe that the races of one planet may be the gods or demons of another, providing they are sufficiently advanced to make the journey and the beings they are visiting are primitive enough to see them as such.

As I was gathering information for this book, I found that our civilization is at a crucial time in its history. For the first time, since humankind's ancestors crawled out of the primeval slime, we have begun to visit other worlds. And because we are just beginning to flex our wings and could within the next hundred years be seen as gods ourselves by some sentient beings in a far solar system, we have much less respect or awe than our forefathers for alien visitors. Where some primitive might have seen a light in the sky, sank to his knees in terror, and told this story as the appearance of a god, today you won't see that happening. Our governments and military have a much different approach to dealing with visiting extraterrestrial races or Nonterrestrial Lifeforms. The current military response to a UFO encountered in American airspace is to make two attempts at communication, order the object to land,

and if it does not respond, shoot it down.

We have only been able to meet and deal with UFOs on their own turf, in the air, for the past 80 years or so. We have walked this earth as a human species for more than 200,000 years and as a quasi-simian life-form at least for the last three million years. And so I found that to even begin to understand what was going on at the Carp landing and the Long Island crash in terms of the type of aliens these could be, I would need some working knowledge of the history of UFOs and extraterrestrial visitors. Then I would better be able to correlate and compare these events with other UFO sightings throughout history.

I sent my assistant, Deborah Parker, to a score of libraries, and then set her loose on the computer networks to search out all major databases for UFO information. Deborah is painstakingly thorough, and if it were possible to gather information on all major UFO sightings from the beginning of time in just a few weeks, she would be the one that could do it. Deborah arrived at my house with an armload of books and several boxes of computer disks.

"Sheesh!" she said. "Did you realize how much information there is on this stuff?" She lay the stack of books on my coffee table. "There's a lot more in the car. More than a hundred books and at least as many floppy disks." She smiled. "The librarians all hate me now. I bugged them all to death. But they were pretty helpful. You would be amazed how many people are really seriously interested in the UFO phenomenon."

I picked up a book by Whitley Streiber.

"Yes," Deborah said, nodding toward the book in my hand. "You should read that, too. Pretty interesting. Talks about this woman who was kidnapped and then raped by aliens."

I laughed. "That's 'abducted,' Deborah, and I don't think they were raped. More like aliens experimenting with strange unusual toys and inserting them into every orifice of her body." Actually the thought made me shudder. Especially when I thought about the ones that were supposedly inserted up nostrils and then sliced off tissue samples. "Tom and I used to talk about that. Little gray men running around some woman's bed at night terrorizing her."

"Sounds like you." She grinned. She held out a book titled *Chariot of the Gods,* which had several torn paper markers in it.

"You better unplug your phone for the weekend and get used to me being here. We have a lot of ground to cover." She sighed. "A lot. And I mean to read you aloud most of what I have marked. See what you think of it."

With her help, the almost Herculean task of plowing through all this information might even be possible. "You're here for the weekend. So what have you got for me first?"

Deborah cleared her throat and then continued. "Looks like extraterrestrials have been visiting us for a hell of a long time. Their visits definitely predate human history, at least the written human history. There are some pictographs that I found that really go back. Can you think of any other evidence I might have missed?"

"Well, for starters," I said, "physical evidence, such as the remains of alien craft, maybe a pyramid which by its very design and structure would preclude existing savages from having built it, and possibly some type of fossil evidence or cave paintings depicting unusual humanoid-type creatures.

"Any one of these would indicate we had been visited by extraterrestrials before recorded human history."

"I think I have something like the last thing you mentioned, strange humanoid pictographs. That happened about 50,000 years ago." She put a the disk in my 486 and pulled up WordPerfect. "Okay, now listen to this . . . The earliest evidence we have of alien contact was uncovered by Tschi Pen Lao of the University of Peking. He discovered astonishing carvings in granite on a mountain in Hunan Province and on an island in Lake Tungting. These carvings were estimated to be at least 47,000 years old, and they show people with large trunks. Breathing apparatus? Or 'elephant' heads shown on human bodies? Remember, the Egyptians often represented their gods as animal heads on human bodies."

Deborah grabbed a large book, opened it, and pointed to a color photo.

"This one is from Africa," she said. "Look at these guys." There were a group of figures sculpted from rocks. They appeared to be human beings, but they had strange, round heads. "These sculptures are dated about eight thousand years ago and were found on the Tassili plateau in the Sahara Desert. Some anthropologists call them 'sun' heads, but they could also be helmets of some kind."

"Let me show you something," I said, leaning over and pulling out a slide projector and carousel from underneath the coffee table. "Hit the lights, I just show this on the wall."

"Oh no," said Deborah, groaning. "Slides from Europe."

"No, no, not Europe," I said. The wall was covered with an unusually clear shot of dense jungle and a pyramid. "I took these while I was in Palenque on a dig."

"A dig?" said Deborah, giving me an odd look.

"Yes, I was working in archaeology with the Mexican government at a temple complex located in the southern part of the Yucatan Peninsula. A dig is another name for excavating a site. They were very short on funds and this particular area"—I clicked the projector remote, and the picture changed to what appeared to be an oriental temple with the same pyramid as we had seen before to the right—"is almost 36 square miles of ruins, of which maybe four to five percent is actually excavated. The Mexican government is even more careful about its archeological treasures than Egypt or Greece. So, our basic agreement was that we could poke around, catalog items, try to decipher the Olmec pictographs, pretty much do what we pleased, as long as anything we found would go directly to the Museo del Archeologico in Mexico City.

"Anyway," I said, clicking for another slide. "Here is a picture of the surrounding jungle area. You'll notice the tops of several pyramids poking up through the vines."

"So, what's your point?" Deborah said. "I mean, that is all very interesting, but what has any of that to do with extraterrestrials?"

"A lot," I said defensively, and clicked the remote. A huge monolith filled the screen. I showed what appeared to be an Indian sitting on a seat, and below the seat were what appeared to be rocket engines and flames. In front of him was a control panel.

Deborah walked up to the wall studying the picture. "Impressive. So when did they carve this?"

"Oh, less than a thousand years ago. Actually it's fairly recent in terms of archeological time," I said.

"Well," said Deborah, taking a book from the top of the stack on the table. "The Olmecs weren't the only ancient people to run into UFOs and aliens. This book is full of them." She held up a copy of the Bible.

"You serious?" I said.

"Absolutely," she answered. "Now listen . . ." She thumbed through the pages. "Okay . . . this is from Ezekiel. This guy must have lived at least a thousand years before Christ. It begins here in Chapter I."

And I looked, and, behold, out of the north, a whirlwind came out of the north, a great cloud, and a fire enfolding itself, and a brightness was about it, and out of the midst thereof as the color of amber, out of the midst of the fire.

"Okay, so there's your fire in the sky, now listen to this."

And in the midst thereof came the likeness of four living creatures . . . as for the likeness of the living creatures, their appearance was like burning coals of fire, and like the appearance of lamps; it went up and down among the living creatures and the fire was bright, and out of the fire went forth lightning.

"I would say that's a major energy disturbance and four aliens. But it gets better. All we need now is a flying saucer, or better yet, several flying saucers."

Now as I beheld the living creatures, behold one wheel upon the earth by the living creatures . . . The appearance of the wheels and their work was like unto the color of beryl . . .

"So, what color is beryl?" I interrupted.

"I looked that up," said Deborah. "Beryl comes from beryllium, and that is steel gray. So looks like our 'wheels' here are metallic. Now, I have some other places I found, but I don't know if you want to use them. Some people might not like having these parts interpreted as NTLs. The oldest biblical reference I could find was in Genesis. It's here in the sixth chapter."

That the sons of God saw the daughters of men that they were fair; and they took them wives of all which they chose . . . There were giants in the earth in those days; and also after that, when the sons of God came in unto the daughters of men, and they bare children to them, the same became mighty men which were of old, men of renown.

"That was just before the Flood. Interesting thing about all that is that right after these NTLs came down and enhanced the genetic pool, people started living a very long time. In fact, right after that Noah lived to be 950 years old, and then they decided they were gods and started building that tower. So it looked like the human race was beginning to worry, whatever race was watching us, and it says here in the eleventh chapter.

And the Lord said, Behold the people is one, and they have one language, and this they begin to do; and now nothing will be restrained from them, which they have imagined to do. Go to, let us.

"Well anyway, whoever 'us' is scrambled their language." She closed the Bible. "I have noted at last 27 references where NTL- and UFO-type things happened. In fact, you know the star over the manger? Well, remember it moved when the wise men followed it."

Deborah sighed.

"I think," I said, "people would be even more disturbed to find out that the entire human race is one incredible, long-term genetic experiment that NTLs have been overseeing for tens of thousands of years. And suppose that they just came back recently to check on their experiment?"

sixteen

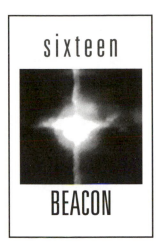

BEACON

As I gathered more and more information concerning the recovery and confinement of the surviving alien at Brookhaven Lab, I began to notice much information that was originally classified appearing in articles in local newspapers and on TV. Despite the sincere efforts of the CIA and other government intelligence agencies to cover up UFO incidents, many films and books written about UFOs contain classified or restricted information.

The following incidents continue the narration describing the recovered living alien and the analysis of two other dead alien bodies. It is certainly not unique in that dozens of alien bodies and living aliens have been found by the military in the last fifty years, since the first well-documented case in Roswell, New Mexico. Despite an "older guard" in the CIA and military that still echoes some of the hard-line attitudes of the Cold War era, a growing number of individuals are attempting to take a more humane approach in our contacts with alien races. In the past, aliens were vivisected, dissected while they were still alive, without any anesthetic or consideration to the terror and agony the alien must have experienced. In the last five years, the government has tried to at least communicate with aliens held in captivity. Most of this is purely for the military to gather information on their intentions and defensive strengths and weaknesses. No alien, except for the one described in this narration, has survived the scrutiny or living in conditions so different than their home environment. The information and events described here were gathered from three separate individuals who either work at or have been inside Brookhaven Lab.

I personally reserve judgement, seeing as the events described are so incredible. Yet, I have verified through separate sources the basic information given on the autopsy and general description of the aliens. There are also several government-funded classified projects developing means to communicate with alien races, SOPs for encounters with aliens, and even a detailed defense strategy to be used if the alien forces turn hostile. It has been stated by one source in the Defense Department that we have been in a hostile, nondeclared war with the "Grays" for the last six years. This is certainly not one sided, in that several American craft have been shot down. Yet, all of the evidence I have been able to uncover indicates these confrontations were provoked by the U.S. military and only defensive action was taken by the UFOs.

We continue now where Sorenson is chewing out one of the Brookhaven personnel for the missing slide that contained alien DNA.

"So, precisely how much material from the alien autopsy is missing?" Sorenson looked at Carol, the pathologist, menacingly. "You realize it was your responsibility to keep the lid on this. Why in the hell did you label the damn slides?"

"I didn't label them," said Carol. "In fact, I wasn't even in the lab when the tissue samples were taken, nor was I even aware that they were here. You must realize a considerable number of people come in and out of this lab. There are dozens of separate projects and pathologists working here.

"Listen," she continued. "I have had it up to here with this cloak-and-dagger stuff anyway." She turned to an old, white-bearded man who was flipping through the notes on the autopsy. "And you, Carter, I mean, I am honored to meet you. You are a legend in the field of forensic medicine, but I had no idea how crazy these CIA people were."

"The CIA is not crazy," said Carter, laying the sheaf of papers on a shiny chrome table. "Just a little over zealous at times. It's a matter of national security. We have no idea what the public reaction will be if this information should leak out. You know from the autopsy what we are up against here from this NTL. They appear to be much more highly evolved than us. They are much more intelligent, have developed superior craft and weapons, and we still are not certain of their intentions. You must realize how serious the situation is."

"Just how serious is it, Carter?" Sorenson grabbed the autopsy report and began thumbing through the pages. Sorenson had no medical background. The strange lists of molarities, organs, weights and microtome slice analysis were meaningless to him.

"They certainly are more advanced physically and intellectually than we are," said Carter. "These creatures may be bipedal, have two eyes, and have fingers and toes, but I would guess they are hundreds of thousands, if not millions, of years ahead of us on the evolutionary tree. For one, they have two brains. At least both of the hemispheres are so developed that the corpus callosum is literally split."

"English, please," said Sorenson, feeling the same way he had while reading the report.

"See the fissure here," said Carter. He walked over to a shelf that held a large jar containing the alien brain. It was overly large and much paler than a human brain. "Goes almost all the way to the brain stem. Also, they have two hearts, a digestive system that is so atrophied it is hardly recognizable. Their nasal filtration system, you know, sinuses and so forth, simply does not exist. Apparently, they live in such a controlled environment, completely sterile environment, they have no need for it."

Sorenson grunted. "Well, none of this sounds particularly menacing to me, Carter."

"If you understood what he's saying, it would," Carol interrupted. "In terms of brain capacity, we are as far behind these creatures as a stone axe-carrying Neanderthal was to modern Homo sapiens. They're ability to process information, communicate, and analyze data must be incredible."

"They can't be all that incredible," said Sorenson. "We shot down three of their ships and recovered not only the craft, but have one additional NTL alive in the lab below us. Despite all this so-called intelligence, the creature hasn't uttered a sound and has made no attempt whatsoever to communicate with us at all."

LINDA KING sat looking in the alien's eyes. It had large, liquid, almost reptilian eyes. They would stare back at her, unblinking, and seemed to look far deeper inside of her than she was comfortable with. Yet this creature seemed incredibly at peace, unafraid, unresisting to wherever it was taken, whatever was done to it.

"If I had known what this was all about, I would have never come here," said Linda. But that was a lie. In fact, if she had known that she would be working with an NTL, she would have been even more insistent that she be involved in the project.

The huge, dark eyes looked down on the surface of the shiny table between them. Linda King knew that the creature wanted her to see it look down. When the creature was more active, it could turn its head so quickly that she could hardly even see it move. It would appear that suddenly the creature's head was at a different angle, but she never would see it turn to get there. Now it was looking at the translator symbol board. She had spent several weeks going over the symbols, trying somehow to convey what they meant to the creature.

The creature was by no means motionless. Its head seemed to turn from left to right in a slow repeating rhythm, and its arms and hands would move about the air without any apparent purpose. This was very disturbing. It was one of the things besides appearance that made this creature so alien. It simply did not move the way we do. Linda wondered whether the gravity where this alien came from was much greater than our own, because when it walked it almost seemed to glide across the floor.

Linda was completely unprepared when it took one single large finger and pressed three symbol buttons.

<SPACECRAFT> button with a symbol resembling the smaller UFO that had crashed
<MOVING>   walking figure indicating movement, coming, or going
<LABORATORY> the symbol for Brookhaven Laboratory

She realized then that the creature had known all along how to use the symbol board. For some reason, it was either not capable of human speech or simply preferred talking in symbols.

"Do you understand what I am saying? Have you understood all along?"

<NOD> The creature pushed the symbol of a head nodding yes.

Linda grinned. She wondered how she must appear to this creature. It was quite possible that she looked as primitive to it as Brutus, the ape, did to her.

<NTL> symbol for alien
<ARMS CROSSED> cares for—likes—loves
<HUMAN>

Linda just stared for a moment, trying to comprehend what this meant. She had thought she understood when Brutus had typed in the same symbols, that the creature in some sort of primitive way had affection for her. But to this creature, its kind many thousands of years ahead of the human race, what exactly did those symbols mean? It was strange, because as it pressed the symbols she also felt an indescribable feeling of warmth and peace. Even more disturbing, when she wasn't watching the alien, the symbols still appeared in her mind, as if the symbol board were really not that necessary. The creature continued.

<HUMAN> <ARMS CROSSED> < NTL> <NTL > <MOVING> <SPACECRAFT>

Linda stared for a second and then grinned with a wave of comprehension. "You want to go back," she said. "You're saying, if I care about you, then I will help you escape so you can somehow get to your ship. But your ship is destroyed. That is not possible."

<NTL> <MOVING> <SPACECRAFT> The creature repeated on the symbol pad.

<NTL> <MOVING> <NTL>

"Another ship is coming," Linda whispered. "When?"

The alien remained still. There was probably no symbol to convey the period of time before the ship would arrive. Yet inside, she felt that it would be very soon, maybe less than a few hours. There was no real choice. Linda being Linda—the zoologist, the caring person, the lover of animals—could not endure standing by while the creature was eventually vivisected on some cold chrome table by military doctors. And that's what would happen. Linda was the only one the creature would 'talk' to. After several months of refusing to communicate with anyone else or give them any useful information as to its origin or purpose, it would be terminated and then autopsied.

Linda exited the lab and headed toward the elevator. As she came to the end of the hall, she could see Bob Whitaker lying back, fast asleep.

"Ahem." Linda cleared her threat.

"What!" said Bob, sitting bolt upright. He looked at Linda, trying to figure out who she was, and at the same time trying to wake up enough to figure out where he was. "What the hell do you want?" he said, glowering at her.

"Sorry to disturb you," said Linda. "It's just that I'm really hungry and there's no one to cover for me in the lab. Could you be a real sweetheart and get me something in the cafeteria? Here," she said, holding out a twenty. "Get yourself something, too. I'd really appreciate it." She remained silent and then leaned close to him her face only inches from his. "Please," she said.

"Oh, alright," said Bob. "I'm pretty hungry myself. Want me to bring it to the lab? I could meet you back there and we could take our break together."

Linda frowned. "No, no." She handed him a folder she had been carrying. "And could you take these to Dr. Harding's office?"

"Damn," he said. "What do I look like, Federal Express?" Bob scowled but reached out and took the document anyway.

"Thanks," Linda smiled. "Okay, bring the food to the lab. We can talk for a while. I would like that."

"Catch you in a few," said Bob, grabbing the folder and heading down the hall.

Linda estimated it would take Bob at least 15 minutes, counting the detour to drop off the papers at Harding's office. Just enough time to get the NTL out of the facility and into the woods surrounding Brookhaven Lab.

seventeen

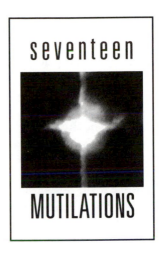

MUTILATIONS

"*They cut the rectum out, and I had to kill the cow*," *said Leonard Jarmon of Hopewell.*

The paper in Deborah's hands was the Decatur *Daily*. It came from Blount County, Alabama. It mentioned a strange mutilation that occurred on January 5th.

> *In northeast Blount County, a farmer suspects someone doing rituals was responsible for a strange mutilation of one of his cows on Jan. 5. "It was cut as smooth as if it was surgery." He said whoever did it wanted the cow's sexual organs. Jarmon said an investigator found an arrow on his land, unlike arrows used by bow hunters. It was something like a poison dart, and he said it might have been how they drugged the cow," Jarmon said.*

Deborah grimaced. It was still early in the evening, but we had been through several dozen books and as many floppy disks on the history of UFO sightings, abductions, and landings. She methodically checked off "cattle mutilations" on her list of "Things to Cover."

"You think that's bad?" she said, continuing to read. "Listen to this."

> *"I had to kill the cow," the farmer said. "Its rectum and sexual organs were cut out but it was still alive."*

"Pretty gruesome," I said, looking at the still photo of the animal taken by the farmer. "So what is this supposed to indicate . . . little green surgeons with scalpels?"

I was amazed at the large stack of materials that dealt with cattle mutilations. Obviously, this was only the tip of the iceberg. From her notes, which I scanned as she read, there were tens of thousands of reported cases to local law enforcement agencies and the government.

"Well, actually," said Deborah, "there is quite a raging debate going on. You have experts who swear this stuff was done with very high-tech lasers. Lasers much more sophisticated and portable than anything we have now. But then there are other experts who think it is all hype. I did a follow up on the FBI guy you mentioned to me last week. You know, the name that Kathryn Kaycoff, one of the directors of "Encounters" gave you. Well, he's pretty convinced there's nothing to it. I talked to him on the phone yesterday. He said we could print this."

Kenneth Rommel, a former FBI agent and author of a 297-page federally funded report on the subject, is skeptical as well. Cattle mutilation claims, says Rommel, are "a bunch of garbage, a bunch of very creative writing on the part of the media, and a lot of statements made by law enforcement officials and others that are totally unsupported by fact." Indeed, Rommel's report, written in 1980 for the state of New Mexico, found only natural causes, including predator/scavenger action, at the root of mutilation claims.

"Yes," I, said grinning. "Sounds like the government was pretty sure that report would close the chapter on cattle mutilations. Yet, last week I spoke to John Altshuler. He's a highly qualified pathologist. Very sharp. It's here in my notes . . . let's see . . ." I thumbed through a manila folder and handed a laser-printed page to Deborah.

A medical report on tissue samples taken from five mutilated animals last March revealed the following informa-

tion. This report, conducted by pathologist/hematologist John H. Altshuler of the University of Colorado in Denver, indicated that the cuts to the tissue were made "at a temperature of at least three hundred degrees Fahrenheit in less than two minutes."

"Pretty confusing." Deborah took another sip of her espresso and sighed. "Kenneth Rommel was pretty insistent that all cases could be explained by predators. He said that eagles could be very precise, almost surgical, in removing a specific organ, especially an eye or tongue. He said beak punctures could resemble those of a surgical instrument. Anyway, here is a more complete list of some of the reported mutilations. You'll notice it includes our farmer, Jarmon."

ALABAMA
Cullman County. Source—Cullman Times. December, 1988. Dog parts found. Dog was cut in half. Found in city of Vinemont.

Cullman County. Source—Cullman Times. January 26, 1989. Calf found dead. "Possibly Shot."

Cullman County. Source—Cullman Times. February 2, 1989. City of Bremen. Cow found mutilated. Milk sac and rear end cut out. Between Jan. 31 and Feb. 1.

Blount County. NE Blount County. Source—Decatur Daily. Mr. Leonard Jarman. Rectum cut out "as smooth as surgery." Strange dart found. Witness never saw a dart like that before.

COLORADO
Calhoun County. 30 Miles East of Colorado Springs. Bill & Linda Dzuris. September 16, 1982. Mutilation found 5 P.M. 4 hrs after last seeing cow alive. Rectum carved out. Udder cut out.

Calhoun County. Fall 1979. 2 heifers mutilated 100 ft. apart. Udders cut out.

San Luis County. Kings Ranch area. September 1957. "Snippy" an Appalachian Mare. Stripped of flesh from the neck up.

Larksville County (?). July 1979. C.E. Potts Rancher. Cow mutilated. Sex organs, eyes and eyelashes cut off.

Logan County. 1976. Former Sheriff reporting. Cow mutilated. Rectum and sex organs gone. Tripod marks found in hard ground. 17 ft. apart. 3 depressions.

Elbert County. 1975-1976. Bill Waugh former undersheriff reporting. Numerous cattle mutilated. Sex organs, rear ends and udders gone. Orange Ball of light sighted over a mutilation area from ground and air.

Costilla County. City of San Luis. Steve Benavidez Sheriff reporting. September 29, 1979. Circular cuts on eyes and abdomen of cow.

NEW MEXICO
Dulce. October 6, 1979. Manuel Gomez reporting. 6 mutilated cows. No tracks. No blood found. Tripod tracks in triangle shape found.

WYOMING
Sweetwater. Fall 1983. 3 cows mutilated.

"I like the tripod one in Dulce," I said. "Tripod tracks to be more precise. Three-legged little green men. Now that's a first."

What impressed me, though it really wasn't that clearly stated in the reports or by the witnesses, was how disturbed some of these farmers were by the unusual mutilation cases. No doubt, being in the cattle business, they had quite a knowledge of damage done to their cattle by predators, possibly even enough knowledge to know by the teeth marks or beak marks what type of predators had done that damage. Yet, in most reported cases, the wound or mutilation was something they had not seen before and was something so profoundly different, that they felt a need to report it to the local police.

"You know, Deborah," I said. "I wonder if anyone has ever seen one of these mutilations in progress. It would seem with all of the thousands and thousands of incidents, someone somewhere would have witnessed something like this while it was happening."

"They have," said Deborah. "In fact, not only have they witnessed it, they have been taken up with the animal into a UFO. I have a case here of a woman who was actually abducted by the aliens who mutilated the cattle. Let's see," she said, rummaging through the disks. "Yes, this was on the network."

A Judy Doraty, while under hypnosis related an incident where she had been abducted by aliens. It was during a visit to Dr. Leo Sprinkle. She had gone to the hypnotist to try to find the cause for a series of severe recurring headaches she had been experiencing.

She related that in 1973, she and her five year old daughter Cindy, had been taken aboard a UFO and examined by extraterrestrials.

Judy Doharty was in her car when she saw a beam of light coming down from a UFO. She stated that the light had an unusual quality to it, it seemed to have some sort of substance in it. The beam moved across the ground in a nearby field and as it passed on a calf that was grazing there, the animal began to rise into the air. The calf struggled frantically trying to free itself as it was lifted up into the space craft.

While on the UFO, she observed the calf being dissected by the aliens. Its eyes, tongue, and sex organs were removed, and then the calf, still alive was returned to the same spot where it had been taken from.

Doharty said that the aliens were able to communicate with her telepathically. She was told that she was under no circumstances to tell anyone what she had seen. Some type of memory block had been imposed, and until she had been hypnotized, Doharty had no recollection of

the incident whatsoever.
    She described the extraterrestrials as short males. She
said they had very large eyes, oddly shaped hands and long
fingernails.

"Creepy," said Deborah, closing the window on the computer. "Another thing I came up with is that often animals are returned to places they couldn't normally climb to, such as isolated tops of buttes with sheer rock faces. Look here." She handed me a short printout. "We have a hunter by the name of Jack Anderson who found a group of mutilated sheep in a very inaccessible place. This happened in the Mormon Mountains. That's a desert range about 60 miles southeast of Las Vegas. Pretty deserted country. Bighorn sheep," she said. "Thirteen of them. No bullet wounds, and this place was extremely difficult to get to. The wildlife officials said the sheep had been dead at least six months, maybe a year, and that they had all been killed at the same time. Because of the remoteness of the spot, their report said they believed the carcasses had been dropped there by a helicopter. Finally," Deborah said, handing me a slip of paper, "Here is the number of Bob Oeschler. He is the UFO researcher that has been investigating the Carp landing. You know that film you've been raving about. I think you should call him."

In a few minutes I had Bob Oeschler on the line. I put him on the speakerphone so Deborah could hear the conversation. Since Bob had been working on the Carp case for many years, I had sent him the so-called "debunk report" from Canada, which labeled the UFO as a helicopter. What I hadn't known before was that Bob was quite knowledgeable on UFO mutilations.

"Deborah and I have been wading through this material on cattle mutilations. Kind of hard to piece it all together, no pun intended. I was wondering if you could give us a Cliffs-notes version?"

"Sure," said Bob.

I was actually somewhat relieved to be delivered from the task of plowing through more mutilation material. I knew that Bob was an excellent researcher, as well a concise and logical communicator, and he would give me precise, condensed information.

"One of the first reported cases was a horse. The animal was found drained of blood. One of most interesting observations that is characteristic with many of the abductions was that there was no blood found anywhere around the carcass."

"None?" I said.

"Not a drop. It would appear that the animal had been operated on somewhere else and then the body had been dropped from the air. Over the years," Bob continued, "there have been hundreds of such cases. The cow you may have read about in Blount County, and the Judy Doharty case, which has been covered in some detail by several researchers. Just recently, a pathologist named John Altshuler did a pretty sophisticated series of tests on some cattle-mutilation tissue. The results were very impressive and he has slides and even tissue samples that show the difference in the tissue slices."

One thing kept sticking in my mind. The FBI investigator had been so positive that all mutilations—and he had been pretty inclusive in his statement were the result of predators.

"So what about Kenneth Rommel's statements that all we have here is a bunch of hungry eagles and scavengers?"

"I'll put it this way," said Bob. "When an animal is torn by scavengers and bleeds, cardiovascular collapse occurs. That means that as the blood drains, all the veins and capillaries flatten out. I have seen cross sections of some of these animals. Under magnification you can see the blood vessels are still open. This would indicate that these animals were bled while alive and that they were somehow sedated so they felt no pain or fear. They also found traces of ultraviolet homing paint on some of the specimens."

None of this seemed to conform to the formally issued government report that intentionally had omitted what seemed to me to be highly relevant evidence.

"You know, Bob, this is much too similar to the pat government study explaining Carp, the explanation that the Roswell crash was a weather balloon, and the Long Island fire department that still insists there was never a fire in Southaven Park on November 22, 1992. It simply doesn't make any sense."

"It does to me," said Bob. "The officer who did the report on Carp told me, hell, I can't report this as a UFO." He paused. I can explain it to you in a single word. Cover-up."

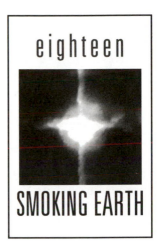

eighteen

SMOKING EARTH

The following documents were received from Bob Oechsler, UFO investigator and analyst, by personal fax on April 10, 1994. They were sent to the author and are reprinted here, intact, unedited, and exactly as received.

GUARDIAN CASE

The Guardian Case is simply one of the most important investigations in UFO research. My involvement in the investigation began in February of 1992 with the receipt of a video tape and documents sent by an anonymous individual using only the name Guardian. The video represents a remarkable improvement in the quality of UFO photographed images. It shows an unmistakable three dimensional image of a structured craft with extraordinary luminosity characteristics. Further images on the video have proven to be the first authentic images of alien beings associated with such events.

The subsequent field investigation efforts yielded gross physical effects at the landing site which was witnessed by several credible individuals. A Canadian Government official who resides in the area of the landing was taken on-board the craft and claimed to have interacted with the occupants, one of whom was a Chinese man in a black business suit. The witness' testimony was subject to polygraph examination. The results proved positive.

This one case has under gone more diversified scientific analysis than any other case in history. This due largely to the abundance of physical evidence found at the site. The case has been popularized with international publicity including segments on NBC's "Unsolved Mysteries" and Fox's "Sightings." We are currently in production involving a documentary on the case to be broadcast during ratings week in February 1994.

[Note from author: This was broadcast on "Encounters" February 22, 1994. I was also interviewed on this program, as was Bob Oechsler, and according to the director, Kathryn Kaycoff, the ratings went 'through the roof.']

The following document was sent to me by Bob shortly after the fax on the Guardian case. He requested I put it out on the network, which I agreed to do, and also included it in this book. It is in his words.

CARP SURVIVES DEBUNKING ATTEMPT

Bob Oechsler RE: CARP : FINAL WORD 04 APR / AVR 94 Leblanc : O.C.I.P.E.

Background :

In order to qualify my response to the rather authoritative commentary published recently by Benjamin Leblanc (Co-director of O.C.I.P.E near Montreal), it will be necessary to provide some insight into my philosophy on analysis and reporting of UFO case investigations. First, let me establish some basis for authority regarding my qualifications in submitting this report. I have no idea what Mr. Leblanc's qualifications may be as he failed to report any such information in his submittal - CARP: FINAL WORD.

My active involvement in the research and investigation into the UFO phenomenon dates back fourteen years, five years in which I served as the host of what became a nationwide radio broadcast called : UFO Today. Anyone who spends 250 hours a year chatting over the telephone with UFO specialists and witnesses is bound to get an incredible education. Add to that another 1,000 hours a year looking at UFO photos, and videos in the company of Ph.D. level technologists and you've got a good basis for fundamental analysis training. When you couple those credits with several weeks a year of field investigations, diplomatic and intelligence agency contracts, former NASA engineering credentials and acclaim as a robotics innovator, you have Bob Oechsler, investigations analyst, biographical information sheet available via fax.

With regard to the CARP / GUARDIAN Case Investigation, I have a particular level of expertise that warrants elucidation under these specific circumstances. My involvement commenced with the receipt of a video tape of a landed craft and some crude, but elaborate, manufactured documents detailing what is on the video and expressing ideological concerns arising out of the history of alien events reported locally over two decades. The package arrived postmarked from Ottawa with no return address and only the designation Guardian on the videotape accompanied by a fingerprint. I researched the history of previous claims by the same source which detailed events in the West Carleton township area just 30 miles west of Ottawa, Ontario. The town of Carp is located several miles to the north of the area where the landing reportedly occurred on August 18, 1991.

Since beginning the Guardian video analyses process in February of 1992, I have visited the Ottawa area conducting field investigations and research on at least nine occasions. I have invested almost three months time on location and thousands of dollars in expenses which include costly electron scanning microscope and x-ray analysis of contamination and control field samples collected at the landing site.

Over the course of my two years of investigation into the mysterious Guardian Case, I have consulted on no less than three major network television broadcasts on the case in question and have included in my investigation three top Canadian Government Agencies, RCMP Federal Investigations Unit included. My investigation has involved more Ph.D. level scientists in varied disciplines than any other case in civilian history to my knowledge. While I feel confident in certain findings and assessments derived from these efforts, it would be premature and inappropriate for me to offer a final conclusion. I cannot even eliminate with 100% certainty that the whole thing was an elaborate fabrication, although I believe it would be an extremely remote possibility.

RCMP GRC - INVESTIGATION REPORT

The investigation conducted by the Royal Canadian Mounted Police (RCMP), Federal Investigations Unit was the basis of the report recently filed by Mr. Leblanc of O.C.I.P.E. (Organization de Compilation et d'Information sur les Phenomenes Estranges). Since the Guardian investigation is a significantly complex one, I'll confine this rebuttal to the issues raised in Mr. Leblanc's report with specific attention to the RCMP investigation cited. Readers can write to the referenced address for more detailed information on my investigation regarding the Guardian Case.

Although I was intimately involved in the RCMP Investigation following a complaint filed by a resident concerned about the low level helicopter flights in the area and perplexed about the reports of a UFO landing nearby, the RCMP refused my written requests for a copy of their final report citing internal regulations. Therefore, in spite of Mr. Leblanc's arrogant perplexity at my failure to publish the RCMP report, this was the first time I've actually seen it. Nonetheless, I was familiar with much of the contents and am aware of the identities of most of those interviewed along with their comments. Consequently, I am fully prepared to respond to the arguments raised.

The primary issues raised in the RCMP Investigation centered on the reports of potentially illegal helicopter air traffic operations in the West Carleton township. As a result of my investigation on the same issue with the Department of National Defense (DND), the RCMP contacted me regarding my investigations into the videotape of a reported landing of an unusual aircraft on private property. That's how the UFO issue got pulled into the investigation.

When I was contacted by RCMP Constable Dennis De Haitre, he was interested in what information I might have to help in his investigation. I agreed to participate on an information exchange basis which was honored in principle. Cst. De Haitre made it clear to me that his investigation of adverse public relations concern regarding the investigation of a reported UFO incident. I indicated to him that my investigation was initiated with the conviction that the event most probably was some sort of military operation. There appeared to be enough evidence on the video to detect military pyro-

technic flare residue at the landing site. The laboratory results proved negative on required detectable elements and most likely eliminated military involvement. Thus began the scramble at RCMP HQ to come up with a viable explanation for the craft in the Guardian video, namely a helicopter. It seemed to be the optimum solution for them since there were so many reports of helicopters in the area, yet the DND report concluded the object in the video and the helicopters unidentified.

When it became evident to Cst. De Haitre and his superiors that I was prepared to put my technical experts with impeccable credentials up against his experts for a meeting at RCMP HQ, they declined my invitation and terminated the case investigation. Cst. De Haitre scheduled one final meeting with me at RCMP HQ in Ottawa to return some investigation exhibits which were loaned to him for his investigation. During that meeting I was permitted to review a letter in the file from an individual at another Canadian Government Agency. The letter detailed the author's expertise and indicated that based on several points (which will be addressed in this report) he concluded the object in the Guardian video was a Sikorsky S-76 helicopter.

The specifics cited from the Guardian video suggesting a helicopter include a presumed relationship between the rapidly strobing blue light on top of the craft which reflects off of a curved surface and the masthead light which is a white light shining "up" through the control rods at the rotor assembly on a helicopter. This is a ludicrous assumption that is easily refuted as the premise for the explanation of the object depicted in the video. The first problem with the hypothesis exists in the RCMP concession that the rotor assembly is operating at 360 to 400 rpm. Any rotation of the rotor assembly would visibly affect the pyrotechnics smoke which is drifting toward the object at 7 to 11 knots, which incidentally matches the meteorological report for the date and time period. No such effect is visible on the video tape.

Another issue associated with the helicopter hypothesis and the rotation of the rotor assembly involves the analysis of the audio track from the Guardian videotape. The RCMP investigation revealed that a sound could be heard on the tape that is consistent with the sound of rotating chopper blades. I retained the services of an acoustical physicist to conduct an audio analysis. One of several *stops involved in the analysis required dubbing the audio track from the Guardian videotape onto a digital audio tape recording (DAT). The sound attributed to the helicopter hypothesis was not on the DAT and therefore it could only be attributed to video noise associated with the bright bursts of light coming from the blue strobe. The video noise need not be a product of the audio track in order to be audible.*

Frame by frame analysis of the Guardian videotape refutes another factor in the masthead light issue in the helicopter frequency of the flashing "blue" (white shows up white on video, never blue) strobe light in the video. RCMP analysts concluded that the rotor assembly would need to operate at 360–400 RPM. With the masthead light turned on, the control rods might give the impression of a strobe effect. There are several problems inherent with this theory. The masthead light would have to be of tremendous luminosity in order to match the video image and the control rods no matter how thick could not totally blank out the scatter effect of the constantly burning light. And there is nothing to account for the reflection of the strobe on the lower surface area of the craft. RCMP declined a suggested demonstration with Sikorsky S-76 helicopter. The Sikorsky Aircraft Corporation reviewed the Guardian video materials and could find no one who could agree with the RCMP interpretation.

SUMMARY

Clearly RCMP would have been better off concluding that the object in the Guardian video was a model constructed for an AT&T Corporation advertising campaign. At least that hypothesis had some eyebrow raising coincidences that proved difficult to accept. Perhaps they were on the right track in looking in the direction of the Sikorsky. After all, the Sikorsky Aircraft Corporation was named as a U.S. defense contractor researching electro-gravitics disc programs in the 1950s according to Wright-Patterson AFB Technical library documents. Maybe the object in the Guardian video was a new kind of helicopter, without the rotor and blade assembly.

Perhaps a touch of professional protocol might be advisedly exercised by Mr. Leblanc regarding his commentary following his research on this case to offer academic conclusions. He certainly did not bother to contact me for comment upon receiving the RCMP report, in fact he didn't bother to send me a copy of his submittal nor alert me to its posting. Every single assertion made by Leblanc is wrong. Comments in the RCMP report that he attributes to me where actually made by the Guardian suspect who has refused even simple methods of proof that he is not Guardian.

Is it possible that O.C.I.P.E. is really an organization whose objectives are to debunk UFO cases? Is the organization capable of conducting competent investigations? Consider the following factual scenario. O.C.I.P.E. collaborated on an investigation involving a report from Guardian regarding a 1989 event which he called a UFO landing in the swamp. The investigation correspondence was published as a crash and probably a "hoax" in Leonard Stringfield's July 1991 Status Report VI. The problem with the assessment is that their investigation located three independent witnesses who triangulated a UFO sighting and other details that matched precisely with the Guardian report. To my knowledge they didn't even bother to spend $12.00 Canadian to obtain date before and after aerial photos of the area available from Energy and Mines. I have great difficulty giving credence to any individual or organization publishing articles with the title : FINAL WORD.

The RCMP investigations report does have some merit in retrospect. They provided a resident with a video camera who recorded a helicopter dive bombing the residence of one of the eye witnesses to the UFO landing reported and videotaped by Guardian. I personally inspected the roof area where shingles were clearly blown off. The fact that the helicopter was attempting to intimidate the witnesses was overshadowed by the fact that DND declined to confirm identification to RCMP. And the revelation by one resident that odd grass formations, ten feet in diameter, have been observed for years is an interesting oddity that seems common in areas of UFO activity. The Guardian videotaped UFO landing investigation has proven to be a very complex endeavor. Confirmation of the landing site with gross physical effects and elemental deposit anomalies, multiple independent eye witness accounts, and meteorological and topographical consistencies all tend to support the analysis and authenticity of the Guardian video. Will we ever know for sure what landed in the fields of West Carleton? Perhaps the answer will never be proven to everyone's satisfaction, but many will go away dazed by the testimony of a Canadian Government Official who claims to *have been taken aboard a craft that night in August of 1991 at the site where Guardian filmed his video. The witness passed two lie detector tests administered by a Canadian polygrapher trained by the U.S. Military. The story is one of intrigue that involves telepathic dialogue with nonhuman entities and extraordinary identification details of the entities depicted in the Guardian video.*

Anyone wishing more detailed information on the Guardian Investigation can write to me at the address below. If you would like a videotaped report of the summary of my findings including a complete copy of the Guardian video, send a postal money order in U.S. funds in the amount of $35 (Canadian Order $40 CPMO) to Bob Oechsler at 136 Oakwood Road, Edgewater, Maryland 21037. Examine the evidence, review the findings and evaluate the analyses before drawing your own conclusion; that is, if one can be reached within our self imposed limits of reality.

Cheers . . . Bob Oechsler, Investigations Analyst

nineteen

RESCUE

The number of aliens who have been able to escape from the military once placed in confinement is very few. One could probably count such cases on the fingers of one hand. Although there are frozen alien remains in the U.S., Russia, South Africa, and the U.K., it is extremely rare for an alien to survive the rigors of captivity. The craft retrieved at Southaven Park and Carp have been broken up into pieces and shipped to various military and research centers throughout the United States. For numerous reasons, such craft are rarely kept intact, nor is any attempt made to fully construct a working prototype. One the other hand, alien tissue, far less identifiable in microtome slices and organ cross sections, is much more common.

The following is the last narration from inside Brookhaven concerning the rescue of the Gray alien. There were two witnesses to this scenario, neither of them known to each other. Perhaps our military and intelligence people learned from this encounter.

Todd was cold. It was four in the morning, bitter cold, and they were standing in a small clearing in the woods in back of Brookhaven Lab. Richard stood next to Jennifer, looking through binoculars at Brookhaven Lab. It was pitch dark, and there was an icy, clear sky above them. Jennifer nervously scanned the trees with her flashlight.

"That's not such a good idea," said Todd nervously. "Didn't you say they have increased security and added more cameras? They are sure to spot that light. Why are we here anyway? It's freezing."

"I'm not sure," said Jennifer. "Alison called me just before I called you. You know, that woman that helped us at Brookhaven when the guard was chasing us. She met a new girl named Linda who is working in the secured area. Linda just called Alison and wanted her meet her out here, but Alison can't go because she's sick. She wanted us to come in her place. She said to bring a camera, which I did, and we might see another UFO."

"Really?" said Richard. "Now that would be cool. I have had a few dreams about the other one I saw. Even drawn a few pictures. I wonder if this one will look the same or be different."

Jennifer turned off the flashlight and looked upward at the sky intently.

"The UFO will probably be similar to the others we saw," said Jennifer. "Alison said it is the same type of aliens as the one they have in the lab."

"Sure," said Todd, expecting to see nothing at all.

"WE HAVE a major problem here, sir." The Specialist 7 communication tech gave the colonel a worried look. "I got four bogies coming in from the north and they are moving very fast, I estimate Mach 4 to Mach 5. Do you want to send a scramble to air base?"

"Yeah, go ahead," said Sorenson, who was standing next the colonel, looking at the radar images.

"If you don't mind, you're in my turf and I'm in charge here," said the colonel. "Initiate a level four scramble."

"We both know who's in charge," said Sorenson. He grunted as a tall, thin man in a lab coat entered. "You got any input for me on this situation, Earl?"

Earl Voyt gave the radar screen a cursory look and frowned.

"We can't use the Q6 beam. Not after what happened last time. It was a wonder that when you used it the first time you didn't turn half the state into fire and brimstone."

"Well, hell," said the colonel. "We got a scramble on at the air base. Even if we could catch them, I doubt our missiles are going to do much. Are you sure about that laser beam?"

"Quite sure," said Earl. "And it's not a laser beam. It's a particle beam."

Sorenson tapped his pencil nervously on the counter. "A tactical nuke?" he said somberly. "What do you think? Maybe two-and-a-half to four megaton mobile launch?"

The colonel shook his head.

"No good. We are near a heavily populated area here. Even if we could hit them over the water before they come in, you're gonna contaminate half of Long Island. Five Star would have a shit fit."

Sorenson was pacing as the phone rang.

"It's for you, sir," said the comm tech, handing the phone to Sorenson.

"What?" Sorenson yelled into the phone. "They what?! Get four SWAT teams over here by chopper now! Jesus Christ, what a bunch of fuck-ups."

The colonel stared at Sorenson, amazed. He had never seen him lose his temper.

"The bogies are reducing speed, sir," said the comm tech. "They're down to Mach 1 and continuing to slow down."

"Just keep your eye on them," said Sorenson.

"Well," said the colonel. "What is it?" He looked at Sorenson, who was obviously distraught.

"That zoologist just took our NTL right out the front door, right past the security guard." Sorenson turned toward the Colonel. "What is the ETA on those SWAT teams?"

"About 10 to 15 minutes max," said the colonel.

"A nuke is out of the question," said Earl. "We just can't risk it."

Sorenson looked grim. "Well, I can tell you one thing. That NTL has seen the inside of our facilities, has probably picked up a lot of information. That to me makes him one big security risk. There is no way in hell we are going to let him get back to one of those ships."

"I see," said the colonel, smiling.

"Yes," said Sorenson. "They've come to rescue him, and there is no way that we can allow him to rendezvous with the alien craft."

MIKE PARENTE had never read much about UFOs. He led a normal life, went to school, worked a part-time job at a fast-food place, and had never really seen anything paranormal or out of the ordinary. Now, as he stood outside his car looking up at the sky at four brilliant UFOs moving slowly toward him, that would all change.

The UFOs moved in tight formation toward the park. He watched as they descended from the sky. The objects moved soundlessly through the air. Suddenly there was a crackle and then a hum, and a beam of light projected from one of the objects to the treetops. It did not go all the way to the ground, but stopped 20 to 30 feet above him. The beam seemed to swirl, be dense, almost solid, sweeping across the woods.

"They're looking for something," he said as he watched them move over the park and then retrace the same path they had traveled several times. Finally the craft froze, motionless in midair.

"And it looks like they've found it."

Linda knew something was wrong. She could not see who or what was observing her, but she knew she was being watched. She also knew that whatever was in the trees had its sights pointed at her and the NTL.

"Run!" said Linda, pushing the alien ahead of her. He did not hesitate, but moved quickly, seeming to almost glide across the ground. High in the sky were several stars much brighter than the rest, and unlike the others around them, these were moving, and growing larger and brighter by the second.

"Not today," said Sorenson, grabbing Linda's shoulder and pulling her back out of the clearing.

Linda screamed, but the sound of her scream was muffled by Sorenson's hand, which was clamped tightly over her mouth.

The NTL had not stopped moving toward the center of the clearing.

Jennifer, Richard, and Todd, only several hundred yards away from the clearing, saw a squadron of black unmarked helicopters coming from the north.

"I can't even believe this," said Todd as the four bright UFOs moved up from behind them and hung motionless over the clearing. As the first helicopter touched down, soldiers in black, with black ski masks, jumped to the ground, ran several hundred yards, and then took cover at different positions around the clearing.

Sorenson grappled with Linda as his communication device hissed with static.

"Target is in sight and range, sir. Bravo team leader is closest and in position."

Linda freed herself and ran toward the center of the clearing where the creature stood. It remained perfectly still, its wide, dark eyes watching the men circling around it.

"No!" she screamed.

The creature's arms flew up in the air as it was riddled with dozens of bullets. Its body jarred violently with the impact of the shells and then it slumped to the ground. Two of the SWAT team grabbed Linda and hurried her, struggling and shrieking, toward one of the helicopters.

Tears streamed down Jennifer's cheeks as she watched from the safety of the bushes.

"That was horrible," she choked. The two boys near her were not crying, but they were very close to it. So close that neither spoke. They just stared at the body of the alien lying on the ground in the distance.

Sorenson looked up at the alien craft. He was preparing to die. Obviously, the prime objective had been to terminate the alien. It could not be allowed to return with whatever knowledge it had gathered during its captivity at the facility or in its encounters with the military. He could not even imagine what type of weapons now had them in their sights. In a few moments the immediate area would be bathed in some high-energy beam, and they would all be reduced to ashes. Yet they had accomplished their objective, the nation's secrets were secure—and that was enough for Sorenson.

There was an incandescent blaze of light and a deafening hum as the beam descended over the fallen creature. And then it and the creature was gone.

"What now?" said Jennifer, looking up nervously. "I won't be surprised if they zap all of those jerks down there with some type of death ray."

"They deserve it," said Todd, his throat still tight, making it very hard to speak.

Suddenly there was a deafening magnetic hum, and their skin tingled with the feeling of static electricity. All four UFOs shot straight up, became pinpoints of light in the night sky, and then vanished.

Linda watched from the helicopter as the UFOs departed. She was crying when all of sudden a tremendous feeling of peace came over her, as if some unseen arms were holding her, some unseen presence comforting her. The symbols were bright in her mind, shining. The symbol for the alien, the crossed arms for affection, and the symbol for the human.

"You're still alive," she whispered.

twenty

ALIEN ENCOUNTERS

"*W*hat exactly do these things look like?" Deborah opened a window on the computer screen and loaded a document from a disk. "Here is a message I picked up on the network from Taylor Holmes, the friend of an abductee. It presents a little different perspective on the Grays, the alien race thought to be responsible for many of the abductions."

The Grays are able to transcend different levels or densities of matter at will, and each is as real as your third dimensional reality is real to you. Further, they do not make distinctions between these different dimensions as we make the distinction between our waking and dream state. In fact, they consider our waking reality more of a "dream" state and say that we exist in our dream state all the time, we've just been conditioned to believe that the things that happen in our dream state cannot happen in our "waking" reality.

As for only taking persons who consent to be abducted, remember we ARE dealing with an alien mind that is quite different from ours. So when they contact humans they do so in the state of consciousness that they think is the most open and normal, which to us, is our dream state. Since we are more open and receptive to the Grays' dimensionality in the dream state, we are more apt to give them permission to be a part of their hybrid experiments. As I said, our waking state seldom remembers giving permission since we just pass if off as a "dream" and forget about it.

The vast majority of the Grays (there are many different types) do not harm the humans that are taken aboard their ships. Their technology is hundreds of years above ours and they are able to perform their examinations and genetic activities without any harm to the individual. However, problems do arise, but they're mostly due to our fragmentation of different states of consciousness.

For example, occasionally a person will come out of his/her dream state during the procedures and become frightened and try to escape. The Grays will usually induce, through mental projection, an altered state of consciousness so the procedures can continue without the individual feeling fear.

As for the irritations, physical symptoms, such as marks on the body, nose bleeds. These are not caused by the procedures themselves, but rather it's the body's way of telling the person that something has happened that cannot be remembered in their waking state. The body generates the trauma to signal the repressed memory. That's why hypnotic regression is so useful in helping the individual consciously remember the experiences and integrate them into his/her waking consciousness.

They consider us more like brothers because we are of the same origin, we are genetically linked.

As I stated before, many years ago they used to took like us. However, through the misuse of atomics they were forced to live underground and over thousands of generations mutated into their present form. They are, in a sense, our past and our future. They have the ability to time travel and in their, and our future, there is already a race of hybrids called Essasani.

Though the abduction experience can be frightening, there are also those who feel a sense of love and connection with the little guys. A feeling that reaches into the depths of a person's soul and transcends rationality.

"Well," I said, "that makes them sound a lot less hostile. But I really don't buy the fact that the procedures done to abductees are all that benign. I have heard some real horror stories."

Deborah laughed. "Well, here's a horror story for you. Seems there is another race besides the Grays. These are more a 'To Serve Man' bunch. You know, like in the old 'Twilight Zone' where this spaceship lands and they discover that book in the craft, and it turns out to be a cookbook. I picked this up on the net, supposedly based on the information of another abductee. These aren't pale skinned and friendly. These are lizardlike and very carnivorous. They look on mankind as a vast cattle yard."

From: Nevada Aerial Research

For the most part, we are dealing with another species, humanoid in shape but reptilian in heritage. Their leader-elite are the "Draco." They are cold-blooded and have to balance their surrounding environment to maintain body temperature. They are suited especially for space travel, as they have the ability to hibernate. The "reptoids" have scales which protect them from losing moisture through their skins. They have no sweat glands. The scales are much larger on their backs, making the skin more waterproof. The scales on their face, neck, chest, and hands are smaller and more flexible. They have three fingers, with an opposing thumb. All have large cat-like eyes and twin nose holes at the end of a short, stubby muzzle.

They are mostly meat-eaters. Their mouth is more like a slit, but they have teeth differentiated into incisors, canines and molars. They average six to seven feet tall. These reptilian beings direct the efforts being called the GRAYS, EBEs, etc., and form the largest category likely to be encountered by surface humans. They are really an order of "cross-breed" or Hybrid between Homo-Sapiens and the reptilian species. There are several other lines of "cross-breeds" which have been bred for various characteristics.

Some even appear more or less human. Some of the reptilians and cross-breeds have sensory pits (near the eyes) that act as an extra sense and can "see" heat. Some have a pineal eye and are telepathic. These beings can operate effectively in the dark. Their eyes are more sensitive to ultra-violet light. They can control their heartbeat. The Grays have a high metallic content in the skin, as well as an unusual cobalt pigmentation. Many have no external sex organs, but some have been bred to have them.

Government authorities; agents disguised as civilians and others seek to learn more about these beings. It should be noted that not all the cross-breeds are hostile. There is an order of small humanoids

(2–4 feet tall) that work with the beings that resemble humans, except close examination will reveal unusually shaped ears.

The most prevalent of these have blond hair, large foreheads, and a medium dark or light complexion. The reptilian cross-breeds are potentially dangerous. One variety (working with the "Draco") has come from a system with a light source that subjected them to a high level of radiation. It is the minds of these beings that would be considered most strange by terrestrial standards.

They are hive-like (robotic) and demented. They are considered detrimental beings (DEROS). These beings do not eat (as we know the term). Some use substances that are synthetically produced, mixed with blood from living animals and humans. This is sometimes mixed with hydrogen peroxide, which kills the foreign bacteria in the mixture. They may also be feeding off the "life essence" of these substances. They also seem to "feed" off nuclear energy, and have apparently manipulated humans into developing sources of radio-active power.

"Not a pleasant thought," I said. "Although, if there are such things, I cannot see the Grays being hooked up with them."

"It's possible they aren't hooked up together," said Deborah. "And despite the fact that many of the reports deal with the Grays, I still found several others talking about these reptile aliens. Here's another that was posted by John Powell on the network."

Or, most infuriating of all, we are assured that there are no actual aliens, that our experiences spring from our own subconscious turmoil or from our need for fantasy fulfillment. Never mind that many abductees are young children, too young to be suffering from such psychological disturbances. Well, then, the resourceful researcher counters, the imagined aliens must spring from some collective human super-psyche that is mirroring our failures and dangers back to us. This particular theory adores the archetypal gray ET, because it resembles some sickly fetal form of humanity and must therefore be an objectified warning of what our species is in danger of becoming if we don't mend our ways. Never mind that many, many abductees have no dealing with grays, but instead are victimized by robust reptoids and insectoids. Not to mention the totally human-looking blond beauties and black-headed, black-robed clan with the widow's peak hairline.

"But I haven't even got into the best stuff yet," said Deborah, holding a large book with an alien face on the cover. The book was *Communion,* by Whitley Strieber, "The firsthand accounts of humans in modern times who have been taken aboard alien spacecraft. Abductions."

twenty one

CHANNEL

The following is highly controversial material that describes a human who claims to be able to receive communications from aliens telepathically—a channel. Just as there are reliable and unreliable sources in every field, there are what appear to be valid channels and then others that are almost laughably fake. In the course of my investigations, I have received several calls from individuals claiming to channel for the Grays. Most of these contacts were amusing, poorly made up science fiction, except one call that I received at 2 A.M. one morning and found particularly disturbingly.

The question I have been often asked is why they selected me to contact. I would assume that the very fact you are reading these words would explain that. Their intent is to send a message to a large number of people. Yet, they are not as interested in contacting government heads, military officers, or people in positions of power, but rather humankind as a whole. After speaking to a channel concerning all this, it would appear that at least two races of alien life-forms plan to make contact in the next two years. This will not be an isolated landing in some obscure location, but a major media event. Hopefully, as more and more information reaches the public, their craft will be able to land in safety and our heads of government will restrain themselves from blasting them and their occupants with whatever new weapons we may have.

I first came in contact with the channel, who would give me a great deal of information on the aliens and their intentions, from Kenny Lloyd, whom I later did an interview for on the Intergalactic Television Network.

"You might find this interesting," said Kenny. As a talk-show host for the Intergalactic Television Network, he specializes in phenomena and is a talented interviewer. "You know those aliens you are writing about, the ones that were taken to Brookhaven? It seems one of them survived and has a message for you, Mr. Michaels. They want to speak to you."

I laughed. I mean, what else could I do? So far, I had been able to separate my personal evaluation of what was happening, trying to keep things on an objective level. Although I had interviewed hundreds of witnesses who had either seen UFO landings, been abducted by aliens, analyzed mutilated cattle, or stood in the center of highly radioactive crop circles, I still had remained basically a skeptic. I wasn't one of the UFO investigators who was sure the CIA was tracking me, or that a hit man had been hired to go across the country and poison my toothpaste. In fact, in contrast to the vast majority of people in the field, I had found the government to be cooperative, intelligent, and helpful in my work. They had sent me reams of information, specifics on Brookhaven Lab, and even annotated publications and periodicals with circles and arrows highlighting key information.

I had been fortunate enough to actually get through to one of Hillary Clinton's aides, talk to a public relations person at the White House, and even had a personal chat with one of the president's Secret Service men.

All this ran through my mind as I pondered Kenny's statement, thinking that were I to come forward with such a claim, I would no doubt be considered for a padded cell, possibly with four-point restraints. And so I laughed. It seemed an appropriate, safe response. But not wishing to offend a very helpful and friendly Kenny Lloyd, I qualified that laugh.

"Sorry, Kenny," I said. "But you realize how off the wall that sounds. So far, I have focused on hard-core physical evidence, testimony, videos, and documents. I am a little hesitant to get into the channel aspect of this. Yet, I am willing to hear you out. What exactly do you mean, this alien wants to talk to me?"

"I understand," he said, not sounding the least bit offended. "But you must be aware that your writing and media appearances are reaching many, many people. I understand the producer of the 'Encounters' show told you that the ratings for their first show 'went through the roof.'"

This was true. I had begun to realize this when talking to Kathryn at Fox. Not only the American public, but the global community is interested in the UFO phenomenon and what appeared to be imminent contact with an alien civilization, and that is reflected by dozens of new shows and movies.

"Go on," I said, activating the recorder.

"The extraterrestrials are aware of what you are doing," he said. "It is that simple. And they want to initiate communication with you. In fact, they may even want to meet with you."

I choked. "I really don't want to go out to some isolated butte in New Mexico and stand on top of a mountain with a flashlight," I said. "And worse, suppose I bring the media with me and the aliens don't show up. Are you serious?"

"I have interviewed two channels who I feel are credible," said Kenny. "There is a woman who gives her entity name as Salurah. I want you to talk to her."

I consented, still feeling very skeptical.

The following is the text of the basic conversation I had with Salurah on May 16, 1994, beginning at 10:07 A.M. The interview lasted almost an hour. I am still investigating some of the facts and information I recorded in this interview. The communication through Salurah allegedly comes from the Ashtar Command, which is a governing body for a "Federation of Planets" or known worlds with intelligent life. It is primarily representing two civilizations from the Antares system, the Antarians and also a group from the Pleiades. There were also communications with a third "renegade" group commonly referred to as the Grays, who stated that they were from the Sirius star system.

JB: Can you tell me exactly what groups have been visiting this planet recently? Are we dealing with a single civilization or are there several different races of aliens involved?

Salurah: We represent several different races. I and the group who recently visited are Antarian. If you wish to visualize the Antarian appearance or understand our essence, we were instrumental and indirectly assisted in a film released to the American public called *Cocoon*. We can take on human form, but are a much more highly evolved life-form. Our true bodies are not physical, but resonate on a higher vibratory plane, one you might conceive as fifth dimensional. The race from the Pleiades is also a highly developed life-form. They have followed a developmental path somewhat different from ours, yet are still much more advanced in the "heart" or spiritual focus rather than intellectual.

The race that we consider interlopers or who have committed acts that we consider unacceptable are the Sirians. You also refer to these as the Grays. While you might feel comfortable with our true appearance, you perhaps would find the appearance of the Grays much more frightening, perhaps even terrifying. They are reptilian, possess very subtle scales, and the heart organ function is vestigial.

JB: I would assume that the Grays are responsible for the majority of the abductions and cattle mutilations I have encountered in my research.

Salurah: Your assumption is correct. Although the intent of the Grays is not hostile, they have no plans of invasion or colonization of your planet, they are conducting numerous experiments on many terrestrial life-forms. They have been conducting such experiments for many millennia, and many of these experiments are done without consideration as to their effect on your species or culture. Some attempts have been made to mask these encounters by memory-suppression techniques. Often, over time, this masking becomes ineffective and the persons upon whom the procedures were preformed will recall the incident.

JB: What kinds of experiments are being performed? Are they simply gathering information or is there some type of goal or purpose to these experiments?

Salurah: The Grays have experimented with the majority of life-forms on your world as well as inorganic chemical and mineral substances. They dissect, take tissue and plant samples, as well as genetically alter and relocate species. Some efforts are made to avoid detection of their craft or direct encounters with members of your species. Unfortunately, there are groups who choose to operate in the more deserted areas that are far less careful and are frequently observed. They also dispose of animal and human bodies without taking adequate precautions to avoid detection.

They are not primarily concerned with the feelings or emotions of humans who are abducted. It is felt that since the painful memories of the procedures done upon humans will be erased or at least sublimated, it is not necessary to use any type of anesthetic or psychologically calming substances.

Recently they have increased their experimentation in the areas of implanting or impregnating females of your species. In the majority of these implantations, they reabduct the female and recover the fetus before the child is born. We understand that within the last year, there have been at least two fetuses they failed to recover and that at least one such child, produced by such a procedure, is currently alive.

JB: So are you, the Antarians, different? Why exactly are you here?

Salurah: Our intent within the next few years is to initiate contact with your people. The fear created by the Grays is a major obstacle to this. We wish to selectively encode a number of humans so that they can reach a higher vibratory level of existence and establish a more productive level of communication.

JB: I don't want to be cosmically rude here, but don't you think you are a bit out of touch with the human emotional and thought process? There are a few factors you seem to have overlooked. One, we do have something called a government. It is fine to set up little private communications with individuals and talk about vibrating on a higher level, but for the most part, the government and the common person are not going to have any idea what the hell you are talking about. You have creatures, and I will call them creatures, because anything that looks reptilian, has huge eyes, is three feet tall and proceeds to ram rotating sharp objects up my nose and rectum, I don't consider particularly friendly or anyone I really want to know that much more about.

Also, as peaceful and loving as you say you Antarians are, why in the world are you allowing these Grays to use my species and the earth in general as an endless supply of "slice and dice them any time you feel like it" lab animals? The next time a UFO gets even close to Southaven Park, I can guarantee you, unless there is a major communication with my government and military, they will just shoot it down again.

Salurah: We know this. That is why we are talking to you. Obviously, our attempts at communication and dealing with these problems have not been effective. There are internal problems with the Grays that you would not understand. We have had our conflicts before and we do not wish to renew these conflicts. There are mountains nearby where you live. We would like you to find one that is fairly remote and that will make our next communication easier. I want time to meet with our leaders and then prepare my thoughts on this.

JB: I'm sorry. I am going to have to end this. My tape recorder is going crazy, my monitor is flickering, and I don't want to lose the data on my hard disk.

Salurah: Yes, we understand. Please remember that fear is the greatest barrier you and your race must overcome for us to make contact. We have a great compassion and empathy for your kind. Your species is on the verge of a time of great knowledge and understanding. It is our intention to help in any way we can.

Blue light produced as laser was focused on
Guardian at the Carp landing.

Landing at Carp.

Carp signal flares (left) and craft (right).

PICTURES REPRODUCED WITH THE PERMISSION OF THE AUTHOR

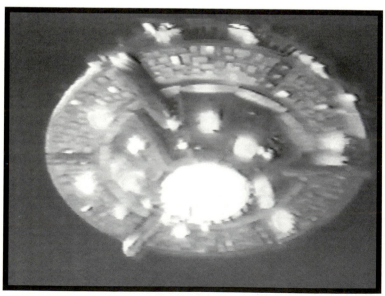

UFO landing.

PICTURES REPRODUCED WITH THE PERMISSION OF THE AUTHOR

UFO after landing.

Crash site at South Haven Park.

Recovered NTL.

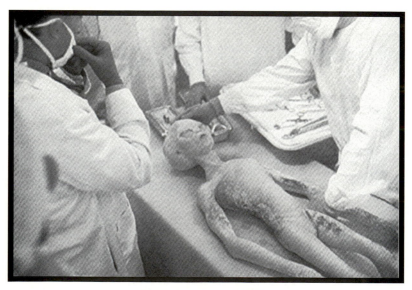

Examination of NTL.

The UFO in an underground military facility.

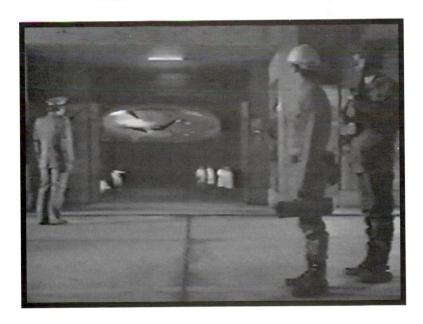

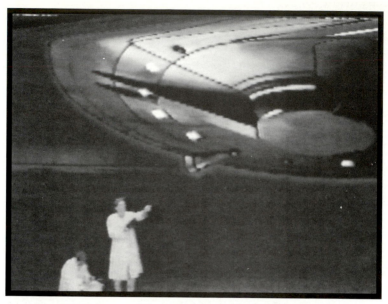

The UFO in a military hanger and lab technicians.

The military meeting the NTL.

NTL in the lab.

Closeup of the NTL.

twenty two

WATCHING AND WAITING

"Like I really don't know I'm being followed."
Linda King smiled. She sat on a bench, the same bench where she had daydreamed about being in Africa a few months ago. Before she had gone to Brookhaven to work with the NTL. Before it had been gunned down like an animal in the clearing by the SWAT team. Across from her sat Alison and Carol, who had flown out from New York. And just down the path, sitting at another bench was a young man in a suit, wearing dark sunglasses. He was eating popcorn and trying to look inconspicuous. Yet how many young men wearing a suit in 80-degree weather and eating popcorn could look inconspicuous?

"So what did they tell you after they whisked you off in the helicopter?" said Alison.

Linda remained silent for a moment, thinking about what had happened that night when the NTL had been killed. She had watched from the helicopter as the UFOs hovered above, beamed up the bullet-riddled body of the creature, and then took off. She had cried for the entire journey as the helicopter made its way to a nearby military base. She was crying not so much from grief, although she felt devastated that they had killed the creature that had become her friend. She cried from shame. Shame at how the aliens had watched as her kind mercilessly gunned down the NTL.

Sorenson and his assistant had met with her a short time after in a small, too brightly lit debriefing room. He had quite simply stated that she had two options. She could continue doing her work at the zoo in animal communication, receive a new grant from the government, which Sorenson would expedite, and then be recognized and honored in her field for her work, or there would be a tragic accident at the lab when one of the orangutans went berserk and attacked her. Of course, this would happen after an injection of a new substance that they had discovered to produce aggression in humans and apes, and no doubt Brutus would then be destroyed. Sorenson made it very clear that, should she go to the press or talk to anyone about what had happened, she would most certainly be increasing the odds of option number two.

So Linda lied. She promised she would discuss it with no one, go back to her job, and forget it had ever happened. And only moments after she was released, she was on the phone to her friend Alison at the lab, asking her to fly out to California as soon a possible. Now the three women sat, on a warm spring afternoon, trying to figure out what, if anything, to do about what they knew.

"They told me to keep my mouth shut, basically, or they would see to it I had an accident with the animals," said Alison.

"That Sorenson is an asshole," snorted Carol. "I can't stand him. Told me the same thing basically, but there's not much he can do about the subjects I work with." She grinned. "They are not really all that revivable."

"Oh, you never know with Sorenson." Alison grinned. "In fact, he looks so much like the bad guy in *Terminator II*, I keep expecting him to melt down in a puddle and ooze under the door."

All three women laughed. Carol stood up and began to pace back and forth. She looked at the man who was watching them from the bench, and he guiltily looked away.

"I went back over the notes from that autopsy. The government took all the frozen slices and specimens. I am sure the alien body is still packed in liquid nitrogen somewhere. I had heard that they took it to a secret lab, underground in Southern California." Carol paused, and then turned to face Linda, who was looking very sad. "You really liked that creature, didn't you?"

"Yes," said Linda, her voice breaking. "I really did. I felt something from it, a feeling, I can't really explain it. But it was very intense, very good."

Carol reached over and touched Linda's shoulder, giving it a squeeze. "Well, tell you something that might make you feel better. When I was doing the tests on the tissue sections, I found some of them had resumed their cellular functioning. They do not metabolize oxygen the way we do, and the individual cell organelles appeared much more highly developed, so much so that I believe each cell could function independent of the others. My point is that, even in the preservative solution, the cells were attempting to resume their life function."

Linda brightened and, digging in her purse, produced a photograph. It showed the alien, wide, dark eyes, a hand with long thin fingers gesturing in the air.

"That's some picture," said Alison, looking at the photo. "It's kind of cute. Is it a he or a she?"

"I don't know," said Linda. "But I kind of feel it was a he. I took that picture on the night shift when no one else was there in the lab."

"So you know what I'm trying to say," said Carol, leaning over Linda and looking at the picture.

"Yes," said Linda, "but I felt that already. That the NTL isn't dead and survived our primitive attempt to kill it."

"It would take a lot more than a few bullets to kill this lifeform," said Carol. "From what I saw while running the tests, as long as there is some viable tissue left for a template, the organism can completely repair itself, even from major trauma. In fact, this creature would be very difficult to kill. I suspect the military would find that very disturbing."

"I'm sure they would," said Linda.

MIKE CHRISTOL took a long swig of his Budweiser and pulled the curtains closed. His room looked rather crowded with all the video players, monitors, and computers, but he liked it that way. It felt comfortable. There was really no reason for closing the curtains. Once the government had taken his camera and the film in it, they had pretty much lost interest in him. After all, whatever he and the teens had seen of the UFO crash in Southaven Park was useless without the film to prove it.

Unfortunately, for them anyway, they had not been following him the next morning when he had gone to a local Photomat, went for an hour for some coffee, and then headed out for the long drive back to Kentucky. He had learned after decades in the UFO business that anytime you get a really good film, the first thing to do is make a copy, and the second thing to do is hide the copy.

Mike lay back, took another sip of his beer, and watched the video screen. He could see the treetops of Southaven Park, the glowing UFO crash, and flames reaching up to the sky above the trees.

"I'VE PATCHED INTO the space shuttle," said the Specialist 4 communications tech. "Our people are getting a little edgy up there. They saw four UFOs that are maintaining a distance of about ten miles but traveling at the same speed and velocity as the shuttle."

The colonel frowned, and Sorenson tapped his fingers nervously on the computer monitor top.

"Do we have them on visual from the Hubble satellite?" said Sorenson.

The screen changed as the technician's fingers flew over the keyboard. The new view, was much clearer, and the saucer-shaped object filled the screen.

"Son of a bitch," said the colonel. "I thought Hubble was for photographing star clusters?"

Ignoring the colonel's remark, Sorenson anxiously watched the screen and then turned toward his assistant, Karen.

"Yes," she said, anticipating his question. "I am linked in and capturing it to CD. Great resolution since they fixed that lens."

"Extremely good," said Sorenson. "We can spot a dime on the sidewalk from a hundred miles up, and with the right atmospheric conditions can even read a newspaper. I don't like what I'm seeing here. We have a definite problem.

The colonel's pocket phone rang, and he put it to his ear, grunted, and then disconnected.

"Russia's got the president on the horn. They want to fire a missile from their platform. They are trying to clear it so the U.S. won't get spooked," said the colonel.

"Kind of a bow shot to make the UFOs leave," said Sorenson.

The colonel shook his head. "I don't think so," he said. "I think they want to take one of the craft out. Apparently they have done this kind of thing before. They are seriously concerned about the shuttle. There is a Russian on board and he's doing some very classified stuff up there."

Sorenson was tired. He had been jetting back and forth, trying to deal with a rash of UFO problems including the Long Island crash and recovery, the escape of the NTL, and finally the unfortunate incident where the SWAT team had gunned down that same NTL right in front of his own people, risking not an international, but an intergalactic incident. Fortunately, the aliens had not retaliated. Sorenson had no doubt that had they so desired, they could have crisped his entire party, Brookhaven, and probably the greater part of Long Island. Despite over one hundred incidents that Sorenson had been involved in, or been closely connected with, there was not a single instance of alien hostile activity toward any military or civilian craft.

There were numerous and increasing incidents of human abductions. There were several human female/alien implant pregnancies, and even the birth of a hybrid in Puerto Rico. Cattle mutilations were on the rise, and the media were being swamped with more and more firsthand sightings and encounters with NTLs.

According to the reports Linda King had done before she had helped the alien to escape, the Grays—the alien race to which the alien belonged—had no intention of taking over or invading the earth. Yet, they had no aversion to experimenting with humans. In fact, Linda had stated that from what she could infer, this had been going on for possibly hundreds of thousands of years. There was a definite interaction with the alien race and human culture, but it was a very controlled and regulated interaction.

The thing that bothered Sorenson the most was that the aliens were becoming less and less careful about being seen or tracked by the military. Yet they would not acknowledge messages sent to them or respond with even any mathematical or symbolic code. It was clear the time for the first open encounter with the NTLs would be in the very near future. And the prospect of controlling the dissemination of such information, which could easily throw the entire world and most governments into panic, was unnerving.

"I'm patched into SAC," said Karen. "They are coordinating with the Russians to monitor the launch."

She quickly typed two series of passwords to preserve her connect. "Okay," she said. "Watch the screen. We have an estimated time to target of 40 seconds."

The central UFO that filled the screen suddenly brightened and seemed to shimmer. The four UFOs began moving in relationship to each other, then suddenly shot up at a 90-degree angle to the earth and quickly vanished into the black sky.

"We didn't even have to launch," said the colonel. "They must be monitoring our communications so thoroughly that they knew what was up."

"That is not a comforting thought," said Sorenson. "I am beginning to realize they are probably fully aware of all our defense capabilities and weapons."

"No," said the colonel. "That is not a very comforting thought."

Part III

ABDUCTIONS

twenty three

NIGHT VISITORS

In the winter of 1930 in Canada, trapper Arnaud Laurent and his son observed a strange light crossing the northern sky. It appeared to be headed for the Lake Anjikuni area. The two trappers describe it as being alternately bullet shaped and cylinder shaped. It can be assumed from this that it was an object of irregular configuration that was tumbling as it moved.

Another trapper named Joe Labelle had snowshoed into the village of the Lake Anjikuni people, and been chilled to discover that the normally bustling community was silent. Even the sled dogs, which would normally have bayed welcome, were silent.

The shanties were choked with snow, and not a chimney showed smoke. The trapper found the village's kayaks tied up on the shore of the lake. Inside the shanties the trapper found a further surprise: there were meals left hanging over fires, long grown old and moldy, apparently abandoned as they were being cooked. The men's rifles were still standing by the doors. This really scared the trapper, because he knew that these people would never leave their precious weapons behind.

He reported his discovery to the Royal Canadian Mounted Police, who investigated further. They discovered that the town's dogs had died of hunger, chained beneath a tree and covered by a snowdrift. More disturbingly, the town graveyard had been emptied.

Deborah stared at the computer screen, wide eyed. I grinned, although the image was more chilling than funny. It sounded like a great start for a grade-B Corman horror movie, with alien-possessed bodies wandering through the snowdrifts.

"Don't you think that is really weird?" she said, and then continued to read from the article.

The graves were now yawning pits. Despite the frozen ground, the graves had been opened and the dead removed. The RCMP continues the case opened to this day. A check with their records department indicated that the matter remains unsolved, and despite a search of the whole of Canada and inquiries throughout the world, not a trace of the missing twelve hundred men, women and children has ever been found.

"That is so spooky," said Deborah. "A whole town just vanished." She turned to the computer and pulled up a file listing various incidents where humans had been kidnapped by aliens.

"Abduction. . ." Deborah read from the dictionary. "To carry away wrongfully by force. To kidnap." She smiled. "And I have some big-time kidnapping here. One of the more famous incidents was that show 'Encounters' you were on. That Betty Cash lady." She clicked the mouse and the file came up. "Check this out."

It all began on the evening of December 29, 1980. It was a chilly winter night and clear skies. Betty Cash, along with Vickie Landrum, and Vickie's grandson, Colby Landrum, were driving home from a bingo game to their home in Dayton, Texas. As they traveled through the deserted stretch, they noticed a DIAMOND SHAPED OBJECT hovering, and spitting a jet of searing flame.

Betty stopped the car in order for the trio to escape the heat. After the object flew off, they continued down the road only to see the craft again this time followed by more than 20 helicopters. In the following months, Betty and Vickie have lost much of their hair. As the hair grew back it was much thinner, dryer, and grayer. Holes have developed in Vickie's fingernails. Both Colby and Vickie break out in sores that permanently scar their face.

There's no doubt says the radiologist on the case "that they were exposed to a broad spectrum of radiation, the nausea, the blisters, the hair falling out, it would certainly help with treatment if we could find out exactly what type was involved." At present the information is not available. The government has denied any knowledge of the craft, or the incident. What was the craft they saw that night. Will they be able to get medical attention from the government? Or will this be another case where the truth is never known? Whatever happened, something did occur that cold December night in Dayton, Texas. Something that changed the lives of three citizens of the UNITED STATES, citizens that deserve the answers, the truthful answers.

"I have literally hundreds of reports here." She sighed. "No way we could even begin to dent them tonight. But I did read most of them and I found this posting on the network that kind of sums up common phenomena observed when people are abducted by extraterrestrials."

(3009) Tue 9 Feb 93 21:32
By: John Powell
To: All
Re: Abduction Article II, 2/6

ABDUCTION "CHECKLIST."

If these reports can be believed—and there is no reason to doubt the honesty of the reporters—the abduction phenomenon includes the following details.
—Aliens can alter our perception of our surroundings.
—Aliens can control what we think we see. They can appear to us in any number of guises, and shapes.
—Aliens can take us—our consciousness—out of our physical bodies, disable our control of our bodies, install one of their own entities, and use our bodies as vehicles for their own activities before returning our consciousness to our bodies.
—Aliens can be present with us in an invisible state and can make themselves only partially visible.
—Abductees receive marks on their bodies other than the well-known scoops and straight-line scars. These other marks include single punctures, multiple punctures, large bruises, three- and four-

fingered claw marks, and triangles of every possible sort.

—Female abductees often suffer serious gynecological problems after their alien encounters, and sometimes these problems lead to cysts, tumors, cancer of the breasts and uterus, and to hysterectomies.

—Aliens take body fluids from our necks, spines, blood veins, joints such as knees and wrists, and other places. They also inject unknown fluids into various parts of our bodies.

—A surprising number of abductees suffer from serious illnesses they didn't have before their encounters. These have led to surgery, debilitation, and even death from causes the doctors can't identify.

—Some abductees experience a degeneration of their mental, social, and spiritual well-being. Excessive behavior frequently erupts, such as drug abuse, alcoholism, overeating, and promiscuity. Strange obsessions develop and cause the disruption of normal life and the destruction of personal relationships.

—Aliens show a great interest in adult sexuality, child sexuality, and in inflicting physical pain on abductees.

—Abductees recall being instructed and trained by aliens. This training may be in the form of verbal or telepathic lessons, slide shows, or actual hands-on instruction in the operation of alien technology.

—Abductees report being taken to facilities in which they encounter not only aliens but also normal-looking humans, sometimes in military uniforms, working with the alien captors.

—Abductees often encounter more than one sort of alien during an experience, not just the grays. Every possible combination of gray, reptoid, insectoid, blond, and widow's peak have been seen during single abductions, aboard the same craft or in the same facility.

—Abductees—"virgin" cases—report being taken to underground facilities where they see grotesque hybrid creatures, nurseries of hybrid humanoid fetuses, and vats of colored liquid filled with parts of human bodies.

—Abductees report seeing other humans in these facilities being drained of blood, being mutilated, flayed, and dismembered, and being stacked, lifeless, like cords of wood. Some abductees have been threatened that they, too, will end up in this condition if they don't cooperate with their alien captors.

—Aliens come into homes and temporarily remove young children, leaving their distraught parents paralyzed and helpless. In

cases where a parent has been able to protest, the aliens insist that "The children belong to us."

—Aliens have forced their human abductees to have sexual intercourse with aliens and even with other abductees while groups of aliens observe these performances. In such encounters, the aliens have sometimes disguised themselves in order to gain the cooperation of the abductee, appearing in such forms as Jesus, the Pope, certain celebrities, and even the dead spouses of the abductees.

—Children abductees sometimes show a new and obsessive interest in their own genitalia after alien encounters, saying that their abductors who come at night have been touching these parts of their bodies.

— Aliens perform extremely painful experiments or procedures on abductees, saying that these acts are necessary but giving no explanation why. Abductees' eyes are painfully removed from the sockets, allowing the aliens to scrape the area or implant devices into the area before the eyeballs are replaced, for instance. Some abductees are subjected to painful constrictions, often around the head, chest and extremities. Painful genitalia and anal probes are performed, on children as well as adults.

—Aliens make predictions of an imminent period of global chaos and destruction. They say that a certain number of humans—and the number varies dramatically from case to case—will be "rescued" from the planet in order to continue the species, either on another planet or back on earth after the destruction is over. Many abductees report that they don't believe their alien captors and foresee instead a much more sinister use of the "rescued" humans.

"That is just the tip of the iceberg," said Deborah. "There are other authors, including Whitley Strieber and Bud Hopkins, who have written numerous books on abductions."

"Yes, I talked to Budd Hopkins concerning the Long Island crash case a few months ago. He seemed very intelligent, very thorough, very professional. I wonder if I was ever abducted," I said. "I used to have some pretty strange dreams when I was five years old about these men in a field and this body lying on the ground."

"If you were, you were lucky. I wish I had," said Deborah. "I have something better than that. "Read this. It tells how to know if you've been abducted by an alien."

Space aliens often erase the memories of people they abduct. But you can still determine if you've been taken aboard a starship or examined by extraterrestrials with tips from two of the world's leading experts.

All you have to do is check for the telltale signs of alien abduction, including memory loss, sudden illness, unusual dreams or strange marks on your body.

These symptoms almost certainly indicate that you've been abducted by space aliens.

"Many people have been abducted by space aliens but can't remember anything about their abductions," declared Brad Steiger, author of the best selling book The UFO Abductors. *"UFO abductees often find they have black spots in their memories. In some cases it is simply a tantalizing sensation that there is something they are trying to remember but can't recall."*

Hayden Hewes, executive director of the International UFO Bureau, said: "Abductees frequently have recurring dreams or daytime visions about alien beings, spacecraft or extraterrestrial realms. They often discover unexplained wounds or scars. Or they mysteriously begin to suffer from physical problems."

According to Steiger and Hewes, the warning signs of alien abduction are:

The mysterious onset of illness, including insomnia, loss of appetite, nausea, headaches, a rash or fatigue.

The nagging sensation of having "lost" a period out of your life.

Complete memory loss.

The mysterious appearance of scars, bruises, puncture marks, burns or missing hair suggestive of medical examination by aliens.

Recurring dreams. Some common images include extraterrestrial worlds or landscapes and crystal sites.

Recurring daytime images. Common ones are space aliens, UFO's or extraterrestrial scenes.

If you have experienced one or more of these symptoms, Steiger and Hewes advise you look in your phone book and contact the UFO organization nearest you. They should be able to put you in touch

with someone who can hypnotize and regress you to the time of the
abduction so you can remember it completely, the experts say.

"Here are few more posts I found on the network," said Deborah.
"One was left by David Jacobs, who has interviewed a number of
abductees and has some very interesting things to say. The other
is from the MUFON network in Oklahoma by Ginna Davis, a UFO
investigator."

06-20-90
post on MUFON by David Jacobs

I would estimate that 99.99% of all abductees are unaware of
what has happened to them. Only a tiny fraction of abductees have
systematically explored their experiences with me or with Budd
Hopkins and are fully aware of the situation that they are involved
in. I have handed out a questionnaire geared toward helping me to
gauge how many people might have had abductions. When the pres-
sure gets too great on an abductee and he/she feels that whatever
has happened to them deserves some sort of an explanation, they
characteristically seek help or answers to their questions in three
main areas. The first is in the therapeutic community. They go to
psychologists and psychiatrists in search of help. They think that
there must be something wrong with them because they are having
crazy thoughts about being on board a UFO, etc. The therapeutic
community has not been very much help in this area. The second
area that people migrate to in search of answers is evangelical or
charismatic religious groups or cults. In religion abductees are of-
ten given a "demonic" explanation. They are told to pray and the
demons will be excised. The third area is New Age groups. Here
they encounter channelers, and believers in benevolent space broth-
ers, and higher cosmic consciousness and higher vibrational pat-
terns, and universal love.
*   Generally speaking, we do not know why a particular person is*
abducted. There appears to be no overt similarities, either mental
or physical between abductees. This appears to be a random phe-
nomenon. However, we have found a rather strong generational and
familial link with abductions. Abductions appear to begin in child-
hood and continue throughout adulthood (there are exceptions to

this). We have not found a way to stop abductions.

The main mental procedure is an examination of an abductee's emotional state after observing some sort of mental imagery. In the reproductive area, people report that sperm and eggs are harvested from them. They are also shown odd-looking babies that they are sometimes required to hold.

Abductees are mentally altered during the abduction so that it is extremely difficult to understand what is happening while it is happening. Recovering the memories is a difficult task. Not only is there a certain amount of trauma involved, but often there is heavy confabulation, false memories, incomplete memories, and pseudo-memories placed in the abductee's mind as part of mental procedures. Furthermore, the physical after effects of the phenomenon can be severe—scars, internal scar tissue, eye damage, and so forth. It is, however, the mental effects that are most import and for people's lives—affording the most damage and the most trauma.

Message number 1014 in "CONTACT"
Date: 11-05-91 20:19

From: John Powell
To: All
Subj: Memory Loss Paper

EID: 1013 01318b17
MSGID: 1:19 / 19.19 29174377
    MUFONET-BBS NETWORK-MUTUAL UFO NETWORK

Contributed by: Oklahoma MUFON

MEMORY LOSS OF ABDUCTEES

By Ginna Meyer

[Note: Ginna is an Oklahoma State Section Director and Investigator. She is presently in her last year of a Bachelor of Science in Nursing. While attending school, Ginna worked for two years in a Post Coronary Care Unit and for the past year has been working in the Labor and Delivery area. Ginna's interest in UFOlogy

and abductions stem from her own experience as a seven-year-old
child in the company of five other children. Her encounter is pres-
ently under investigation.]

    Recently I attended a workshop with a panel of recovering burn
patients. While listening to their stories, I noted how each one had
coped with the traumatic experience of being burned. The degree to
which these individuals were injured was severe, yet varied. The way
in which each individual coped with the situation was also dissimilar.
Each had developed a form of amnesia, some for a longer time span
than others. One individual responded with great concern for her
business and those who depended on her. She gave very specific de-
tails to her assistant on how to close down the business and how to
finish her responsibilities to her clients. During this time, the emer-
gency medical team was tending to her second and third degree burn
wounds. She stated that she was totally unaware of the severity of
her situation and did not realize that she had almost died.
    Another burn victim was able to speak of the factual informa-
tion of what had happened to him as witnesses, family and friends
had related details to him. Unfortunately, or fortunately, as he puts
it, he had no recollection from approximately twenty-four hours prior
to the incident until approximately one week before he was dis-
charged from the hospital. He was a patient in the hospital for about
three months. At the time of the narration, he was still unable to
recall anything about that time period.
    After listening to the panel, I started to think about how abductees
cope with their experiences. Some claim to recall eighty to ninety per-
cent of the incident without hypnosis, while others are, allegedly,
walking around not even realizing that they have had an encounter.
I, myself, am frustrated by the fact that I can remember only perhaps
five to ten percent of my own experience without hypnosis. I am sure
that some of you can relate to my situation. As a result of this, I have
done some research. I initially thought this form of coping mecha-
nism might be called Post-traumatic Stress Disorder (PTSD). PTSD
includes certain behavioral symptoms, such as:
    1. Recurrent dreams and nightmares
    2. Acting as if one is reliving the traumatic event
    3. Social numbness, withdrawal, or both
    4. Sleep disturbance

5. *Avoidance of activities perceived to arouse recollection of the event*

6. *Hyperalertness or "startle response"*

It affects the thought process, resulting in recurrent intrusive memories, memory impairment, and trouble concentrating (Haber etal 1987, p. 547). Haber and her colleagues define PTSD ". . . as a reliving of a very stressful experience, with accompanying guilt and personal dysfunction."

As I continued to do some light research on the subject, I discovered another disorder that may be more appropriate: Dissociative Disorder. This, according to Haber etal, is referred to as those reactions in which there is a sudden, temporary alteration in the normally integrated functions of consciousness, identity, or motor behavior. Such individuals block off part of their lives from conscious recognition because of the threat of overwhelming anxiety (possibly related to a traumatic experience). One symptom of the dissociative disorder is amnesia. Amnesia is an alteration in consciousness that may include either a loss of memory for a specific period of time or a loss of all past memories. The forgotten material is still present beneath the level of consciousness though, and is accessible to recall at a later time (Haber etal, 1987, p. 566). My thoughts now are this: There are three theories for the inability of abductees to completely recall their experiences. As some of you know, abductees are allegedly given "hypnotic suggestions" by their abductors, so as not to remember the encounter. This, in itself, may be the only reason why a good many abductees need professional hypnosis to assist them in recalling their event. Personally, I doubt it. It may be more likely that it is a combination of the abductor's hypnotic suggestion and the above described coping mechanism of dissociative disorder, resulting in varying amounts of amnesia. Or, could it be that we are blaming the "little guys" for our inability to cope with their "alien presence" and that we respond with the acquired amnesia and that they are really not giving us strong hypnotic suggestions? I doubt that the latter is true.

d. Haber, P.P. Hoskins, A.M. Leach, and B.F. Sideleau, *"Comprehensive Psychiatric Nursing,"* 3rd edition, and McGraw Hill, New York, 1987.

twenty four

THE MEDIA

The arrival of computer networks and bulletin boards has changed the basic reporting and exchange of information on UFO sightings as much as the development of the printing press took us from passing on stories from oral tradition and legends to the novel and printed history books. Although there have been stories of extraterrestrials and flying saucers for many thousands of years, the radio broadcast in 1938 of *The War of the Worlds* by H.G. Wells illustrated the profound influence of the media on the public perception of UFOs.

Several months ago, as Kathryn Kaycoff, a director for the Fox show "Encounters," and I sat in a seaside restaurant, I became, possibly for the first time, truly aware of that. Since the camera crew had not arrived yet, we had decided to talk a bit, go over some of the questions, and discuss the incidents on Long Island and also Carp. As she sat across from me, I was immediately aware of being in the presence of "the media." She oozed New York in a clean-cut business suit, perfectly styled hair, and a voice that sounded perpetually prerecorded, mixed, and equalized. I was just beginning to understand the implications of a coast-to-coast broadcast with a viewership of up to twenty million, a broadcast that could be seen by one in ten of all the people in the United States.

"So, do you believe in these UFOs? Do you think we really are being visited by alien civilizations?"

She gave no hint of her own belief. Her eyes looked back at me, friendly, aware, yet I could tell that little inner videotape was rolling. No doubt she had interviewed all kinds of people for these docudramas." She probably hadn't decided about me yet. Was I well meaning but only two steps away from the psych ward, or the exception to the rule, a valid UFO researcher with some real, hard-core evidence?

"I'm not sure," I said. "I wasn't when I first started investigating these incidents, and I still haven't reached any written-in-stone conclusions yet." I thought of some of the other UFO researchers I had talked to on the phone. Some of them made grandiose claims and then, of course, kept secret the names of the individuals involved. And when pressed, the key witnesses, the ones with the critical information, had suddenly decided they didn't want to recount their experience to the media. Very convenient. "I have become a little disillusioned by some of the other researchers. I talked to one video expert in British Columbia who had been sent a film, and the researcher had requested that he 'fix it up.' Make it look more believable. When the video expert expressed shock and refused to alter the film, the researcher had said 'Well, no one need ever know.' Of course, I knew. I had looked at the same film. And it definitely needed some kind of help."

Kathryn looked surprised. "You're not saying that a researcher deliberately asked someone to phony a film up and then was going to release it to the media?"

"Unfortunately, I am."

"Who was this person?" said Kathryn. "Do I know them?"

I told her. "I'm afraid I could never put the name in my book or even cite the organization or the film involved." I sighed. "Besides, I am trying to avoid these personal UFO-researcher wars. Seems to be more fun to some of these people to thrash each other than the actual research itself."

Kathryn shook her head and nodded as the waitress lay down a steaming plate of seafood.

"So tell me about Fox," I said. "Sounds like you are doing quite a bit in the UFO field."

"Well, you know we did the 'Sightings' programs. This episode I am interviewing you for is for the 'Encounters' series. First episode," said Kathryn. "We are covering a lot of ground: the Long

Island crash, the Carp case, Puerto Rico. Should be an interesting show."

"I can't believe the growing interest in UFOs," I said. "Really, almost everyone I talk to is interested in what I am working on and wants to know more about it."

Kathryn's beeper went off. She picked it up, read the number, and smiled.

"They're here," she said. "So, are you ready to tell the world what you have found out about the Long Island crash?"

"I can hardly wait." I grinned. "It's quite a story."

RADIO AND TV, of course, have been around for many decades now. Yet the new emerging entities, the computer network and BBSs (bulletin board systems) have only been truly active for less than fifteen years. Kathryn and Fox represent a major medium: network television. But I had first learned of the Southaven Park crash from a much more powerful source of information, the thousands of boards around the world with UFO reports, e-mail, and the sysops (system operators) who run these boards.

One such personality, Mike Christol, runs a BBS in Kentucky called Space_Link. He has been researching and gathering information on UFOs since his teens. His board contains not only thousand of text files on dozens of topics, but also GIFS (computer pictures) of aliens, UFOs, and assorted phenomena.

I spent many long hours talking to Mike. He was invaluable in gathering information on Carp and other UFO cases.

"So, how did you get interested in UFOs, Mike?" I said.

"Well, my first encounter was investigating this crop circle."

"And just what are those?" I said.

"It's a burned or depressed circular area. Sometimes they can be rather complex geometric patterns." He sighed. "Anyway, there was this large circle in a field and that was my first real investigation. It was pretty exciting."

"So now you have set up a network in Kentucky called Space_Link or KUFON where people can call and report sightings?" I said.

"Yes," said Mike. "I have talked to a lot of people over the years, In fact, I even wrote down a little document about interviewing people. I thought you might be interested in it."

I had downloaded (called Mike's BBS and transferred) the file to my computer the night before.

"I read it," I said. "Mind if I use it in the book?"

"Sure," he said. "It's nothing really serious. But I think it gives you some idea what we're up against talking to these different people and also shows the different types of people we talk to."

UFO'S AND THE MAN ON THE STREET

What does the average man on the street think about UFO's? To find out, let's take a stroll down Main Street USA and talk to those men, women, and children with whom we come in contact.

Me: Good afternoon Sir, I'm taking a poll on UFO's, and would like to get your opinion. First of all, what is your name?

Man: My name is Harry Feet.

Me: Ok. Mr. Feet. What is your opinion of UFO's? Do you think they exist?

Harry Feet: Nah. Them UFO's is just somebody's 'magination runnin' wild, from watchin' too much television. Why, you know, I was watchin' this here space picture, Ma and me, and it was gittin' real interestin' when all at once I heard this real weird noise out back, ya see? I got up outta my chair and went and looked to see what it was. I saw this big old red light just behind the barn, ya see, and I was thinkin' it was one of them UFO's. I ran and got my shotgun, wouldn' gona let them critters git us, ya know. Hee-hee!

Well, anyway, I got my gun and went out in the yard and watched this red light. It was really flyin' low back there behind the barn. I walked back out in the field behind the barn, and all at once I see'd all these men out in the field, down by the creek. I moseyed on down there, and it seems some fool had got drunk and run his pick-up off in the creek, and them men was using a hello-copter to shine a lite on it so's they could get a chain on it and pull the truck up out of the creek. Hee-hee-hee! Well, they got the old boy out, and his old truck wasn't hurt hardly at all, 'cept muddy up to the doors and water in

*the floor some. But anyhow, that's the only time I ever thought I
saw a UFO.*

*Nah, I really think most of them people what see's them UFO's,
is just like that ol' boy what got drunk and thought he was seein' the
road when he ran that dang truck in the creek.*

*Me: Eh . . . Well, thank you for your opinion Mr. Feet. (Sheeee . . .
what a guy.)*

*As I continued my pollesting of the people on the street, I noticed
that for the most part, the more education a person had, the more
likely he/she was to accept the idea of the existence of UFO's. For
example, I happened to stop this lady and she turned out to be a
physicist who graduated from a reputable technical school in the
North-East section of the USA.*

*Me: Good afternoon Mam. I'm taking a poll on what the average
American thinks about the existence of UFO's. What is your name?*

*Lady: My name is Mary Wisdom. Yes. I feel there is more than ad-
equate evidence to suggest that the UFO phenomena is worthy of
further study by the scientific community. I have talked with many
people during my career who have convinced me that I must keep
an open mind when dealing with this subject. While I do think what
most people see and interpret as UFO's is some form of natural
phenomena, mistakenly identified due to unconventional weather
or atmospheric conditions; certainly, a small percentage of these
cases are of objects worthy of detailed research. I have discussed,
with my colleagues, the possible solution to the questions:*

    1. What are UFO's?

    2. From where do they originate?

    3. What would be the effect of this phenomena on humanity?

    *I personally have not witnessed any such phenomena, but I with-
hold final judgement until we have had an opportunity to review
the evidence available. I certainly think the Universe is an ever ex-
panding macro-cosm capable of producing a variety of life forms.
Some may develop along the same or similar lines as we of planet
Earth, and others may develop from a totally different embryonic
form of gestation.*

Such life forms, if they exist, may have evolved thousands or millions of years before us, and may have developed technology capable of inner galactic travel. I think we as scientists, have an obligation to use the education and technology we have been blessed with to answer this question for the benefit of all mankind, once and for all. If they exist, lets find out and say so. If they do not, likewise, let's say so. As we as a species continue to develop, mentally, physically, spiritually, and technically, we may some day venture into the vast reaches of other Civilizations and become the proverbial "UFO'S" TO THAT CIVILIZATION!

Me: Thank you for your opinion Ms. Wisdom, I'm sure there are many people who would applaud you for your attitude. (Wow! What an interesting lady.)

Interestingly enough, adults aren't the only ones who have an opinion on the subject. Take for instance these two boys who happened to come along while I was talking to a gentleman.

Boys: Hey mister, what about us? Aren't you interested in what we think, or do you think what us kids think is important?"

Me: Why yes boys, I certainly do think your thoughts are important. Tell me, what are your names and how old are you?

Boys: My name is Timmy and I'm eleven years old. This is Billy, and he's ten. We are best friends. Isn't that right Billy?"
Billy: Uh-hun, me and Timmy have been best friends forever! My mommy and Timmy's mommy are sisters.

Me: So Timmy do you and Billy think there are UFO's? If so, what do you think they are?

Timmy: Yah, I think they're . . .

Billy: Flying Saucers . . . That's what they are! I saw them on t.v., and they come from Mars, and they landed in this sand pit over the hill and this boy, he saw them land, but nobody would believe him . . . nobody would listen to him and these Martians, they, they were catching people and taking their bodies . . .

Timmy: Shut up Billy! That's only television. That's not real. That's only in the movies. I . . .

Billy: It is so real! I seen it myself. I seen it down by the 'lectric plant. It was real, real big and it was red and green and . . . *and* . . . *it made this funny whirring sound. I thought it was gona get the men down at the plant and eat them too. But it didn't. It just stayed in the air for a few minutes then took off real fast, zoooommmm, and it was gone outta sight real fast.*

Timmy: Well, he did come running in and tell mom and aunt that he'd seen a flying saucer down by the power plant!? But when we went out and looked down the hill, we didn't see nothing. I don't know what Billy saw, but, ah, he's just a little kid, and his 'magination runs away from him some times . . . *you heard him talking 'bout the t.v. show, and how excited he got. I don't know if he's lying or not. But I think them "flying saucers" might be real. Heck, I heard mom and dad talking after Billy went home and they said that God could have made men and women and little boys and girls like me on some other planet somewhere. God can do anything you know!*

Me: Thank you very much boys. I think your moms and dads have got two very intelligent boys.

Well I've talked to about fifty people in the last four hours. Many more have refused to talk with me. They probably think I'm nuts for doing this poll. I was talking with a gentleman who didn't know anything about the subject, and said he couldn't give me any meaningful answer when an ex-serviceman interrupted us.

Me: Well sir I appreciate you talking to me any. . . .

Intruder: It's people like you that's responsible for the continued perpetuation of all this UFO B— S—! I was in the service of this country for over twenty years, worked in a very sensitive position with top government security clearance and I know for a fact that there are no such things as UFO's!!!

People have seen weather balloons, clouds, high flying planes, stars, planets, satellites, etc. and thought they were UFO's. The problem with people is that they listen to you UFO sensationalists peddle your propaganda and they swallow it hook, line and sinker! These same people probably believe in spirits, witches, devils, and Santa Clause too. Why don't you people quit filling people's heads so full of this S—, and . . .

Me: Just a minute sir. You are entitled to your opinion, but that's all it is as far as I'm concerned, is your opinion! I have had to deal with this gung ho, national security, misidentification crap for too many years, and I'm telling you here and now that you people are the ones who are responsible for the insecurity, fear, and superstition which manifests itself among the peoples of this country. To save your own A—, you continue a tradition started back in the 1940's by a government in chaos, unable to affect the coming and going of these in the least.

Due to an accident caused by a new radar system, capable of a two hundred mile sweep, A UFO CRASHED IN ROSWELL, NEW MEXICO, on or about July 2, 1947, during a thunderstorm. It was subsequently recovered by the military and from that time on, you B—t—s have deceived the American as well as the World populace with your DECEPTION AND INTIMIDATION. You people have heckled, and tormented people for no reason other than they saw something strange, which didn't fit the known spectrum of objects which our technology could produce, then or now. You A— H—think that because you are in a position of security, it gives you the right to deny people their basic rights, both in this country and worldwide.

It's not the average "Joe Blow" who is in need of a change of underwear, it's you self-appointed guardians of "NEED TO KNOW" who fear the most! What have we to fear from the UFO PHENOMENA? It's apparently been with mankind since his beginnings, and yet we still manage to go on, day by day, with our lives, and for the most part remain unaffected by these NEMESIS OF THE UNKNOWN, DESPITE YOU NEOLITHIC GUARDIANS OF MANKIND! Come on, man. Give us, as humans, a little credit. We live in an age of space flight, nuclear weapons, implants, as well as super computers.

We are on the verge of moving our own civilization to other worlds and therefore securing the future of the human race as a species. I could understand the post war attitude of the 1940's, but this is the 1990's. The world is moving forward. Why have you few who think you know what's best for the many, lagged behind?

Man: You mmmmmm mmmmm mmmm . . . (He looked stunned for a moment, turned and walking away, shook his head as he departed.)

Until next time America, this is your man on Main Street, USA, wishing you well, and saying: "Watch the skies."

twenty five

MOONBASE

The U.S. military not only acknowledges that UFOs exist in internal, classified documents and memos, but has detailed protocol for dealing with persons who have touched an extraterrestrial or even been in close proximity to one. Since numerous astronauts have seen UFOs while in orbit, even while landing and walking on the moon, most of these procedures are primarily utilized on NASA personnel and astronauts returning from space. However, entire families have been taken by the government and placed under armed guard. These families, who have reported face-to-face encounters with extraterrestrials, have been relocated to secret camps through the U.S. and overseas, their goods placed in storage, and their homes tented and placed in quarantine. As we began to venture beyond the confines of the atmospheric envelope around planet earth, we have attracted the attention of numerous other races from other solar systems and distant stars.

The following was posted by UFO Joe on InfoNet. This concerns a report that was classified "Above Top Secret." The report states that the crew of the Eagle, which was the first craft to land on the moon, and Neil Armstrong, who took the first step on the moon, saw a most unusual sight. As he turned around he found himself looking at an alien craft at the top of a crater.

The following file was posted on InfoNet, London, Ontario.

ALIEN MOON BASE BY UFO JOE, INFONET

Is there an "Alien Base" on the Moon? More and more people are coming forward with stories of an Alien presence on the Moon. Rumors are that their "Moon Base" is on the dark side of the moon, the side we never see from Earth. Did you ever wonder why the Moon landings stopped and why have we not tried to build a Moon Base? It seems a better and easier idea than a floating space station?

According to Neil Armstrong the Aliens have a base on the Moon and wanted us to get off and stay off the Moon! Milton Cooper a Naval Intelligence Officer tell us that the Intelligence community calls the Alien Base "Luna":

LUNA: The Alien base on the far side of the Moon. It was seen and filmed by the Apollo Astronauts. A base, a mining operation using very large machines, and the very large alien craft described in sighting reports as MOTHER SHIPS exist there.—Milton Cooper

Did Apollo 11 Encounter UFOs on the Moon? from the Book "Above Top Secret" by Timothy Good.

According to hitherto unconfirmed reports, both Neil Armstrong and Edwin "Buzz" Aldrin saw UFOs shortly after that historic landing on the Moon in Apollo 11 on 21 July 1969. I remember hearing one of the astronauts refer to a "light" in or on a crater during the television transmission, followed by a request from mission control for further information. Nothing more was heard.

According to a former NASA employee Otto Binder, unnamed radio hams with their own VHF receiving facilities that bypassed NASA's broadcasting outlets picked up the following exchange:

NASA: What's there? Mission Control calling Apollo 11 . . .

Apollo 11: These "Babies" are huge, Sir! Enormous! OH MY GOD! You wouldn't believe it! I'm telling you there are other spacecraft out there, lined up on the far side of the crater edge! They're on the Moon watching us!

In 1979 Maurice Chatelain, former chief of NASA Communications Systems confirmed that Armstrong had indeed reported seeing two UFOs on the rim of a crater. "The encounter was common knowledge in NASA," he revealed, "but nobody has talked about it until now."

*Soviet scientists were allegedly the first to confirm the incident.
"According to our information, the encounter was reported immediately after the landing of the module," said Dr. Vladimir Azhazha,
a physicist and Professor of Mathematics at Moscow University.
"Neil Armstrong relayed the message to Mission Control that two
large, mysterious objects were watching them after having landed
near the moon module. But his message was never heard by the
public—because NASA censored it. "According to another Soviet
scientist, Dr. Aleksandr Kazantsev, Buzz Aldrin took color movie
film of the UFOs from inside the module, and continued filming
them after he and Armstrong went outside. Dr. Azhazha claims that
the UFOs departed minutes after the astronauts came out on to the
lunar surface.*

*Maurice Chatelain also confirmed that Apollo 11's radio trans-
missions were interrupted on several occasions in order to hide the
news from the public. Before dismissing Chatelain's sensational
claims, it is worth noting his impressive background in the aero-
space industry and space program. His first job after moving from
France was as an electronics engineer with Convair, specializing in
telecommunications, telemetry and radar. In 1959 he was in charge
of an electromagnetic research group, developing new radar and
telecommunications systems for Ryan. One of his eleven patents was
an automatic radar landing system that ignited retro rockets at a
given altitude, used in the Ranger and Surveyor flights to the Moon.
Later, at North American Aviation, Chatelain was offered the job of
designing and building the Apollo communications and data-pro-
cessing systems.*

*Chatelain claims that "all Apollo and Gemini flights were fol-
lowed, both at a distance and sometimes also quite closely, by space
vehicles of extraterrestrial origin—flying saucers, or UFOs, if you
want to call them by that name. Every time it occurred, the astronauts informed Mission Control, who then ordered absolute silence."
He goes on to say:*

*"I think that Walter Schirra aboard Mercury 8 was the first of
the astronauts to use the code name 'Santa Claus' to indicate the
presence of flying saucers next to space capsules. However, his
announcements were barely noticed by the general public. It was a
little different when James Lovell on board the Apollo 8 command
module came out from behind the moon and said for everybody to*

hear: 'PLEASE BE INFORMED THAT THERE IS A SANTA CLAUS.' Even though this happened on Christmas Day 1968, many people sensed a hidden meaning in those words."

Rumors persist. NASA may well be a civilian agency, but many of its programs are funded by the defense budget and most of the astronauts are subject to military security regulations. Apart from the fact that the National Security Agency screens all films and probably radio communications as well. We have the statements by Otto Binder, Dr. Garry Henderson and Maurice Chatelain that the astronauts were under strict orders not to discuss their sightings. And Gordon Cooper has testified to a United Nations committee that one of the astronauts actually witnessed a UFO on the ground. If there is no secrecy, why has this sighting not been made public?

A certain professor, who wished to remain anonymous, was engaged in a discussion with Neil Armstrong during a NASA symposium.

Professor: What REALLY happened out there with Apollo 11?

Armstrong: It was incredible, of course we had always known there was a possibility, the fact is, we were warned off! (by the Aliens). There was never any question then of a space station or a moon city.

Professor: How do you mean "warned off?"

Armstrong: I can't go into details, except to say that their ships were far superior to ours both in size and technology—Boy, were they big! . . . and menacing! No, there is no question of a space station.

Professor: But NASA had other missions after Apollo 11?

Armstrong: Naturally—NASA was committed at that time, and couldn't risk panic on Earth. But it really was a quick scoop and back again.

Armstrong confirmed that the story was true but refused to go into further detail, beyond admitting that the CIA was behind the cover-up.

twenty six

THE ALLEY ABDUCTION

Date: 09-02-94
From: Glenda Stocks
To: All
Subj: alley abduction 1/4

Newsgroups: alt.paranet.ufo
Date: Thu, 1 Sep 1994
From: MR JAMES EASTON <TEXJE@VAXB.HERIOT-
          WATT.AC.UK>
Subject: The Alley Abduction

"The Alley Abduction"

The following article has been reproduced from a recent edition of UFO Magazine (UK). The article, entitled as above, was written by Tony Dodd, the chief investigator of Quest International, publishers of the magazine. Tony Dodd is regarded as one of the most highly respected, experienced UFO investigators in the U.K., if not the world.

It was just another call on the UFO hotline . . .

I asked the caller to relate details of what had happened and the strange circumstances which had befallen Clair and Barbara began to unfold.

"It was the 30th of March 1988. I was forty-five years old at the time, and my daughter was twenty-four. It was 5:25 A.M. when we left my house in Birmingham to go to work at a nearby mill. It was a dark morning and as usual we took a short cut down some nearby alleys to get to the mill which was about 15 minutes away. We had taken this route many times without any problems, but on this morning, we heard a strange distant humming sound but didn't take much notice of it, only to comment that it was unusual at that time of day."

"Suddenly we were both startled by a light which was shining down on us from above. It was like somebody shining a bright torch. We both stopped and looked up and became frightened as the light was getting larger and larger, until it was directly over our heads. I remember holding my daughter's hand and then starting to feel dizzy. The next thing I remember was walking along the alley with my daughter, but something was wrong. We were both in a daze and both walking erratically because we were dizzy. My daughter was wearing a leather coat which was dry when we set off, but now it was wet, yet it hadn't been raining."

"We felt very strange and when we eventually reached the mill gates we were confronted by the security guard who commented that we were very late for work. I don't remember much about that day, neither does my daughter. Since that time we have always been apprehensive about going to work in the morning."

The woman, who was called Clair, and her daughter, Barbara, felt that something had happened to them that morning.

Further questioning revealed that both women suffered from a form of sunburn on their faces and arms after the incident. They also suffered from nose bleeds and a strange naval discharge. Barbara stated that a small patch of hair was missing at the nape of her neck.

The women agreed to undergo hypnotic regression. Arrangements were made for this to take place on the 12th of March 1994. It was decided that Clair would be regressed first. This was conducted out of sight and sound of her daughter. Under hypnosis she was taken back to the morning of the incident. She was invited to

remember all the events of that day, from that point and then left to
tell her own story.

"We have closed the door and are walking down the street, not
in any hurry, we have plenty of time. It's dark and quiet and we are
talking about everyday family matters. We are turning into a nar-
row alley, it's our shortcut to work. I can hear our footsteps as we
walk. I can hear another sound, it's strange . . . never heard it before, it's like a low humming sound . . . seems to be above us. There's
a light in the air, it's like a torch shining down on me, it's getting
bigger. We're frightened, holding each others hand. I feel strange,
the light is now below us, we're looking down on the light. There's a
moon above us, we're moving towards it."

There now followed a long pause and she started to talk again,
she had a bewildered expression on her face.

"Where am I? A room, it's all white, everything is white, it seems
to have a window all the way round it. I'm laying on a table, can't
move. I've got no clothes on. There's a netting cloth over my legs, it
feels wet. I can see Barbara, she's laying on a table next to me, she
has no clothes on, there's netting over her legs as well, what are they
doing?"

At this point I asked her "What is who doing?" She answered,
"The little men." I asked her to tell us what they looked like and she
said, "They're strange, only small, they've got tiny ears and big black
eyes. They're very thin, they've got three very long fingers." Questions were then raised over the figures clothing. "They're not wearing any clothes and their skin is white. There's some around my
table and some around Barbara's."

Now she started to show fear in her face, and said, "They're
touching my stomach, they feel cold. They're looking at my hands
and feet. They've got a long glass tube, it's only thin. They seem to
be pushing it into my stomach through my navel." I asked her if she
was feeling any pain, and she replied, "No, but they have left the
tube sticking out, they are now looking at my hair. It feels as though
they are pulling it. They have gone back to my stomach. They are
pulling the tube out, it's got fluid in it. I think they are taking eggs
from me,"

Clair started to show anxiety for her daughter, saying things
like, "please don't hurt her." She went on to reveal that the small
figures placed a cup-shaped object over her head. Some time later

she was allowed off the table and taken to a wall where a large television-like screen appeared. One of the figures pushed some buttons. Symbols lit-up on the screen, including triangles, squares and wavy lines. The screen then changed, television-type pictures of wars, fighting and explosions appeared. She continued:

"It's strange, everything I touch seems wet. There are some other people standing at the back of the room. They are very tall, not like the small men. One is standing closer than the others, he has got long blond hair. He seems to have blue eyes. He is wearing a silver suit with a blue badge on the left of his chest. The badge is a circle with a triangle next to it, with two zig-zag lines next to the triangle."

After this she was allowed to put her clothes back on and began to feel dizzy and disoriented. She suddenly found herself back in the alley with her daughter who looked dazed. She grasped her leather coat and asked "How has my coat got wet?"

They continued their short journey to work. Neither person had many memories of the rest of the day, but Clair said "It was as if we were working in a daze." They noticed what appeared to be sunburn on the faces and other parts which had not been covered by clothing.

Clair was eventually brought out of her hypnotic state and taken to another room to rest.

Barbara was now brought to the room and put into a hypnotic state—taken back to the date of the incident, to the point where she and her mother were leaving home to go to work. At this stage she was asked to recall the events of the day.

Barbara related how they left home in the dark to walk to work. In the alley they heard the strange sound. She then started to show signs of fear as she described the light shining down on them from the sky and how she first thought it was a helicopter. The light seemed to come down on top of them and they were holding each other in fear. At this point her speech became disoriented and difficult to understand. She was showing signs of stress. There was then a long pause before she continued. "I'm laying on a table without my clothes, I can see my mum, she's laying on another table."

She then started to cry, saying, "I want my mum, I want my mum." She was comforted and told that nothing could hurt either her or her mother, and to continue to describe what she saw. After a pause she sobbed, "I've got no clothes on, I can't move . . . there's a *cloth over my legs, it's wet, it's like netting. I can see my mother, they're looking into her mouth." Asked who was looking into her mother's mouth she replied, "Small people with big eyes, they have no clothes on. They have wrinkly skin. They walk funny, they waddle and they have only got two fingers." We asked her to describe what else was visible, and Barbara responded:*

"There is something like a big camera on a long arm, it's hanging above me, there seems to be a window which goes all around the room, everything seems to be white. The little people are around my table, they are looking at my hands and feet. Now they are looking into my mouth. I can feel one of them touching my stomach."

"One of them has got a thin rod, it has a silver ball on the end, he's pushing it up my nose." She felt no pain and went on to say that when the rod was removed, the silver "ball" was missing.

Other statements soon followed:

"They are placing an object like a piece of wire into my ear. I can feel them moving it about. They've now taken it out. I can hear a whistling sound in my ear."

"They're now touching my stomach. One of them has got a glass tube, he's pushing it into my stomach, near my navel." She was showing signs of anxiety, but we quickly comforted her and told Barbara that nothing could hurt her.

"They're pulling the tube out of my stomach, it's full of fluid, they're putting it into a dish. They have got two wire things, they've pushed them into my cervix. I can feel it. They've removed the wires, there's something on the end of them, they're putting it into a dish. They have got something like a very large glass cup, they're putting it over my head."

There was a long pause before she said:

"They've taken the thing off my head. They're turning me over. I can feel them examining my back and legs. They are now touching my hair at the back. It feels like they placed a small circular object on my hair at the bottom of my head. It's pulling my hair, I don't like it. They've turned me over again, they're standing near my feet. They are looking at our packets of cigarettes, they must have taken them from our pockets."

She recalled how she was taken off the table and moved to a large screen in the wall. At the base of the screen were banks of red buttons. She remembered that the "man" taking her to the screen

*was touching her arm, his skin was cold and felt wet. He pressed
some of the buttons and the screen lit-up; an array of symbols,
including triangles and squares could be seen. Her abductors
removed Barbara to another room where there was a strong smell
of burning. She was shown some small biscuit-like objects which
were apparently food. The creatures asked her to take one, and
accordingly put a small piece in her mouth. The biscuit tasted horrible and she soon spat it out.*

*Following this incident she was then taken back to the original
room where she saw her mother, now dressed, standing beside a
very tall beautiful woman who had long blond hair and blue eyes.
She smiled. The figure appeared to be wearing a type of silver-
coloured suit; a blue badge with a triangular and circular insignia
was positioned on the left of her chest. After dressing, Barbara was
handed back her leather coat; one of the little figures kept rubbing
it in his face as if feeling the texture. After feeling dizzy, she recalled
being back in the alley with her mother.*

*This concludes the report which narrates the events described
during the hypnotic regression of Clair and Barbara.*

Part IV
HYBRID

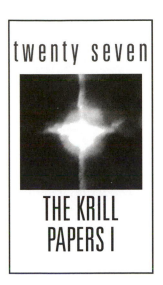

twenty seven

THE KRILL
PAPERS I

$\mathbf{T}$he Krill papers are documents that were uploaded to the network from an anonymous author and have been
the subject of intense debate for several years.

There is a great deal of information to support the fact that
aliens landed at Holloman Air Force Base in the '60s. This scene
was very similar to the landing in Spielberg's *Close Encounters of
the Third Kind* and, as in the movie, communication was established between the United States government and the aliens. A
treaty of sorts was "signed," and diplomatic relations between the
two races initiated. It was said that the aliens left one of their kind
with the U.S. and took one of ours as a gesture of mutual good
faith. The name of the alien was KRLL (also spelled KRYL). In
this document we will use the name KRLL. The military code name
for KRLL was "Cril." The "O.H." in this document stands for "Original Hostage."

The following information was gathered over several years. It
is a synopsis of facts gathered from the alien KRLL. This alien was
only able to survive a short time, and after a few years sickened
and died. There are a number of theories as to why the alien died,
seeing as its normal life span was several hundred years. The primary theory is that it simply could not fight off certain viruses to
which it was exposed in its interaction with humans.

CONFIDENTIAL

A SITUATION REPORT ON OUR ACQUISITION OF
ADVANCED TECHNOLOGY AND INTERACTION
WITH ALIEN CULTURES
JANUARY 1988

Throughout the forty year period when UFO have been actively observed in our civilization, a lot of data has been gathered—data which has often pointed to aspects of the phenomena that have been suppressed. As a result of the suppression and compartmentalization of the information, our culture has been fragmented into several levels of "reality" which both co-exist and oppose each other. Part of our culture does not or will not believe in the existence of other species; part of our culture acknowledges their existence or the probability of their existence; part of our culture is actually interacting with the other species. These simultaneous realities contribute to the condition of extreme confusion in which we find ourselves.

Research into UFO's follows a similar pattern. Some view the matter in a completely empirical perspective; others search for patterns and functional relationships in events; still others go out and ask the right questions at the right time and get answers. Some of those answers that have appeared are, to some people, quite disturbing and fantastic.

All in all, we are dealing with new concepts in physics, new concepts in psychology, and the gradually growing awareness that we are not only not alone here, but we have never been alone here. As if that were not enough, it turns out that factions of our society have known this, and apparently have been interacting with some of these alien species for quite a while. The bottom line is that all along, humanity has been led down a false path, a path that has been plagued by layer upon layer of conspiracies and disinformation. Technological knowledge and absolute power have been the motives on the human side. Survival has been the motive on the alien side, off at least as far as the predominant alien visitors are concerned. The intent of this paper is to bring much of the details regarding this into the open. You are not being asked to believe it, but to consider it in the light of what has happened, what is hap-

pening, and what may be developing right under our very noses. If you find that you cannot stomach such thoughts, or that you cannot deal with it, read no further.

It is quite evident, or it should be, that the UFO situation is both complex and dangerous. The UFO problem is a multi-situational and multi-dimensional phenomena. We have established the following as having a basis in fact:

- Craft from other worlds have crashed on Earth.
- Alien craft are from both ultra-dimensional sources and sources within this dimension.
- Early U.S. government efforts at acquiring alien technology were successful.
- The U.S. government has had live alien hostages at some point in time.
- The government has conducted autopsies on alien cadavers.
- U.S. intelligence agencies, security agencies, and public agencies are involved in the cover-up of facts pertaining to the situation.
- People have been and are currently abducted, mutilated, murdered and kidnapped as a result of the UFO situation.
- There is a current active alien presence on this planet among us that controls different elements of our society.
- Alien forces maintain bases on Earth and on the Moon.
- The U.S. government has had a working relationship with alien forces for some time, with the express purpose of gaining technology in gravitational propulsion, beam weaponry and mind control.
- Millions of cattle have been killed in the process of acquiring biological materials.
- Both aliens and the U.S. government are responsible for mutilations, but for different reasons.
- We live in a multi-dimensional world that is overlapped and visited by entities from other dimensions. Many of these entities are hostile. Many are not hostile.
- The basis of our genetic development and religions lies in intervention by non-terrestrial and terrestrial forces.
- Actual technology far exceeds that perceived by the public.
- The United States space program is a cover operation that exists for public relations purposes.
- People are being killed in order to suppress the facts about the

*situation. The CIA and the NSA are involved so deeply that expo-
sure would cause collapse of their overt structure.*
•Facts indicate alien overt presence within five to ten years.
*•Our civilization is one of many that have existed in the last bil-
lion years.*

Animal Mutilations and UFOs

General Chronology
    *In the middle of 1963, a series of livestock attacks occurred in
Haskell County, Texas. In a typical case, an Angus bull was found
with its throat slashed and a saucer-sized wound in its stomach.
The citizenry attributed the attacks to a wild beast of some sort, a
"vanishing varmint." As it continued its furtive forays through the
Haskell County outback, the bloodluster assumed somewhat more
mythic proportions and a new name was destined to endure: The
Haskell Rascal. Throughout the following decade, there would be
sporadic reports of similar attacks on livestock. These attacks were
occasionally described as "mutilations." The most prominent of these
infrequent reports was the mutilation death of "Snippy" the horse
in southern Colorado in 1967, accompanied by area UFO sightings,
a Condon Committee investigation and worldwide press coverage.*
    *It was in 1973 that the modern animal mutilation wave can be
said to have begun in earnest. That year is generally thought of as
the year of the last concerted UFO flap, although there may be reason to question that contention, given the events of two years later.
In 1973 and 1974 the majority of the classic mutilation reports origi-
nated in the central United States. In 1975, an unprecedented on-
slaught spread across the western two-thirds of the United States.
Mutilation reports peaked in that year, accompanied by accounts of
UFOs and unidentified helicopters. In 1978, the attacks increased.
By 1979, numerous livestock mutilations were occurring in Canada,
primarily in Alberta and Saskatchewan. Attacks in the United States
leveled off.*
    *In 1980, there was an increase in activity in the United States.
Mutilations have been reported less frequently since that year,
though this may be due in part to an increased reluctance to report
mutilations on the part of ranchers and farmers. The mutilations
still continue. Over ten thousand animals have died in the United*

States; although the mutilations have been occurring worldwide, the same circumstances are always present.

General Observations

Any investigation which intends to probe the systematic occurrence of the mutilation attacks upon livestock and other animals must include within its purview certain factors which may or may not be directly related to the acts of mutilation themselves. These mutilations—the killing and furtive removal of external or internal parts—have been directed at literally thousands of animals (primarily livestock) since the 1960s. The surgery on these animals is primarily conducted with uncanny precision, suggesting the use of highly sophisticated implements and techniques. The numbing and persistent regularity of the mutilations and the seemingly casual disposal of the useless carcasses all hint at extreme confidence—even arrogance—of the mutilators. It is an arrogance which appears to be justified by the freedom and impunity with which these acts have been carried out.

The pertinence of a specific element of the problem is shortly revealed in the course of any thorough investigation into the mutilations. I refer to the appearance of unmarked and otherwise unidentified helicopters within a spatial and temporal proximity of animal mutilation sites. The occurrence of the two has been persistent enough to supersede coincidence. These mystery helicopters are almost always without identifying markings, or markings may appear to have been painted over or covered with something. The helicopters are frequently reported flying at abnormal, unsafe or illegal altitudes. They may shy away if witnesses or law officers try to approach.

There are several accounts of aggressive behavior on the part of the helicopter occupants, with witnesses chased, "buzzed," hovered over or even fired upon. At times these choppers appear very near mutilation sites, even hovering over a pasture where a mutilated carcass is later found. They may be observed shortly before or after mutilations occur—or within days of a mutilation. The intention here is merely to stress that the "mystery helicopter" element is a part of the issue which deserves scrutiny.

The idea of "mystery helicopters" did not develop concurrently with the animal mutilations themselves. Such helicopters—

unmarked, flying at low levels, soundless (or sounding like helicopters)—have been reported for years, and have been linked to an even more widespread phenomenon—the "phantom" (fixed wing) aircraft. The helicopters themselves have been seen in areas where UFOs were reported, in many countries. In some of the more interesting accounts, the mystery helicopters were seen with UFOs, or shortly after the UFOs were sighted.

The most apt case I can think of, but certainly not the most isolated, is a case described by Virgil Armstrong in his lecture on "What NASA Didn't Tell Us About the Moon." He discusses helicopters and UFOs in general. Armstrong describes a friend of his that had invented a special camera arrangement with the idea that it would increase the chances of getting good pictures of UFOs. The camera was mounted on a gunstock along with a laser. The idea was to fire the laser at the UFO, if one appeared, and hopefully the UFO would come to a halt, enabling him to take some quality pictures.

Not too long after they were set up in the desert, a UFO did in fact appear, and they fired the laser and the disk stopped in a hovering mode. They took quite a few good pictures of it. Shortly thereafter, the disk flew away. Within minutes, they heard the unmistakable sound of helicopters coming their way. The helicopters landed strategically around their group, and out of the choppers came a group of Black Berets, which are strategic Air Force security forces. The commander of the Berets walked up to the group and said, "What are you doing here?" "Obviously, we are photographing flying objects, and we just saw a flying saucer and we got some very very good pictures of it." The commander then asked the leader of the group if he knew where he was. The group leader replied "No." The commander then said, "We suggest you get out of here right now!" The group leader then asked, "What right do you have to tell us to get out of here? Is this government land?" The commander of the Black Berets replied, "Indeed it is. It is Andrews Air Force Base, and if you are not out of here in ten minutes, you are under arrest." With that, the Berets removed the film from the camera, and the group left.

Not only does this illustrate one kind of instance where UFOs are seen in relationship to helicopters, but it also illustrates the fact that either some of the disks are ours, or we have a military/government relationship with those who fly them. The helicopters men-

tioned above are not the mystery ones, but were United States military ones. Another case of military helicopters and United States-owned disks comes from the book UFO Crash at Aztec, by Wendell Stevens. In the book he relates the incident where an Indian was backpacking in the mountains in the vicinity of Area 51, Groom Lake, on the Nellis AFB range north of Las Vegas. He heard approaching helicopters and hid out of sight. The helicopters were broadcasting a warning over public address systems for anyone in the area to show themselves because they were going to conduct a "dangerous military test." The Indian maintained his hidden posture, and the helicopters flew overhead and back down toward the Groom Lake facility. Minutes later, two helicopters were seen flying up the canyon with a black disk flying between them and slightly above them. They flew overhead and then the helicopters turned around and flew back towards the base, followed shortly afterward by the disk. The individual's name and how to contact him for further details is given in the book.

The Mystery Choppers

Situations involving the mystery helicopters appear to be a little more insidious. A good example is an event which occurred in Madison County, Montana, between June and October of 1976. Twenty-two confirmed cattle mutilations had occurred during that period, and they were accompanied by reports throughout the county of silent, unmarked, jet-black helicopters, flashing or steady anomalous lights in the air and near the ground, unmarked fixed- wing aircraft and white vans in remote and previously inaccessible areas.

Toward the latter part of this period, in early autumn of 1976, a hunter from Bozeman, Montana, was out alone around 3:00 P.M. one day in the Red Mountain area near Norris. He watched as a black helicopter without markings flew overhead and disappeared below a small hill. The curious hunter climbed to the top of the hill. There was the black chopper (a Bell Jet Ranger, he thought) on the ground, the engine still running. Seven men had apparently exited from the craft and were walking up the hill toward the observer. As the hunter advanced toward the seven, he waved and shouted congenial greetings. It was then that he realized there was something about the men—they were all Oriental. They had slanted eyes and olive skin and were jabbering among themselves in some indeci-

*pherable language. They wore "everyday" clothes, not uniforms.
Suddenly they began to return to the helicopter. The hunter, still
waving and shouting friendly greetings, started after them. The
Orientals quickened their pace. When the hunter approached within
five or six feet, they broke into a dead run, crowded into the chopper
and took off.*

*In a documented "mystery helicopter" wave in England, accounts
place Oriental-appearing occupants in an unidentified chopper.
Slant-eyed, olive skinned, Oriental-seeming occupants have been a
staple at the heart and at the periphery of UFO accounts for years.
Significant numbers of the infamous "men-in- black" (MIB) have a
similar appearance, but very often they are seen as very pale and
gaunt men who are sensitive to light. In STIGMATA No. 5 (Fall-
Winter 1978) Tom Adams outlined the most prominent speculative
explanations accounting for the mutilation / helicopter link, including the following:*

*• The helicopters are themselves UFOs, disguised to appear as ter-
restrial craft.*
*• The choppers originate from within the U.S. govemment / military
and are directly involved in conducting the actual mutilations.*
*• The helicopters are govemment / military and are not involved in
the mutilations but are investigating them.*
*• The helicopters are government / military, and they know about
the identity and motives of the mutilators and by their presence,
they are trying to divert attention to the possibility of involvement by the military.*

*The answer, as far as Tom Adams is concerned, could be a com-
bination of the above explanations. There also has been speculation
that they are involved in biological experiments with chemical or biological warfare or the geobotanical pursuit of petroleum and mineral
deposits. On one occasion, an army standard-type scalpel was found
at a mutilation site. Since the disks have been mostly involved with
the mutilations, it is thought that this was a diversionary event.*

*These events, or the discussion of them, is just the precursor to
the actual revelations of what is behind the mutilations: alien
acquisition of biological materials for their own use. To discuss this
in a logical and sequential manner, we must review what has been*

really happening right under our noses: direct interaction with extraterrestrial biological entities (EBE's). To discuss that, however, we must attempt to start at the beginning with what we now know to be true.

The Saga Begins (MJ -12)

It seemingly all began thousands of years ago, but for the purposes of this discussion, let's start with some events that we all are familiar with. In 1947, two years after we set off the first nuclear explosion that our current civilization detonated, came the Mantell episode, where we had the first recorded incident of a military confrontation with extraterrestrials that resulted in the death of a military pilot. It is quite evident now that our government did not know quite how to handle the situation. In 1952, the nation's capital was overflown by a series of disks. It was this event which led to the involvement of United States security forces (CIA, NSA, DIA, FBI) to try to keep the situation under control until they could understand what was happening. During this period, the government established a working group, known as Majestic Twelve (MJ-12).

The original members were: Admiral Roscoe H. Hillenkoetter, Dr. Vannevar Bush, Secretary James Forrestal, General Nathan P. Twining, General Hoyt S. Vandenburg, Dr. Detlev Bronk, Dr. Jerome Hunsaker, Mr. Sidney W. Souers, Mr. Gordon Gray, Dr. Donald Menzel, General Robert M. Montague, and Dr. Lloyd V. Berkner.

The MJ-12 group has been a continuously existing group since it was created, with new members replacing others that die. For example, when Secretary Forrestal was upset at seeing the United States sold out in World War II, he wound up being sent to a Naval hospital for emotional strain. Before relatives could get to him, he "jumped out a 16th story window." Most persons close to him consider his suicide contrived. When Forrestal died, he was replaced by General Walter B. Smith.

In December of 1947, Project Sign was created to acquire as much information as possible about UFOs, their performance characteristics and their purposes. In order to preserve security, liaison between Project Sign and MJ-12 was limited to two individuals within the intelligence division of the Air Material Command whose role it was to pass along certain types of information through channels. Project Sign evolved into Project Grudge in December, 1948.

Project Grudge had an over civilian counterpart named Project Bluebook, with which we are all familiar. Only "safe" reports were passed to Bluebook. In 1949, MJ-12 evolved an initial plan of contingency called MJ-1949-04P/78 that was to make allowance for public disclosure of some data should the necessity present itself.

Majestic Twelve was originally organized by General George C. Marshall in July, 1947, to study the Roswell-Magdalena UFO crash recovery and debris. Admiral Hillenkoetter, director of the CIA from May 1, 1947, until September, 1950, decided to activate the "Robertson Panel," which was designed to monitor civilian UFO study groups that were appearing all over the country. He also joined NICAP in 1956 and was chosen as a member of its board of directors. It was from this position that he was able to act as the MJ-12 "mole," along with his team of other covert experts. They were able to steer NICAP in any direction they wanted to go. With the "Flying Saucer Program" under complete control of MJ-12 and with the physical evidence hidden away, General Marshall felt more at ease with this very bizarre situation. These men and their successors have most successfully kept most of the public fooled for 39 years, including much of the western world, by setting up false experts and throwing their influence behind them to make their plan work, with considerable success. Until now.

Within six months of the Roswell crash on 2 July 1947 and the finding of another crashed UFO at San Augustine Flats near Magdalena, New Mexico, on 3 July 1947, a great deal of reorganization of agencies and shuffling of people took place. The main thrust behind the original "security lid," and the very reason for its construction, was the analysis and attempted duplication of the technologies of the disks. That activity is headed up by the following groups:

- *The Research and Development Board (R&DB)*
- *Air Force Research and Development (AFRD)*
- *The Office of Naval Research (ONR)*
- *CIA Office of Scientific Intelligence (CIA-OSI)*
- *NSA Office Of Scientific Intelligence (NSA-OSI)*

No single one of these groups was supposed to know the whole story. Each group was to know only the parts that MJ-12 allowed them to know. MJ-12 also operates through the various civilian intelligence and investigative groups. The CIA and the FBI are manipulated by MJ-12 to carry out their purposes. The NSA was created in the first place to protect the secret of the recovered flying disks, and eventually got complete control over all communications intelligence.

This control allows the NSA to monitor any individual through mail, telephone, telexes, telegrams, and now through on-line computers, monitoring private and personal communications as they choose. In fact, the present-day NSA is the current main extension of MJ-12 pertaining to the "Flying Saucer Program." Vast amounts of disinformation are spread throughout the UFO research field. Any witnesses to any aspect of the program have their lives monitored in every detail, for each has signed a security oath. For people who have worked in the program, including military members, breaking that oath could have any of the following direct consequences:

•A verbal warning accompanied by a review of the security oath.
•A stronger warning, sometimes accompanied by a brow-beating and intimidation.
•Psychologically working on an individual to bring on depression that will lead to suicide.
•Murder of the person made to appear as a suicide or accident.
•Strange and sudden accidents, always fatal.
•Confinement in special "detention centers."
•Confinement in "insane asylums" where they are "treated" by mind-control and deprogramming techniques. Individuals are released with changed personalities, identities, and altered memories.
•Bringing the individual into the "inside," where he is employed and works for "them," and where he can be watched. This is usually in closed facilities with little contact with the outside world. Underground facilities are the usual place for this.

Any individual who they perceive to be "too close to the truth" will be treated in the same manner. MJ-12 will go to any length to preserve and protect the ultimate secret. As we will see later, the characteristics of what this ultimate secret would turn out to be would change drastically, for it was something even MJ-12 could not predict—actual contact with alien groups.

How the actual contact between the government and aliens was initially made is not known, but the government was made aware that it could be done by a civilian using the right equipment. Dr. Paul Bennewitz, civilian scientist, did so using computer equipment and informed the government he had done so, not realizing that by then, in 1983, that the government was in truth as deep into dealing with the aliens as his communications with them revealed. Dr. Bennewitz lives next to Manzano Weapons Storage Area in Albuquerque, New Mexico. He observed UFOs constantly over the area and initially decided that they were a threat to the installation. He proceeded to figure out a coding system and attempted and was successful in communicating with the aliens that were flying over that area.

What he found out is that after initial contacts with the aliens years ago, we agreed to provide them with bases underground in the United States in return for certain technological secrets which the aliens would reveal to us. The aliens would also be allowed to carry out certain operations, abductions, and mutilations without intervention.

The original contact between the government and the extraterrestrial biological entities, who are grey in color and about 3.5 to 4.5 feet high (hereafter referred to as the Grays), was achieved between 1947 and 1951. We knew that the Grays were instrumental in performing the mutilations of animals (and some humans) and that they were using the glandular substances derived from these materials for food (absorbed through the skin) and to clone more Grays in their underground laboratories. The government was also aware that the Grays performed some of the abductions to secure genetic materials. The government insisted that the Grays provide them with a list that would be presented to the National Security Council.

Through all this, the government thought that the Grays were basically tolerable creatures, although a bit distasteful. They presumed at the time that it was not unreasonable to assume that the public would and could get used to their presence. Between 1968 and 1969 a plan was formulated to make the public aware of their existence over the succeeding twenty years. This time period would culminate with a series of documentaries that would explain the history and intentions of the Grays.

The Grays assured us that the real purpose of the abductions was for the monitoring of our civilization, and when we learned that the abductions were a lot more frequent and insidious than we were led to believe, the government became concerned. Their concern was also based on additional information regarding the purposes for the abductions:

- *Insertion of a 3mm spherical biological monitoring device through the nasal cavity into the brain of the abductee.*
- *Implementing subliminal posthypnotic suggestions that would compel the abductee to perform some specific act at a time to be within the next two to five years.*
- *Genetic crossbreeding between the Grays and human beings.*
- *Insertion of discoid monitoring devices into the muscle tissue of the abductees. Presence of these has been verified by x-ray.*

By the time we had found out the truth about the intentions of the Grays (they intend to stay here and stay in control of our world) it was too late. We had already "sold out" humanity. Not that it would have made any difference, because they were here doing what they were doing anyway.

In 1983, a story was outlined by government sources that said that the Grays are responsible for our biological evolution through manipulation of the DNA of already evolving primates on this planet. Various time intervals of the DNA manipulation were specified for 25,000, 15,000, 5,000, and 2,500 years ago. Originally, the government thought that the Grays meant us no harm, but today, in 1988, the picture that is emerging is exactly the opposite. The story now is one of great deception at several different levels: the Grays Trojan Horse-style manipulation and lying which allied MJ-12 forces with them four decades ago; the government's disinformation of the subject of UFOs in order to perpetuate the agreement with the Grays free of public scrutiny; the lies to the abductees; the Grays on-going abduction of people and mutilation of animals in order to harvest enzymes, blood and other tissues for their own survival needs; and a genetic blend of the Grey race and a tall Nordic race to enable Grey interface with humans to be done with greater ease.

Information from a source at a southwest Army base reveals that these multiple levels of deception are true. It is also indicated that the goal of SDI (Star Wars) is actually to follow through with an attack, proposed by the Grays, on the Nordics when they arrive en masse between now and 1992. This time schedule seems to match with the posthypnotic programming of many abductees for actions between the next two to five years. The same source see the world dominated and controlled by the Grays in a way similar to that portrayed in the "V" television series—they are concerned only for their own survival agenda, and this agenda requires biological substances from other life forms on our planet.

The apparent reasoning for the Grey preoccupation with this is due to their lack of a formal digestive tract and the fact that they absorb nutrients and excrete waste directly through the skin. The substances that they acquire are mixed with hydrogen peroxide and "painted" on their skin, allowing absorption of the required nutrients. It is construed from this that some weaponry against them might be geared in this direction.

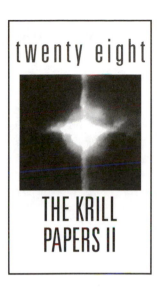

twenty eight

THE KRILL PAPERS II

Observations by a Visiting Nordic

*In October, 1987, UFO researcher George Andrews was success-
fully able to contact one of the Nordics not associated with the Grays,
through a woman in California. What follows are the comments
made by the alien:*
"Were you a culture about to invade, you would not do it with a
flourish of ships showing up in the heavens and undergo risk of
being fired upon. That's the type of warfare slightly less evolved
beings get into. You would create intense confusion and disagreement with only inferences to your presence—inferences which would
[in turn] cause controversial disagreement. "The Grays are insidious little fiends. They did exactly [to us] what they're doing here [to
you]. You are not on the verge of an invasion. You are not in the
middle of an invasion. The invasion has already taken place. It's
merely in its final stages. "What would you invade? [Here he
describes the operational plan of the Grays from the beginning.]
You would go to the most secret of communities within a society. In
the case of the United States, you would go and infiltrate the CIA.
You would take over some of them and you would take over part of
the KGB. "You would create great dissension and disagreement
between factions of the public at large—some groups saying they
have seen UFOs, others saying 'No, no, this is not possible.' You*

*would involve two major countries in an ongoing idiotic philosophi-
cal disagreement so that while the Soviet Union and the United
States constantly battle back and forth about who has which piece
of territory or whether one invades Iran or whether one invades
Afghanistan or whatever . . . whether one dismantles one nuclear
warhead or (the other dismantles another group of warheads—you
would sit back and laugh if you had the capacity to laugh. "You
would present yourself indeed to some in a group who would protect you [CIA or MJ-12] thinking they had a secret more secret and
more perfect knowledge of something than anyone else on this planet
had, and they would covet you and you would trust their own greed
and you would trust their own mass stupidity to trap them. And
you'd do it on both sides. "You'd show yourself to some of the mass
populace to further involve [factions of] the government in an attempt to shut them up, to keep them even more busy quieting them
and trying to 'stop more information about UFOs from getting out.'
You'd have the mass populace to a state where they distrusted the
government. 'Oh, why don't they believe us? Why can't they understand that these things are really happening? We're not crazy!' "So
you would have battles constantly about whether UFOs exist or they
don't exist. You would have the public and the government at each
other's throats. You would set two major superpowers at each other's
throats. And you would have set up groups like 'haves'—the wealthy
but contented—and the 'have-nots.' You would plant the seeds of
massive discontent. "Eventually you might have some show of ships
landing in the 1990s. One or two. By the time they have landed, be
assured they will be in complete control. You will start doing cross-
breeds and more crossbreeds, generation after generation. "You bribe
the government with a few tidbits—a Star Wars system. You tease
and tempt the Soviet Union with a laser system far finer than any
of their own scientists could think of. And you always have that
subtle inference—just on the borderline of consciousness so that
UFOs don't seem to believable, yet you keep it couched in secrecy
and make it seem quite so insane that no one would believe them.
On top of it, you would unleash forces that would want to kill them
[UFO contactees] if they disclosed that the CIA is dealing with the
exact same things the [contact victim] is. "Maybe one or two hundred years from now, some of the Grays will even physically mingle
and you may have some creatures walking around who are pretty*

much hybrids between Grays and your own race. For now, anything that walks around will look much like yourselves. It's simpler. It holds down on mass panic. "Everyone who has experiences with them [Grays] will be at odds with the government. To add to that, we will go into a complete phased of earthquake after earthquake and upheaval after upheaval. "The inner core of the CIA is deeply controlled by the Grays. The CIA sees interaction with the Grays as a path to greater scientific achievement. "One reason you are seeing so many different kinds of UFOs is that other cultures are watching with extreme interest. Scientists from other cultures arrive to watch. The Grays have not only taken over the intelligence agencies, they have also taken over what those agencies call 'lunatic fringe groups.'"

Well, that's what Nordic had to say. The source of this also makes the following commentary:

"The ultimate evil is that masked form of psychological complacency that leads one to adhere to a group philosophy rather than eke out one's own horizons. As soon as you acquire an awareness of being a so-called 'chosen special group,' you are on the way to a fall. That is the seed of destruction in any society and any culture and it leaves it vulnerable. It will be the eventual undoing of the Grays as well. They see not their error—it is the very weakness they seize upon that is their own inherent weakness. To try and change a Grey, or a cultish type of 'Star Person,' or a CIA member is futile. It will happen, but all in its own good time . . . it is the spirit that makes anyone stand up and disagree with something that is untrue and incorrect that will be the thorn in the side of the Grays, and the other forces that have allied with them."

During the occupation of the Grays, they have established quite a number of underground bases all over the world, especially in the United States. One such base (among others in the same state) is under Archuleta Mesa, which is about 2.5 miles northwest of Dulce, New Mexico. Details about that base have come across by way of two sources, The first source is by way of an abduction of a woman and her son who witnessed the pickup of a calf for extraction of biological materials. "In May, 1980, a most interesting case occurred in northern New Mexico. A mother and her son were driving on a rural highway near Cimarron when they observed two craft in the process of abducting a calf. Both of them were then abducted and *taken on separate craft to the underground installation, where the woman witnessed the mutilation of the calf. It was alleged that she also observed vats containing cattle body parts floating in a liquid, and another vat containing the body of a male human. The woman was subjected to an exam and it was further alleged that small metallic objects were implanted into her body as well as into her son's body. More than one source has informed us that catscans have confirmed the presence of these implants."*

The above extract is from a transcript of a conversation between Jim McCampbell and Dr. Paul Bennewitz on July 13, 1984. Bennewitz reports that through regressive hypnosis of the mother and child (required only in about 30% of abduction cases) and his own follow-up investigation (including communications receive via his computer terminal, which are ostensibly from a UFO-related source), he was able to determine the location of the underground facility: a kilometer underground beneath Archuleta Mesa on the Jicarilla Apache Indian Reservation near Dulce, New Mexico (since 1976, one of the area of the U.S. hardest hit by mutilations). Bennewitz' information is that this installation is operated jointly as part of an on-going program of cooperation between the U.S. government and EBEs. There are also underground bases at Kirtland AFB and Holloman AFB, as well as at scores of other bases around the world, including Bentwaters, England. Back to the base under discussion. . . . After Bennewitz briefed Air Force officials on what he had found, a trip to the area revealed the following data: The base is 2.5 miles northwest of Dulce, and almost overlooks the town. There is a level highway 36 feet wide going into the area. It is a government road. One can see telemetry trailers and buildings that are five-sided with a dome. Next to the domes, a black limousine was noted—a CIA vehicle. These limos will run you off the road if you try to get into the area. To the north there is a launch site. There are two wrecked ships there; they are 36 feet long with wings, and one can see oxygen and hydrogen tanks. The ships that we got out of the trade are atomic-powered with plutonium pellets. Refueling of the plutonium is accomplished at Los Alamos. The base has been there since 1948. Some of the disks are piloted by the NSA. The base is 4,000 feet long and helicopters are going in and out of there all the time. When it became known that Bennewitz was familiar with this, the mutilations in the area stopped. In 1979, something happened and the

base was temporarily closed. There was an argument over weapons
and our people were chased out. The aliens killed 66 of our people,
and 44 got away. One of the people who in fact got away was a CIA
agent who, before leaving, made some notes, photos, and videotapes,
and went into hiding. He has been in hiding ever since, and every
six months he contacts each of five people he left copies of the material with. His instructions were that if he missed four successive
contacts, the people could do whatever they want with the material.
This agent calls an individual known to MUFON. Somehow, a
description of the "Dulce Papers" was issued, and was received in
December, 1987, by many researchers. The "Dulce Papers" were com-
posed of 25 black and white photos, a videotape with no dialogue
and a set of papers that included technical information regarding
the jointly occupied (U.S.-Alien) facility one kilometer beneath the
Archuleta Mesa near Dulce, New Mexico. The facility still exists
and is currently operational. It is believed that there are four additional facilities of the same type, one being located a few miles to
the southeast of Groom Lake, Nevada.

"A GENERAL DESCRIPTION of what these papers contain is that they
contain documents that discuss copper and molybdenum, and papers that discuss magnesium and potassium, but mostly papers
about copper. Sheets of paper with charts and strange diagrams.
Papers that discuss UV light and gamma rays. These papers tell
what the aliens are after and how the blood (taken from cattle) is
used. The aliens seem to absorb atoms to eat. They put their hands
in blood, sort of like a sponge, for nourishment. It's not just food
they want; the DNA in cattle and humans is being altered. The 'Type
One' creature is a lab animal. They know how to change the atoms
to create a temporary 'almost human being.' It is made with animal
tissue and depends on a computer to simulate memory, a memory
the computer has withdrawn from another human. Clones. The
'almost human being' is slow and clumsy. Real humans are used
for training, to experiment with and to breed with these 'almost
humans.' Some humans are kidnapped and used completely. Some
are kept in large tubes, and are kept alive in an amber liquid. "Some
humans are brainwashed and used to distort the truth. Certain male
humans have a high sperm count and are kept alive. Their sperm is
used to alter the DNA and create a non-gender being called 'Type

Two.' That sperm is grown in some way and altered again, put in wombs. They resemble 'ugly humans' when growing but look normal when fully grown, which only takes a few months from fetus-size. "They have a short life span, less than a year. Some female humans are used for breeding. Countless women have had a sudden miscarriage after about three months' pregnancy. Some never know they were pregnant, others remember contact some way. The fetus is used to mix the DNA in types one and two. The atomic makeup in that fetus is half human, half 'almost human,' and would not survive in the mother's womb. It is taken at three months and grown elsewhere."

WELL, THAT'S WHAT the "Dulce Papers" review says. There are some pen and ink reproductions of some of the photos made in the laboratories (3), an illustration of what one of the wombs looks like (2' x 4'), an illustration showing one of the tubes where one of the "almost humans" is grown, a page showing a simple diagram of crystalline metal, pure gold crystal, and what looks like either a genetic or metallurgical diagram or chart. Also attached is what looks like an x-ray diffraction pattern and a diagram of hexagonal crystals, with a comment that they are best for electrical conduction. It would appear that the last half of material in the "review" applies to the supercrystalline metal used for hull structure, or something along that line.

OBVIOUSLY, THIS IS all rather bizarre from a certain point of view— any point of view, in fact. Nevertheless, material that is supported by years of descriptions and multitudes of corroborations must mean something, especially when bumped against what is seen to be going on. It is apparent from this and other data that has been accumulated over the years, that there are underground bases and tunnel complexes all over the world, and that more are being constructed all the time. Many of you may recall the "Shaver" mysteries and inner-earth city stories. Well, all that is true. There are cities down there, amongst other things, and some of them have nothing to do with the main subject of this paper. They've been there for a long time.

Let's change direction for a moment. One individual by the name of Lew Tery has been working on some ideas regarding UFOs and geomagnetic anomalies. I will go into what he has discovered (although the concept of the relationship is not new) and let you judge that for yourself. After purchasing aeromagnetic and gravitational anomaly maps from the United States Geological Survey, it becomes evident that there was indeed a valid connection between these areas and UFOs. Mr. Tery gave a lecture in Arizona about that relationship, and was subsequently harassed by the FBI, and told that the information is "sensitive." Mr. Tery took the hint and declined to talk publicly about it to the degree that he had been doing. Both the aeromagnetic and gravitational (Bougier Gravity) maps indicate basic field strength, as well as areas of high and low field strength. Interestingly enough, the areas of maximum and minimum field strength have the following:

• All have frequent UFO sightings.
• All are either on Indian Reservations, government land, or the government is trying to buy up the land.
• Many of them, especially where several are clustered together, are suspected bases areas and/or areas where mutilations and abductions have historically taken place.

In these observations, Mr. Tery has gone far, but he has gone a little farther in noting that there are times when the UFOs are seen in these areas. Through painstaking research, Mr. Tery found that the sightings, as well as many abductions and mutilations, occur:

• On the new moon or within two days before the new moon.
• On the full moon or within two days before the full moon.
• At the perihelion (moon closest to earth) or within two days before the perihelion.

A glance at the nearest farmers' almanac will give you the information you require as far as the days for this year or any other one. There seems to be no concrete explanation for the coincidence of the times and the events, but it is true.

The Men in Black

All things considered, UFO research has become pretty much of a circus today, and the most intriguing and controversial sideshow skirting the edges is the question of the "silencers," or the mysterious "Men in Black." There is a strong subliminal appeal in these accounts of visits by mysterious dark-suited figures (I have been visited myself, as have others I've known) attempting to silence UFO witnesses. A typical situation would be that a witness has a UFO sighting or UFO-related experience. Shortly thereafter he is visited by one or more "odd"-looking men who relate to him the minutest details of his experience, even though he has as yet told no one for fear of ridicule or other reasons. The men warn him about spreading the story of his experience around and sometimes even threaten him personally, sometimes obliquely, sometimes directly. Any evidence, if it exists, is confiscated in one way or another. Sometimes the visit is for some totally meaningless reason and the subject of UFOs is hardly mentioned, if at all. But again, the men all seem to look alike. We actually seem to find ourselves in close proximity to beings who obviously must be directly connected in some way with the objects themselves or the source behind them, yet they seem to be functioning unobtrusively within the framework of our own everyday existence. The classic conception of an MIB is a man of indefinite age, medium height and dressed completely in black. He always has a black hat and often a black turtleneck sweater. They present an appearance often described as "strange" or "odd." They speak in a dull monotone voice, "like a computer," and are dark-complected with high cheekbones, thin lips, pointed chin, and eyes that are mildly slanted. The visitors themselves are often on absurd missions. They have reportedly posed as salesmen, telephone repairmen or representatives from official or unofficial organizations. Their mode of transportation is usually large and expensive cars— Buicks or Lincolns, sometimes Cadillacs, all black, of course. I might note at this point that their physical appearance also has included beings that have pale-grayish skin, and that some of them have been seen to have blond hair, yet they wear the clothing and drive the cars previously described. Their cars often operate with the headlights off, but ghostly purple or greenish glows illuminate the interior. Unusual insignia have been seen emblazoned on the doors and the license plates are always unidentifiable or untraceable. The fabric of their clothes has been described as strangely "shiny" or thin, but not silky—almost as if they have been cut from a new type of fabric. Their often mechanical behavior has caused them to be described by some as being like robots or androids (think back to *the Dulce lab). A lot of descriptions of some of these "folks" are pretty bizarre. A businessman's family in Wildwood, New Jersey, was visited by an unusually large man whose pants legs hiked up when he sat down, revealing a green wire grafted onto his skin and running up his leg. There are other cases of MIB appearing on the other side of a wet, muddy field after a heavy rain, but having no mud whatever on their brightly shined shoes and in the bitter cold, out of nowhere, wearing only a thin coat. Their shoes and wallets all seem new and hardly broken in. They are not alone. They seem to have faceless conspirators in the nation's post offices and phone companies. Researchers and witnesses often report their mail going astray at an unusually high rate and being bothered by bizarre phone calls where they are spoken to by metallic, inhuman-sounding voices. Unusual noises on the phone, intensifying whenever UFOs are mentioned, and voices breaking in on conversations, have all led many people to suspect that their phones are being tapped. One can't discuss the MIB for long without mentioning the name of John A. Keel, an author who has written much about them. Keel has done more than any other writer to publicize this bizarre aspect of the UFO situation. Keel suggests that the UFO are part of the environment itself and conic from another time-space continue, that most of the UFO phenomena is psychic and psychological rather than physical. Well, I personally would not define it that way, although those two components are certainly deeply involved in what's going on. The first noted appearance of the MIB was in 1947, at the scene of the Maury Island incident, where some debris was ejected from a disk, and subsequently recovered by officials, who loaded them on an Army bomber which crashed on takeoff.*

To illustrate a little how bizarre some of the incidents are regarding the MIB, I have assembled a short list of some of the more interesting factors in some cases:

- *An ex-Air Force man is gassed and interrogated by MIB after he has learned classified NASA secrets.*
- *Close-up photos of UFOs were seized from a teenager who is also directly threatened by MIB.*
- *MIB sighted in the lobby of the U.S. State Department leave a mysterious artifact.*
- *MIB pose as Air Force officers to silence witnesses.*

*MIB tries to buy before-hours Coke and sings to birds in trees.
*MIB disintegrates a coin in a witness' hand and tells him that his heart will do the same if he talks.

THROUGHOUT ALL THIS information, I have neglected to mention some aspects of the psychology of the Grays. Dr. Paul Bennewitz, in his original report to the government entitled "Project Beta," goes into some detail, which I will now discuss:

*The alien, either through evolvement or because the humanoid types are "made," will exhibit tendencies for bad logic. They appear to have more frailties and weaknesses than the normal Homo Sapiens.
*They are not to be trusted.
*Because of the aliens' apparent logic system, a key decision cannot be made without higher clearance. All are under control of what they call "The Keeper," yet it would appear that even this is not the final authority. Delays as long as 12–15 hours can occur for a decision.
*Because of this apparent control, individual instantaneous decision-making by the alien is limited. If the "plan" goes even slightly out of balance or context, they become confused. Faced with this, possibly, the humanoids would be the first to run.
*Psychologically their morale is near disintegration. There is pronounced dissension in the ranks—even with the humanoids.
*Because of their own internal vulnerability mind-wise to each other, there is a basic lack of trust between them.
*They appear to be totally death-oriented, and because of this, absolutely death-fear oriented. This is a psychological advantage.
*The prime, and weakest area discovered, probed and tested is exactly what they have used, thinking it their key strength— that being the manipulation of and control of the mind. Manipulated in reverse-psychology they face a situation where they have a vulnerable, integrated weakness.
*They totally respect force.

Grey Physiology and Anatomy
     The approximate height of most specimens is between 3.5 and 4.5 feet. The head, by human standards, is large in comparison

with the body. Facial features show a pair of eyes described as large, sunken or deeply set, far apart or distended more than the human, and slightly slanted as Oriental or Mongoloid. No ear lobes or apertures on the side of the head were seen. The nose is vague. One or two holes have been mentioned. The mouth area is described as a small slit or fissure. In some cases there is no mouth at all. It appears not to function as a means for communication or for food. The neck area is described as being thin, in some instances not being visible at all because of the tightly-knit garment. Most observers describe these humanoids as being hairless. Some of the bodies recovered have a slight hair-patch atop the head. Others have what appears to be like a silver skullcap. There were no breathing attachments or communications devices. This suggests telepathy with higher intelligence. In one instance there was an opening in the right frontal lobe area, revealing a crystalline network. This network implies the development of a third brain. The arms are described as long and thin, reaching down to the knee section. The hangers each contain four fingers, with no thumbs. Three fingers are longer than the other. Some are very long. Some are very long. Others are very short. No description is available of the legs and feet. Some pathologists indicate that section of the body was not developed as we would anticipate, showing that some of these beings were adapted to life in the water. There was a webbing effect between the fingers on most of the specimens. According to most observers, the skin is grey. Some claim it is beige, tan or pinkish-grey. No reproductive organs or capabilities were discovered. No phallus. No womb. Conforms cloning mentioned by other sources. The humanoids appear to be from a mold, sharing identical racial and biological characteristics. There is no blood as we know it, but there is a fluid which is grayish in color.

The "Taxonomy of Extra-Terrestrial Humanoids," another offering by George Andrews, yields some other observations:

- *Working under the instructions of the humanoids from Rigel (the Grays), CIA and former Nazi scientists have developed and deployed malignant strains of bacteria and viruses, including AIDS, in order to exterminate undesirable elements of the human population.*
- *The Grays are almost entirely devoid of emotions, but can obtain*

a "high" by telepathically tuning in the different kinds of intense human emotion, such as ecstasy or agony. (Does that explain why UFOs have always been seen in regions of war and human conflict?)

• There are over 1,000 humans in the United States alone who are the offspring of intergalactic or extragalactic beings and terrestrial humans. (The son of an acquaintance of [deleted in original] is one.)

• Throughout recorded history, as well as during prehistoric times, there has been constant genetic manipulation of and interbreeding with humans in order to breed out the less evolved simian traits. The Nordic races have participated in this from the beginning, and we are as much a part of them as we might suppose.

• Grays have the ability to camouflage themselves as tall Blonds through mental energy projection. Blonds never project themselves as Grays. Some Blonds seen with the Grays are physically real, but are prisoners of the Grays who have either paralyzed them or have destroyed their ability to teleport through time and other dimensions. Note: A lot of the material obtained by George Andrews has as its source a Blond that is a time traveler that escaped the Grey takeover of their system.

• Both Blonds and Grays have the ability to disintegrate matter into energy and then reintegrate the energy back into matter. This ability allows them to pass through walls and to transport abductees out of their cars with the doors still locked.

• The original Rigelians were the Blonds until they were invaded by the Grays, a parasitic race, who took over and interbred with them. The original Rigelians were the ones who seeded the earth. It is because of this common ancestry that terrestrial humanity is of such interest to both the Blonds and the Grays.

• Terrestrial human females can be impregnated either on board ship or while they sleep in their homes. Males need not be manifested in visible form for this to occur.

• The Blonds now habitate the Procyon system. The conflict between the Blonds and the Grays is in a state of temporary truce, although the conflict between the Rigelian and the Sirius system is being fought actively.

• The Blonds with speech abilities will respond violently if attacked or threatened, but the telepathic ones will respond peacefully.

•*Blonds were sometimes mistaken for angels in earlier centuries. They do not seem to age, and consistently appear to be from 27 to 35 human years old.*

CONFUSED? *Well, now you can see why the natural diversity of the way things are hard to sort out for the average researcher. The probability that this information is true or partially true remains fairly high, based on analysis of what we know about abductions and general contact between humans and EBEs that has been documented.*

REAL ESOTERICA—SIRIUS AND THE MIB. *Let's regress for a moment back to the MIB. According to John Keel, the MIB often state that they are representatives of the "Nation of the Third Eye." Based on some of the info we have already researched, it is apparent that Sirius has been in contact with us for a long time. According to George Hunt Williamson (one of the early contactees) in his book "Other Tongues, Other Flesh," the earth allies of Sirius, i.e., the secret societies, use the Eye of Horus as an insignia. This symbol has also been seen on the MIB. Secret societies believe that there is a Great White Lodge on earth. They call it Shamballa— and consider it to be the spiritual center of the world. Now, theosophists such as Alice Bailey say that the Great White Lodge is on Sirius. If the All-Seeing-Eye is a symbol of Sirius' earth-allies and the MIB wear that symbol, and if Shamballa represents the Great White Lodge on earth—then the MIB are emissaries of Shamballa. Sirius and Shamballa are two sides of the same coin. This is verified in the book "The Undiscovered Country," by Stephen Jenkins. Jenkins was told by Buddhist priests that Shamballa was located in the constellation of Orion. The entrance to Shamballa on earth is usually placed in the trans-Himalayan region. Some assert it is in the heart of the Gobi Desert (where there have been allegations of crashed disks and bases). According to the explorer Nicholas Roerich, there are caves in the Himalayan foothills that have subterranean passages. In one of the these passages, there is a stone door that has never been opened, because the time for its opening has not yet arrived. In 1930, Doreal founded the Brotherhood of the White Temple. He says that the entrance to Shamballa is far underground. He goes on to say that space bonds around Shamballa, and that there is a warp which leads into another universe.*

twenty nine

Let's get back to something we can have more of a direct handle on. Many times psychics have been called upon by investigative authorities to evaluate situations, and in many cases what they have contributed has been very helpful. This was done in the case of animal mutilations back in 1980 by Peter Jordan, who engaged several psychics to render their impressions from photos and maps of mutilations and mutilation areas. What follows is a condensation of what was found during this exercise.

Name of Psychic: Ronald Mangravite
- This animal has been dead a few days.
- Some parts are decaying faster than others.
- There is an overload of electrolytes in the body possibly due to injection of a citrate.
- Something wrong with blood. Picking up higher portion of plasma which may be lymphatic fluid.
- Two men working on the animal. Very sharp surgical knives.
- Men dressed in black. Jumpsuits. Shiny black nylon.
- Winch line coming down from chopper.
- Men are skilled ex-military.
- Something is going to be done with the tissue.
- Flurometry connection. Spectrophotometer.
- Choppers are brown or grey.

- Underground implications.
- Experimentation with different analytical techniques.

Name of Psychic: Elisabeth Lerner
- Paramilitary forces.
- A serious invasion of American privacy.
- Non-American Indians part of secret project.
- The word "Annide."
- The word "Carmine" or "Karmine."
- The symbol "dk."
- A new wave of mutilations will strike near southwest New Mexico.
- The Hobart Company is involved in this. (Refrigeration equipment?)
- Three huge, doughnut-shaped objects will be seen in conjunction with these new mutilations.
- Breakthrough in research.
- Muscle relaxant injections.
- Someone with the name "Empeda."
- This is a Mexican operation.
- Names "Kielman" and "Kelman."
- Institution with many Lincoln Continentals and Cadillacs.
- Laboratory underground.
- Lilly Pharmaceuticals.
- Roman numerals IVIII [sic].
- Name "Stephano."
- The number "1714."
- Last name "Audler."
- First name "Mase."
- Last name "Audli."
- Jet rocket labs nearby.
- Domes above the ground.
- Vehicle ID # MP 1936. Small jeeps.
- Last name "Plento."
- Initials "C.B.P." heads operation. Wears brown military shoes. Army.
- Number "1161."
- Around an oil field.
- Place where oil crosses in an "X" pattern.
- Chemical engineering connections.

- Mustard.
- Periscope device on bottom of craft. Chopper called "The Shark."
- Man with blond hair. English features. High forehead. Wears square ring. Insignia reads "C.B.P."
- Has something to do with ammunition. Colonel.

Name of Psychic. Nancy Fuchs
- Dusk scene. Men talking about some animal's throat. Something missing.
- Cylindrical object.
- Long thick object inserted into jugular vein.
- Powerful energy flow emanating from device used to kill cattle.
- Feeling of tremendous anger and hostility.
- Research implication. Minerals needed for research.
- Intimidation of rancher Gomez.
- Embryos.
- Thousands of samples needed for this breeding effect.
- Crossbreeding.
- Animal dies in seconds.
- Jolts of electricity through animal.
- Breeding and genetics involved.
- Army background.
- Liquid-filled shoes leave no prints.
- Marshall. Army. Cap with black rim and gold braid. Pompous. White-haired. Very influential. Walks into Pentagon whenever he pleases. Commission given 15–18 years ago for mutilation project when he was overseas. Grand Marshall. Friend of General MacArthur. Lives in Dakotas. Money invested. High-priority issue. Tall. Heavyset. Only 17 people know of this.
- Project with $2.5 million allocated early in game for breeding experimentation. Late 1960s through Pentagon. More and more money invested every year.
- Land wanted. Want to destroy ranchers prime source of income. John Mitchell connected to this.
- Howard Hughes.
- Uranium connection.
- Picture complex. Faction-ridden.
- Interest in speeding up growth of cattle.
- Importance of pancreas.

The "war on drugs" is in fact a war on the independent drug dealer who constitutes a threat to the monopoly. Comment: Additional ways to subdue the population or eliminate undesirable?

[The following are additional excerpts from the Krill papers which have been condensed and edited.]

Thousands of sightings can be fitted into the "great circle" route, and often the dates are staggered so that it appears that the phenomenon moves systematically from point to point. Every state in the United States has from two to ten "windows." These are areas where UFOs appear repeatedly year after year. The objects will appear in these places and pursue courses confined to sectors with a radius of about 200 miles. The great circle from Canada (not to be confused with the traditional Great Circle) in the northwest through the central states and back into northeast Canada is a major window. Hundreds of smaller windows lie within that circle. Another major window is centered in the Gulf of Mexico and encompasses much of Mexico, Texas and the Southwest. As mentioned previously, many windows center directly over area of magnetic deviation. UFOs seem to congregate about the highest available hills in these window areas. They become visible in these centers and then radiate outward, traveling sometimes 100–200 miles before disappearing again.

Among the great heaps of neglected and ignored UFO data, we find hundreds of "minipeople" accounts. These are very rarely published anywhere because they tend to be so unbelievable. Most of them are identical to the fairy and gnome stories of yesteryear. Witnesses to these events can experience conjunctivitis, akinesia (paralysis), amnesia, and the other effects often noted by witnesses to more conventional events. One notable event is one that occurred in Seattle, Washington, in the latter part of August, 1965.

A woman awoke around 2 a.m. and discovered she could not move a muscle or make a sound. Her window was open, and suddenly a tiny, football-sized dull-grey object floated through the window and hovered over the carpet near her bed. Three legs lowered from the object and it settled to the floor. A small ramp extended from it and five or six tiny people clambered out and seemed to work on some kind of repairs on the object. They wore tight-fitting clothing. When they were finished, they got in and the object took off and sailed out the window. At that point, she was able to move. The case was investigated by J. Russell Jenkins of Seattle. You can readily see why almost none of these kinds of stories ever appear in print, except in occult-oriented literature. Nevertheless, if we hope to assess the true UFO situation, we must examine all these stories. We can learn nothing by considering only those incidents which are emotionally and intellectually acceptable to us.

TIME IS ONE of the most important aspects of the UFO thing. It plays a strange but significant role. Part of the answer may not lie in the stars but in the clock ticking on your fireplace. Our world exists in three dimensions. We can move in many directions within these dimensions. Space does not exist except when we make it exist. To us, the distance between atoms in our matter is so minute that it can only be calculated with hypothetical measurements. Yet, if we lived on an atom, and our size was relative to its size, the distance to the next atom would seem awesome. There is another man-made measurement called time. Unlike the other three dimensions, time has us seemingly trapped. Time becomes very real to us, and it appears that we couldn't live without it. Yet time doesn't really exist at all. This moment exists to us. Does this mean the same moment is being shared by other planets?

The UFO phenomenon does seem to be controlled. It does follow intelligent patterns. If the objects themselves are manifestations of higher energies, then something has to manipulate those energies somehow and reduce them to the visible frequencies. Not only do they enter the visible frequencies, but they take forms which seem physical and real to us, and they carry out actions which seem to be intelligent. Thus we arrive at the source. The source has to be a form of intelligent energy operating at the highest possible point of the frequency spectrum. If such an energy exists at all, it might permeate the universe and maintain equal control of each component part. Because of its very high frequency, so high that the energy particles are virtually standing still, the source has no need to replenish itself in any way that would be acceptable to our environmental sciences. It could actually create and destroy matter by manipulating the lower energies. It would be timeless, because it exists beyond all time fields. It would be infinite because it is not confined by three-dimensional "space." Children figure neatly into this, and they always have. The child's mind, especially before the so-called age of reason when the logic circuits begin to form, is a clear instrument, open and uninfluenced by opinions and conclusions.

This is an important point in the UFO mystery. Perhaps if we were in a pure energy state, each particle of energy would itself serve as a synapse, and information could be stored by a slight alteration in frequency. All the memory fragments of a rose, for example, would be recorded at one frequency, and the whole energy form could tune into that memory by adjusting frequencies, as we might adjust a radio receiver. In other words, no complex circuitry would be required. No body would be necessary. The energy patterns would not need material form. It would permeate the entire universe. It could surround you completely at this very moment and be aware of all the feeble impulses of low energy passing through your brain. If it so desired, it could control those pulses and thus control your thoughts. Man has always been aware of this intelligent energy or force. He has always worshipped it.

Our first conclusion is that the UFOs originate from beyond our own time frame or time cycle. Our second conclusion is that the source has total foreknowledge of human events and even of individual lives. Since time and space are not absolutes, these two conclusions are compatible. It is that all human events occur simultaneously when viewed by a greater intelligence. If a greater intelligence wants to communicate with a lower form, all kinds of problems are presented. The communication must be conducted in a manner which will be meaningful and understandable to the lower life form. An acceptable frame of reference must be found and utilized. UFO phenomenon, especially the "soft" ones, are frequently reflective; that is, the observed manifestations seem to be deliberately tailored and adjusted to the individual beliefs and attitudes of the witnesses. Contactees are given information which, in most cases, conforms to their beliefs, UFO researchers who concentrate on one particular aspect or theory find themselves inundated with seemingly reliable reports which seem to substantiate that theory.

John Keel's extensive experiences with this reflective factor led him to carry out weird experiments which confirmed that a large part of the reported data is engineered and deliberately false. The witnesses are not the perpetrators, but merely the victims. The apparent purpose of all this false data is multifold. Much of it is meant to create confusion and diversion. Some of it has served to support certain beliefs which were erroneous but which would serve as stepping-stones to the higher, more complex truth. Whole generations have come and gone, happily believing in the false data, unaware that they were mere links in the chain. If it were all understood too soon, we might crumble under the weight of the truth. This earth is covered with windows into those other unseen worlds. If we had the instruments to detect them, we would find that these windows are the focal points for super high-frequency waves—the "rays" of ancient lore. These rays might come from Orion or the Pleiades as the ancients claimed, or they might be part of the great force that emanates throughout tile universe. The UFOs have given us the evidence that such rays exist. Now, slowly, we are being told why.

IT IS ALSO apparent that some entities are having a good laugh at our expense. As mentioned before, literature indicates that the phenomenon carefully cultivated the religious frame of reference in early times, just as the modem manifestations have carefully supported the extraterrestrial frame of reference. The Devil's emissaries of yesteryear have been replaced by the mysterious "men in black." A major, but little-explored, aspect of the UFO phenomenon is therefore theological and philosophical rather than purely scientific. The UFO problem can never be untangled by physicists and scientists unless they are men who also are schooled in the other disciplines. The earth was occupied before man arrived or was created. That's an important point to consider.

The original occupants were paraphysial and possessed the power of transmutation of matter. Man was the interloper. The inevitable conflict arose between physical man and the paraphysial owners of the planet. Man accepted the interpretation that this conflict raged between his creator and the Devil. The religious viewpoint has always been that the Devil has been attacking man (trying to get rid of him) by causing havoc upon him. There is historical and modern proof that this may be so. It is interesting that parapsychologists have long concluded that the paralysis that contactees experience is a contributing cause; that the entity may materialize by utilizing energy from the percipient himself. John Keel has in his files hundreds of cases, some of which have now been investigated by qualified psychiatrists, in which young men and women obsessed with the UFO phenomenon have suffered frightening visits from apparitions, followed up by mysterious black Cadillacs which appeared and disappeared suddenly, and have been terrified into up their pursuit of the UFOs. The phenomenon is again reflective in nature; the more frightened the victim becomes, the more the manifestations are escalated. Think about it.

The Other Side of the Coin.
There is a balance in nature, and there also seems to be a balance in the UFO picture. People have actually died after exposure to the gamma and UV rays from UFOs. But other people have actually had their ailments cured by similar rays. Occult literature is filled with accounts of this type. Except for those who might be specially constructed for incubus-succubus activities, it does appear that our "angels" and "spacemen" come from a world, in many cases, with sex—and very probably, a world without an organized society; a world in which each individual is merely a unit in the whole and is totally controlled by the collective intelligence or energy mass of that whole. In other words, these beings, or some of them anyway, have no free will. They are slaves of a very high order. Often they try to convey this to percipients with their statements, "We are One," "We are in bondage." We face a great task in trying to isolate the UFO phenomenon from the larger and more important "big picture," the overall situation of which the UFOs are merely a small part. Elemental beings are another aspect of the world we live in. Children see them more than adults, perhaps for the reasons described before.

Historical records certainly indicate that the little people have always existed all over this planet; that they possess the power of flight, the power of invisibility, and, to varying degrees, the power to dominate and control the human mind. Accounts of little humanoids with supernatural powers can be found in almost every culture. The manifestations have remained the same throughout history. Only our interpretations of those events have changed. It brought the birth of Spiritualism, which was in its heyday in the 1850s and 1860s, and was just another form of communication between the ultraterrestrials and ourselves. UFO flaps also parallel outbreaks of poltergeist cases. It all tics in together. Assuming that each discovered historical report represents a larger number of unpublished or undiscovered reports, just as today's UFO reports represent on the average 250 unreported or unpublished sightings, we can conclude that a flap condition existed, for example, in the years 1820, 1834, 1844, 1846, and 1849. We also find that there was an outbreak of poltergeists in 1835, 1846, and 1849.

As the 19th century progressed, reporting improved, and we are able to make more precise correlations. A UFO flap took place in 1850, and there was also a series of poltergeist cases. A larger poltergeist outbreak occurred in 1867, following flaps in 1863–64. UFO activity became more intense beginning in 1870, and there were notable flaps in 1872, 1877, and 1879. The 1880s produced a major explosion of all kinds of phenomena, including the sudden disappearance of people. Poltergeist cases were in abundance in that decade, particularly in the big flap years of 1883 and 1885. Astrophysicist Morris K. Jessup labeled the years 1877–87 the "Incredible Decade" after scouring astronomical journals of the period. Astronomers made some remarkable discoveries during those years. The previously unobserved satellites of Mars popped into view in 1877, new craters appeared on the moon, all kinds of strange objects flitted around the upper atmosphere.

THE TRANCE PHENOMENON deserves extensive study because so many aspects of it are directly related to the contactee phenomenon. In both, you will find the same contradictions. There seem to be both good and evil forces at work. The good guys latch onto people with particularly receptive minds and turn them into trance mediums and the bad guys use the same methods to tamper with the minds of contactees and even to commit murder indirectly. Since incidents of these types can be traced throughout history, it seems probably that these forces have always been here on this planet. Do the ultraterrestrials really care about us? There is much evidence to suggest that they don't. They care only to the extent that we can fulfill our enigmatic use to them.

There have been innumerable psychic hoaxes for the past 150 years, and many of these parallel the UFO hoaxes. In ufology we have to contend with the teenager's hot air balloon, and in psychic phenomenon we have to worry about youngsters firing rocks at houses. There are, however, more UFO sightings than there are plastic balloons, and more poltergeists dumping rocks in living rooms than there are wild-eyed youngsters with slingshots. There are also more ultraterrestrial entities than either the occultists or the UFO researchers can dream of. Giant winged beings, usually

described as headless, are an integral part of the UFO phenomenon. Winged human forms have been seen flying over many areas
of the world. John A. Keel wrote a book called the *Mothman Prophecies* and Gray Barker a book called *The Silver Bridge* that go into
some detail. They are usually described as having blazing red eyes
set deep in their shoulders.

ON MAY 13, 1917, three girls in Portugal were in the meadows of a
place called Cova da Iria outside of Fatima, Portugal, when they
saw a flash of light in the clear sky. They ran for shelter under
outside a tree, thinking that was lightning. When they reached
the tree, they stopped in amazement, for there hovering just above
a 3-foot evergreen nearby, a brilliant globe of light hung suspended.
Within this globe there was an entity garbed in a luminous white
robe with a face of light which dazzled and hurt the eyes. The figure stated that it was from heaven, and asked the girls to come
there on the 13th day, for six months in succession. On October 13,
1917, an estimated 70,000 people had gathered at the site. Suddenly the crowd screamed, for something came through the clouds:
a huge silver disk which rotated rapidly as it descended towards
the crowd. It seemed to change color, going through the spectrum.
These gyrations continued for ten minutes.

Miles from there, others were also watching the same object.
The incident at Fatima was obviously a carefully planned and
deliberately executed demonstration. The major prophecies of
Fatima had been written down and sealed in an envelope, and
turned over to the Vatican. They were supposed to be revealed to
the world in 1960. The secret of Fatima? One Pope was murdered
after only 30 days in office when the Vatican thought he would
reveal it. It is said to be a prediction of the end of the world. The
demonstration was therefore a failure as far as the ultraterrestrials
were concerned. Such demos proved highly effective in Biblical
times, but times were changing and new methods were called for.
A similar event such as Fatima took place in Garabandal, Ger-
many, on July 2, 1961. Even more startling, on the entity's right
side they could see "a square of red fire framing a triangle with an
eye and some writing. The lettering was in an old Oriental script."
The Third Eye. Haven't we heard of that before? Remember the
Nation of the Third Eye—the MIB, etc.?

thirty

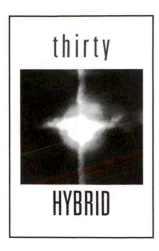

HYBRID

I was soon to find out where one of the alien babies—or hybrids, as they are called—was born. I had been so absorbed in researching the Long Island crash and the Carp landing that I had no idea that all hell was breaking loose in the small area of Laguna Cartagena, in Puerto Rico. At the time, I did not realize that for the aliens, the United States mainland was not necessarily a first choice area to make initial contact with the human race. Besides being heavily defended by nuclear missiles and the Strategic Air Command, any landing of a UFO on the continental United States would be considered an ominous threat and probably would result in an incident in Southaven Park.

Despite the good intentions, or professed good intentions of the Antarians, it was far more feasible that the first contact would be with the Grays. In the remote tropical paradise of Laguna Cartagena, besides making the critical blunder of allowing a hybrid child to be born, the Grays had ceased all attempts to disguise their growing presence at what was rumored to be an underwater base. They were flagrantly abducting dozens of villagers, hovering over dwellings, and even draining power from the local power station. One of my Hispanic friends called me, extremely excited, and sent me file after file of reports of encounters in the town of Caja Roja, just a few miles away from the swamp.

From: Carlos Steffens / Puerto Rico

My mother got up from her bed and went to the kitchen to get the medicine and realized there was a loud humming sound outside. She looked out the window and saw three UFOs hovering a few feet above the posts that carry the electric wires. After a few seconds she realized what they were and ran to our room. She locked herself there with us until morning broke, when she went to our grandmother's. A few days later, there was a news article that the same night she saw them, there were a lot of reports from all over the island of UFO sightings.

She describes what she saw as taking a cup and putting it upside down in a saucer. I don't remember if she said they were red or any other color. However, she did say they were in a "stair" formation. She also spoke of a second UFO sighting. She was coming from a wedding in the SW part of the island, renown for its consistent amount of UFO sightings and abductions. She was driving and one of her aunts was with her. They were coming through the expressway when all of a sudden she realized she wasn't in the expressway anymore. She was in a road that was used about 20 years ago, when the expressway didn't exist. Also she was at the beginning of the road instead of where she should have been had she started there. (What I mean is, she was already an hour into the trip and suddenly she was back in another road and just at the point she would be if she had been driving for only 30 min. instead of an hour).

The most curious thing happened when they looked at their watches. An hour and 45 min. had gone by but as far as they knew, they had only been driving for an hour. Neither of them can account for those 45 min. nor how they went from the highway all the way back to that old road. I suggested hypnosis but she refuses saying that it might be something related to what she saw when we were young and that terrified her too much. She doesn't want to know what happened.

The following article was published by the newspaper *El Vocero* of Puerto Rico and is related to UFO activities. Although I have translated it from Spanish to English, I want to make it clear that I am *not* a professional translator and that English is my second language.

Unlike people's beliefs that UFO phenomena are happening only in a few places on the Island (Puerto Rico), El Vocero learned this week about the strange case of a peasant from Columbia, Mr. Luis Roberto Rodriguez, who says that he was abducted by ETs last April and brought to an alien city on the moon. This writer got permission from the newspaper "Vanguardia Liberal" of Bucaramange, Colombia, to transcribe some details of the interview that Mr. Rodriguez had with their reporter. The peasant, who lives in a small town named Tunja, is 37 years old and the father of several children. He said that he was brought back to earth forty hours after his abduction. He was also given messages for the president and the cardinal of Colombia, Mario Revollo.

This all started on an April morning when Rodriguez went out of his humble home to milk his cow. He said that while riding his horse, a huge ship, as big as a stadium, sent a beam of light onto him. The horse got scared. He dismounted the animal to get protection from the light and he then lost consciousness. When he awoke he realized he was in a strange place. He added that he spoke with two beings who made him undress and examined him carefully. He also said that although he saw a very big ship, he was taken to the moon on a smaller one, which made him believe he was transferred from one ship to another during the trip.

The following is a rough translation copy of the alleged message from the extraterrestrials for the U.S. president.

Space Confederation 1.24 A-25 for the President of the U.S.

Facing the fury of men against men, we are sending this message from the space to make you aware of the evil and destruction you are putting yourselves into. Your power on earth is big but it is not so in the confines of space. That is why your scientific advances will be stopped as well as your nuclear arms, otherwise men will experience a rapid fall into their own abyss. If they do not stop their tendency to destroy themselves, they will see hate, treason, and lies grow, and they will see the seven plagues develop more quickly. Earth itself will punish men. The weak lines of the earth will begin vomiting the fury that man himself has caused. Your fights will bring disasters because men's arms are pointing at each other. There will be powerful nations eating the crumbs of the less powerful and weaker. There will be panic and horror for what is coming but there will also be happiness among those who have suffered.

In many countries bloody wars are coming, but they will start in the countries that have more destructive powers. However, the human race will receive a preparation for its evolution. Mr. President, it is imperative to stop the development of arms on all levels, otherwise earth will increase it's imbalance. Humans will be seeing days and nights passing more swiftly. If humankind would awake from this hecatomb and would listen to this SOS, earth would become the paradise that God gave us since the beginning. You will see a sign of our presence in each place of the earth providing help to those we gave this mission. We will get closer to offer our help. Creator 24-25 Z Peace, happiness, divine integrity, space brothers.

These messages were delivered by Mr. Rodriguez, a peasant with scarce academic knowledge. It would seem that after the numerous sighting and abductions, a growing numbers of UFO researchers and curiosity seekers flooded the Laguna Cartagena area.

LAJAS, Puerto Rico—

UFO buffs, extraterrestrial hunters and the curious are bringing litter and crime with them as they flock to a nearby lagoon where UFOs supposedly fly by, Lajas police said. The gathering of large groups around the Cartdgena lagoon in the eastern part of the island commonwealth to look for UFOs led lo reports of vandalism, littering and public drunkenness, said police Lt. Rafael Rodriguez.

For some time residents of Lajas and Cabo Rojo near the lagoon have reported seeing flying saucers and extraterrestrials during the night, which has sparked the curiosity of thousands of people who come to look for the unidentified flying objects.

Shortly after I had received these articles and many others, which will be published in future research, I received a call from a man in Puerto Rico. After some soul searching, the man had decided to put me in contact with a mother who had been abducted by extraterrestrials several times, had been impregnated, and had given birth to an alien child. He told me that the incidence of sightings in the Laguna Cartagena area had increased to the point where alien craft were being seen coming up out of the ocean several times nightly. He included a videotape that showed close-ups of these craft as well as a clip of a U.S. jet being chased by a UFO.

Yet the thing that kept sticking in my mind was the child. The information from the channel had mentioned two such children, whom the Grays had not been able to remove from the pregnant mothers before they were born. So the Long Island crash and the Carp landing had only been the beginning of my experiences in the field of UFO research. And I knew very soon that I would have to take a trip to Puerto Rico, to capture firsthand what was claimed to be a fleet of Gray ships coming up from the ocean, and most important, to see with my own eyes what very few people had ever seen: a child produced by the impregnation of a human mother with alien DNA—a hybrid.

EPILOGUE

"So that about wraps it up," I said to Tom Theophanis, handing him the manuscript. It was now spring, and instead of the dreary, icy forest, the Canadian countryside had been transformed into rich greens, and the sky was a rich, unbroken blue.

"You realize that a good UFO Researcher would continue this investigation for years. Gather all possible information, interview more witnesses, go over the facts hundreds of times," said Tom.

"Yes, and you've done that, and I assume will continue doing that," I said, "as other researchers on Long Island will continue gathering information on the crash. But I think I have enough facts here to at least prove that some type of craft crashed on Long Island and that something landed in Carp, Ontario.

"I'll leave it to you to fight about the fine points of the data on network TV or on the computer network. My purpose was to bring the public the incredible story of a possible alien spacecraft that was shot down on Long Island and a flying saucer that landed in Canada.

"People who want to learn more or become actively involved in UFO research can find more information at the end of the book. I have listed phone numbers and locations of organizations and computer networks. I've included hotlines for reporting sightings, and have even given credit to a lot of people in the field who have gone unnoticed until now by the general media."

Tom grinned. "Well, yes, I guess you are right. So, tell me, do you believe in UFOs and little gray men yet? Do you think there really are UFOs?"

"Ask me in a few weeks. I was told to go out and stand on top of some mountain and they would land." I laughed. "Or ask them through the channel."

"I have received invitations like that," said Tom, "some of them from very reputable sources. So far I haven't seen any aliens or any craft. Are you going?"

"Why not?" I said. "I'll take my assistant with me, and who knows? Perhaps they have some elaborate Spielberg-quality hoax cooked up. Who knows? It will be worth the show."

He handed me a stack of folders. "Well, here are the reports from Puerto Rico you asked for. I understand that you and Bob Oeschler are going up to Carp to talk to Guardian and look at the site again in July," said Tom. "I would be glad to go with you."

"Sure," I said. "Should be very interesting. You know, no one has ever interviewed Guardian personally except for Fox. This will be a first. And I am really looking forward to seeing the alien child. I am surprised the government hasn't taken it away."

"Yet," said Tom. "Perhaps it is simply a deformed or hydrocephalic baby. You should take a geneticist with you. Run a test for alien DNA."

"Of course," I said. "Now it's my turn." I pulled a video from my briefcase and put it in his VCR. "Crash film, even better quality than the original one shown on Fox of Long Island. See, the UFO is very clear, you can see the trees in the background, even see two aliens burning in the flames."

"You think that is interesting," said Tom, pulling out a videotape from his library. "Wait until you see this."

WITNESSES

During my investigation of the Carp and Southaven Park incidents, I interviewed over two hundred people. The list that follows is not complete. There are several key witnesses who, for their own safety, requested that their names be withheld. These include my sources (there were three) at Brookhaven Lab, the fireman who was at the crash site, and anyone who was in direct contact with the NTL. It is current practice by the CIA and government to quarantine and isolate any person, animal, or that which has been in close contact with an extraterrestrial or UFO. It is rather ironic that the government formally denies the existence of UFOs, and yet has specific policies to deal with those who come in contact with them. I would like to thank the persons on this list and the even greater number not included for their cooperation and help in writing this book. Persons are listed in the order in which they were contacted.

Kathryn Kaycoff—director for the Fox series "Encounters." We spent several hours talking about her show and the UFO phenomenon. I was later on the "Encounters" show, which aired three times on national television in 1994.

Miles Quinn—captain of the Public Safety Department and Fire Department who formally denies there was any fire on the night of the crash. This is the same person who showed me two entries in the logbook documenting these fires, and also the same fire department where I interviewed three firemen who were at the crash site.

Don Echer—host of "UFO Tonite" and a very sharp UFO investigator. We spoke many times. One of the original persons to receive the Guardian documents on the Carp incident. His observations as well as a copy of those documents are printed in this book.

Budd Hopkins—an author and professional investigator of abductions. Quite possibly the inspiration for Whitley Strieber's *Communion*. He personally saw the film of the crash and gave me an in-depth analysis of his observations and comments on the film. He also went over some of his personal work in the abduction field.

Mike Christol—the head of the Kentucky UFO Network, a lifelong UFO investigator, and my friend. He is one of the most interesting people I have ever known and has one the largest UFO video libraries in the world, rivaled only by Video Dave's. Without Mike Christol's help this book could not have been written. For those living in the South interested in UFOs , I would highly recommend his computer network Space_Link. Mike's interviews with several individuals and their views on UFOs have been included in this book.

Tom Theophanis—top UFO researcher, video analyst, and sometimes exacting ex-police investigator. It was Tom who first showed me both the Long Island crash film and Carp landing. These films were sent for graphics analysis at my video studio. Our frequent conversations are chronicled in the book, and it was Tom and his friend Mike Christol who really introduced me to the world of UFOs.

John Ford—the primary and first investigator of the Long Island in crash Southaven Park. He has spent the last two years investigating and gathering information on this incident. He is the head of LIUFON, Long Island UFO Network, and was also on several television programs as well as the "Encounters" show. As per our agreement I have used none of John's material or photos but rather reinterviewed all of the witnesses myself as well as a considerable number of additional ones and got all of my information firsthand.

Mike Strainic—head of MUFON, a UFO Network in Canada. A very likeable and sharp guy, very knowledgeable on UFOs. A friend of Tom Theophanis and well informed on the Carp incident, the UFO landing in Canada.

Bob Oechsler—ex-NASA UFO investigator who investigated

the Carp landing in depth. Discovered the landing site and with a team of technicians ran tests on the soil, vegetation, and even checked for radioactivity in the area. His findings and rebuttals to a rather pointed attempt to discount his finding are included.

Walter Andrus—head of MUFON in the U.S. Another very sharp, lifelong UFO investigator. Has been on several talk shows and appeared at symposia and other UFO events.

Mike Parente—witnessed the arrival of the mother ship, which later confronted the military at Brookhaven Lab. Mike provided sketches of the ship. His brother was later accosted by the police for giving information on what he had seen of the crash while passing the park on his bicycle. Mike had not been that interested in UFOs before that night and clearly observed the mother ship and the small formation of craft flying over the park.

Video Dave (Dave Aaron)—has his own talk show and is an unforgettable character to interview. He owns one of the largest collections of UFO videos in the world and runs the UFO Audio-Video Clearinghouse. His help was invaluable in contacting the other primary video analysts as well as enlargement and capture of some of the photos used in this book.

Joyce Hansen—one of the two women who observed the roadblock on the night of the crash. Extremely interesting person, and a friend of Kathy Kasten.

Preston Nichols—author of the *Mantock Project*, UFO investigator, and astute observer. Because of his active life in the field and frequent travels, a bit hard to contact, but well worth the effort.

Mona Rowe—head of public relations at Brookhaven Lab. Supplied me with considerable material on the lab as well as information on UFO reports over the years involving the lab. She witnessed a formation of UFOs flying over the bay near the time of the crash.

Kathy Kasten—observed the roadblock, special SWAT team, and fire engines the night of the Southaven crash. She is an author currently working on a book on the Roswell incident.

Diane Labanek—witness at the Carp UFO landing. She appeared on the "Encounters" show and related her experience and her feelings as she watched the craft land just hundreds of yards from her farmhouse.

Reverend Kenneth Stanley—car caught on fire at the same time the mother ship was approaching Southaven Park. Taken and mistreated by officials. As per agreement for publishing his experience,

I have included his experience at the hospital. Suit is currently pending against the police department concerning this incident.

Dana Judge—military personnel at base who heard a loud "boom" at the time of the Brookhaven crash. Related that there were no training or other military flights in the area at that time.

Kenny Lloyd—host of the Intergalactic Television Network. I will be appearing on this show sometime shortly after the release of this book. Interesting talk show featuring a variety of unique people and unusual topics.

Larry Fenwick—head of CUFON (California UFO Network).

Graham Lightfoot—with the party investigating the Carp landing in their memorable trek through the swamp.

Linda Howe—writer, director, and producer of "Alien Harvest." The top authority on cattle-mutilation research. She has recently released "Alien Harvest II." Provided a great deal of information on the cattle-mutilation phenomena and why a large part of it could not be attributed to predators.

John Altshuler—highly spoken of in UFO circles as one of the best tissue analysts. He has ascertained through exhaustive studies that many of the wounds on the mutilated animals were produced at very high temperatures. This would indicate that the wounds are the result of the application of some type of laser to the animals rather than the teeth or beak of a predator.

Salurah—direct contact with the alien races that are visiting this planet. Their message, as they wished it to be included in this book, can be found in the channel chapter. More concerning Salurah and the alien child or hybrid that has been born in Puerto Rico will be included in my next book, *Hybrid*.

SPECIAL THANKS TO

Greg Walberg—who has remained a steadfast friend. He also has the courage to go with me to meet the Grays for the first covered-by-the-press meeting of humans and extraterrestrials. I don't know if they'll show-up Greg, but if they do, knowing the government, that will be the last anyone ever sees of us.

Patricia Hansen and Deborah Bell—both of whom believed in me and encouraged me to write.

Cinnamon—who in her own way provided a great deal of inspiration.

NETWORK

The following is a list of nodes for the MUFON network world-wide where you can get more information about and report UFO sightings. Although some of the more basic information about UFOs was taken from the printed page, the majority and best information may be found on the network. You will need a computer and some type of modem. (A modem is a communications device that allows your computer to talk to other computers by phone.)

MUFONET-BBS NETWORK

Administrative System

MufoNet Administrator	512-556-2524	Lampasas, TX
MufoNet Public Relations	501-646-5812	Fort Smith, AR
MufoNet-Databank Direct	512-556-2524	Lampasas, TX
RC North East US	716-225-8631	Rochester, NY
RC South East US	703-768-5649	Alexandria, VA
RC North Central US	913-648-6979	Kansas City, KS
RC South Central US	501-646-5812	Fort Smith, AR
RC North West US	509-758-6248	Clarkston, WA
RC South West US	602-814-1491	Chandler, AZ
RC Canada	514-974-0445	Deux-Montagnes, Quebec
RC Australia/New Zealand	61-3-467-8090	Melbourne, Australia
RC Europe	44-1691-671900	Shropshire, England
RC South America	55-612-437676	Brazilia DF, Brazil

Fax Numbers

Mutual UFO Network (MUFON)	210-372-9439	Seguin, TX
MUFONet BBS Network Admin.	817-628-1031	Lampasas, TX

Numbers for Reporting UFO Sightings

Toll Free * (see note)	800-UFO-2166	toll free in the U. S.
Alberta MUFON	403-289-3552	Alberta, Canada
Canada (Nat'l HQ Vancouver)	604-683-6168	BC, Canada
Centre for UFO Studies	204-956-2830	Manitoba, Canada
MUFONtario	416-828-8018	Ontario, Canada
MUFON-NWT	819-252-3730	NWT, Canada
MUFON Quebec	514-349-4437	Quebec, Canada
Mutual UFO Network	210-379-9216	Seguin, TX
Nat'l UFO Reporting Center	206-722-3000	Seattle, WA
Sask - MUFON	306-745-2483	Saskatchewan, Canada
UFO Filter Center	812-838-9843	Mt. Vernon, IN
Ufo-Bc/MUFON	604-271-6313	BC, Canada
Ufori	506-457-0232	Atlantic Provinces, Canada
Uforic	604-685-1836	BC, Canada

*Sponsored jointly by MUFON International, the J. Allen Hynek Center for UFO Studies, and the Fund for UFO Research, and supported in part by the Bigelow Foundation.

Australia & New Zealand

11th Hour	61-69-311-460	Wagga Wagga
1990 MultiLine BBS	61-9-370-3333	Mount Lawley
A.L.I.E.N. BBS	61-2-743-5871	Concord West
Alternative News Network	61-70-511-845	Cairns
AlphaByte BBS	61-9-227-9540	Carrine
Andromeda Connection	61-3-396-1113	Footscray West
Bridge	61-3-686-6107	Middle Park
Blue Star	61-2-456-2770	Berowra
Christianity Out West	61-68-625-145	Parkes
Clayton's BBS	61-3-328-4927	West Melbourne
Compu-Talk	61-3-379-2097	Strathmore
Computer Addicts BBS	61-3-557-5278	Moorabbin
The CrySTal	61-89-85-5504	Darwin
Magenta Black	61-02-25-4748	Howrah
Mail Fix	61-8-371-0398	Athol
Night Owl Theatre	61-3-802-2332	Blackburn
New World	61-76-362-136	Toowoomba
NTH Dimension	61-7-349-2730	Brisbane
Paradise	61-75-748-611	Worongary
PenRIG Aplha Research	61-59-75-0779	Mornington
P.O.D.S. Australia	61-7-398-5334	Camp Hill
Quickening	61-76-910-363	Southbrook
Soft-Tech	61-7-869-1131	Sandgate
Stringline	61-02-438-604	Risdon Vale
#Vixlab BBS	61-2-873-3201	North Rocks
Zoist	61-3-467-8090	Melbourne

Canada

Chucara File Center	514-974-0445	Deux-Montagnes, QB
Dark Matter	604-534-7667	Langley, BC
Esoterica BBS	514-655-6589	Boucherville, QB
Outback BBS	306-692-6471	Moose Jaw,SK
*TRACE BBS	604-272-0007	Richmond,BC

Europe

Starbase Four	44-1691-671900	Shropshire
CyberTech BBS	44-1734-261424	Reading
Neurology BBS	44-1202-889382	Wimbourne
Amiga Central Line 1	44-1527-585990	Redditch
Amiga Central Line 2	44-1527-585991	Redditch
#Nth Degree BBS	44-1222-224424	Cardiff
ArcForum BBS	44-1506-440367	Livingston
Strange Phenomena Invest	44-1506-857709	Broxburn
Oil Slick BBS	44-1467-633480	Kintore
Phantom BBS	44-1224-709833	Aberdeen
STeelers BBS	44-1475-728430	Greenock
Touchdown BBS	44-1475-7889	Greenock
TBSCNDOS BBS	44-1207-237146	Stanley
AQUA-BOX	49-561-878363	Kassel
Flatline	49-08167-6027	Zolling
Knucklejoint	49-2621-180570	Lahnstein
Magic Lighthouse	49-6151-719363	Darmstadt
NORSK BBS	49-211-9179035	Duesseldorf
Taunus Box Node 1	49-6196-533005	Schwalbach
Taunus Box Node 2	49-6196-533004	Schwalbach
Star Communicator	43-1-749-3086	Vienna
Pyromania BBS II	352-57-4816	Mondercange

South America

ELLA BBS	55-149-21-3945	Botucatu
ERA BBS	55-152-22-1569	Sorocaba
BLASTER BBS	55-31-281-4806	Belo Horizonte
GRALHA BBS	55-41-271-0415	Curitiba
Halifax BBS	55-11-575-6994	Sao Pablo
Kanopus BBS	55-41-225-2582	Curitiba
Linepaths BBS	55-61-368-4142	Brasilia
Navigator BBS	55-61-243-7676	Brasilia
NetServ BBS	55-61-244-4447	Brasilia
ODONTO Line BBS	55-11-521-6555	Sao Paulo
Point BBS	55-61-224-3012	Brasilia
Silver-Net BBS	55-473-22-9603	Blumenau
Top Parana BBS	55-41-272-2382	Curitiba-Parana

=new system—may not yet be on-line with MUFONet
#=system temporarily down or inactive

United States

A & B Express	619-447-2792	El Cajon, CA
Absence of Evidence BBS	410-321-7461	Lutherville, MD
Above Board	703-768-5649	Alexandria, VA
*ADS At The Park	619-281-0123	San Diego, CA
Alien Biker Kat BB S	619-277-4140	San Diego, CA
ALIEN NATION BBS	203-528-7537	East Hartford, CT
Alternative Insights	516-676-3325	Glen Head, NY
ASA CompuHelp	614-476-3723	Westerville, OH
*Astrological Services	816-561-4194	Kansas City, MO
Authors' Area Writers' Forum	513-848-4288	Bellbrook, OH
Baron Carlos' Castle	809-277-0928	Guaynabo, PR
Castle Talamasca	410-398-6971	Elkton, MD
C.O.M.A. BBS	804-971-2498	Charlottesville, VA
Chatter Box	504-775-7825	Baker, LA
Children of Galaexy	718-364-7943	Bronx, NY
*Classic Image	702-247-6393	Las Vegas, NV
Close Encounters Research Ne.	713-558-5342	Houston, TX
COPS-N-HAMS BBS	904-651-8757	Shalimar, FL
Cowford Cargo Cult	904-384-6021	Jacksonville, FL
Crop Circles	412-483-3119	Charleroi, PA
Crow's Nest Amiga BBS (1)	412-929-9083	Belle Vernon, PA
Crow's Nest Amiga BBS (2)	412-929-6557	Belle Vernon, PA
Dallas Remote Imaging Group	214-492-7154	Carrollton, TX
DarkStar	904-244-7495	Mary Esther, FL
Databank	214-681-2218	Dallas, TX
Desert Reef	602-624-6386	Tucson, AZ
Desert Shack	805-940-6826	Lancaster, CA
Dragon's Keep	513-427-2803	Dayton, OH
Dynamic On-Line Service	602-885-4932	Tucson, AZ
Electric Fox	901-327-1008	Memphis, TN
Encounter	602-814-1491	Chandler, AZ
*Far Out BBS	619-581-9049	San Diego, CA
FileBank	303-534-4646	Denver, CO
Fone Emporium	904-676-1142	Jay, FL
Fortean Research Center	402-488-2587	Lincoln, NE
*From The Ashes	916-332-0396	Elverta, CA
Gates of Delirium	916-339-9043	North Highlands, CA
Gray's Anatomy	619-778-1866	Palm Springs, CA
Graveyard Shift	602-290-0463	Tucson, AZ
Grid Epsilon BBS	205-856-9809	Birmingham, AL
Ground Zero	813-849-4034	New Port Richey, FL

#Guru Meditation	317-486-9245	Indianapolis, IN
#Hangar 18	316-251-7460	Coffeyville, KS
Heart Life Communications	303-377-1963	Denver, CO
Heart of the Sun	214-424-2961	Dallas, TX
Highland Lakes	915-388-3209	Kingsland, TX
Highlander OS/2	817-498-7578	Fort Worth, TX
House Atreides Node 1	214-276-7626	Garland, TX
House Atreides Node 2	214-494-3702	Garland, TX
House Atreides Node 3	214-494-8281	Garland, TX
Inn of the Sleeping Cat	301-736-6591	Andrews AFB, MD
Joe's Place	301-736-8839	District Heights, MD
KC GeneSplicer	913-648-6979	Kansas City, KS
Lair of the Feline	703-525-4111	Arlington, VA
Lucky's Fly-In BBS	718-318-8406	New York City, NY
MAGIC Bus	810-544-3653	Royal Oak, MI
Magnetic Inx	503-955-8094	Grants Pass, OR
Maelstrom	904-457-3162	Pensacola, FL
Mainframe	904-581-0150	Mary Esther, FL
#Men's Room	419-865-0355	Holland, OH
MICAP BBS Network	303-985-5903	Lakewood, CO
MICROLINK	303-237-8575	Denver, CO
Moiraine's Playground	817-542-6103	Copperas Cove, TX
MUFON-ATL	404-919-0431	Atlanta, GA
My Blue Heaven	602-750-0716	Tucson, AZ
Necronomicon BBS	407-639-1727	Rockledge, FL
Oregon Desert	503-475-3056	Madras, OR
Pagan's Way	305-925-1620	Dania, FL
Palace Flophouse & Grill	702-265-7674	Gardnerville, NV
Pluto Daily Ledger	904-837-8113	Destin, FL
Prowler's DOMAIN	509-327-8922	Spokane, WA
QST	916-920-1288	Sacramento, CA
Quantum Shift	904-478-1161	Pensacola, FL
Rainbow QuickBBS	501-646-5812	Fort Smith, AR
Random Oblique	904-939-3253	Navarre, FL
Rat's Edge	716-225-8631	Rochester, NY
Realm-FX	305-977-3761	Pompano Beach, FL
Reverse Polarity	203-620-0001	Plantsville, CT
Rick's Fantasy Land	904-664-6582	Ft Walton Beach, FL
Run-Time BBS	602-525-3711	Flagstaff, AZ
Separate Reality Node 1	205-765-2080	Excel, AL
Separate Reality Node 2	205-765-2933	Excel, AL
Serial Port	601-366-1803	Jackson, MS
Sirius UFO Network	612-780-5916	Lino Lakes, MN
Sirius	501-424-6116	Mountain Home, AR
Slacker's Palace	612-884-0575	Bloomington, MN

South Jersey Info Exchange	609-522-6825	West Wildwood, NJ
Southern Coast Online Svcs	609-399-5708	Ocean City, NJ
Space Link	502-683-3026	Owensboro, KY
Spirit	704-297-5973	Vilas, NC
Station 1 BBS	708-258-6475	Peotone,IL
#StarShip 182	317-889-7899	Indianapolis, IN
StarWest	509-758-6248	Clarkston, WA
StarWest Line 2	509-758-9547	Clarkston, WA
Studio PC	813-862-4632	Port Richey, FL
SuperBoard	702-423-4739	Fallon, NV
Tex*Star (MUFONet HQ)	512-556-2524	Lampasas, TX
Tex* Star (MUFON Members Line)	512-556-2728	Lampasas, TX
Thirst For Knowledge	512-454-8065	Austin, TX
Title 14	203-892-4514	Norwich, CT
Twilight Zone	805-258-0413	Edwards AFB, CA
UFO BBS	619-262-2134	San Diego, CA
UFOria	703-803-6420	Clifton, VA
Ursa Major BBS	310-541-5611	Manhattan Beach, CA
Water Works	216-385-0262	East Liverpool, OH
Weird Science	606-932-6606	South Shore, KY
XBN	508-586-6977	Brockton, MA
X-Files BBS	505-891-4499	Rio Rancho, NM